# GREAT
# CATASTROPHE

# GREAT CATASTROPHE

ARMENIANS AND TURKS IN THE
SHADOW OF GENOCIDE

THOMAS DE WAAL

OXFORD
UNIVERSITY PRESS

## OXFORD
UNIVERSITY PRESS

Oxford University Press is a department of the University of
Oxford. It furthers the University's objective of excellence in research,
scholarship, and education by publishing worldwide.

Oxford    New York

Auckland    Cape Town    Dar es Salaam    Hong Kong    Karachi
Kuala Lumpur    Madrid    Melbourne    Mexico City    Nairobi
New Delhi    Shanghai    Taipei    Toronto

With offices in

Argentina    Austria    Brazil    Chile    Czech Republic    France    Greece
Guatemala    Hungary    Italy    Japan    Poland    Portugal    Singapore
South Korea    Switzerland    Thailand    Turkey    Ukraine    Vietnam

Oxford is a registered trademark of Oxford University Press
in the UK and certain other countries.

Published in the United States of America by
Oxford University Press
198 Madison Avenue, New York, NY 10016

Library of Congress Cataloging-in-Publication Data
De Waal, Thomas.
Great catastrophe : Armenians and Turks in the shadow of genocide / Thomas de Waal.
pages cm
Includes bibliographical references.
ISBN 978-0-19-935069-8 (hardback : alkaline paper) 1. Armenian massacres,
1915–1923—Influence. 2. Armenian massacres, 1915–1923—Political aspects.
3. Armenia—Relations—Turkey. 4. Turkey—Relations—Armenia.
5. Memory—Political aspects—Armenia. 6. Memory—Political aspects—Turkey.
7. Turkey—Ethnic relations. 8. Collective memory—Turkey. 9. Genocide—Political
aspects—Case studies. I. Title.
DS195.5.D49 2015
956.6'20154—dc23
2014020230

1 3 5 7 9 8 6 4 2
Printed in the United States of America
on acid-free paper

To my mother, Esther Moir de Waal,
who first taught me about history

# CONTENTS

# AUTHOR'S NOTE

⸺⸻◦◦◦⸺⸻

IN MY WORK IN the South Caucasus in the 1990s, coming from the Russian side, I slowly began to feel the importance of an issue that still had a dark and muffled resonance in the region from three generations before: the fate of the Ottoman Armenians in 1915. It is not an issue to be approached lightly, and it was only after many years and many trips to Turkey that I felt able to do so.

A lot of good histories have been written about the Armenian Genocide, and this is not an attempt to write another one. My aim is to provide a book for the general reader about what came after 1915: how different eras and political agendas shaped the Armenians, changing relations between Armenians and Turks, the politics of genocide, and the dynamic and often more hopeful events of the last 15 years.

I use the term "Armenian Genocide" in the book, having, after much reading, respectfully agreed with the scholarly consensus that what happened to the Armenians in 1915–1916 did indeed fit the 1948 United Nations definition of genocide. At the same time, along with many others, I do so with mixed feelings, having also reached the conclusion that the "G-word" has become both legalistic and over-emotional, and that it obstructs the understanding of the historical rights and wrongs of the issue as much as it illuminates them. As the reader will see, this is one of the themes of the book.

Names are problematic in a book of this kind, and I have tried to be consistent, while not confusing the general reader. I try to use the most commonly used name of a given place at the particularly historical moment; for example, I refer to the cities of "Constantinople" and "Tiflis" until the 1920s, when they became known internationally as Istanbul and Tbilisi. However, of the main versions of the name of the Armenian capital, I have chosen to use Yerevan throughout. The Armenians' homeland, covering the old Armenian plateau and the upper reaches of the Rivers Euphrates and Tigris, has many names. For a long time, Armenians and many Western travelers called it "Armenia" or "Western Armenia." Kurds call its southeastern portion Kurdistan. Here I shall use the less ethnically determined term "Eastern Anatolia," while being aware that this name, too, has political connotations.

Before I reach the last 30 years, where I can draw on contemporary sources and eyewitnesses, I draw on exclusively English- and Russian-language sources, though I am aware that this also gives the book a certain coloring. The story of the divided Armenian Diaspora, for example, is told mainly through the pages of the newspapers *Hairenik Weekly* (later *Armenian Weekly*) and the *Armenian Mirror-Spectator*.

A great number of people have helped me with the book and I am grateful to them all—particularly, perhaps, to those who will not share all of its analysis.

In Washington, I would like to thank Levon Avdoyan of the Library of Congress; my colleagues in the Carnegie Endowment for International Peace Russia Eurasia Program, especially Ann Stecker, and the staff of the library, Keigh Hammond, Kathleen Higgs, and Christopher Lao Scott; Charles King; and Emil Sanamyan.

In Ankara, Tansu Acik and Burcu Gültekin Punsmann. In Istanbul, Cengiz Aktar, Ergun Vartkes Ayik and Pelin Ayik, Burcu Becermen, Tuba Çandar, Andrew Finkel, Sabine Freizer, and Hugh Pope. In Diyarbakir, Serra Hakyemez and Gaffur Ohanian. In Yerevan, Hayk Demoyan, Salpi Ghazarian, Tigran and Nana Kzmalian, Tigran Paskevichian, and Gevorg Ter-Gabrielian. In Beirut, Arda Ekmeji; the staff of Carnegie Middle East Center and especially Jana Momtaz and Ali el Yassir.

In New York, I would like to thank Lauren Bisio and Masha Udensiver-Brenner at Columbia University; and Edward Wilson and Suzy Coue Wilson, who briefly turned part of their Silver Lake House into a "Genocide Studies Center." In Boston, Gerard Libaridian was generous with his insights, and Asbed Kotchikian gave detailed and useful comments on the manuscript. In Ann Arbor, Fatma Müge Göçek generously shared the manuscript of her forthcoming book.

On my 2012 trip to Turkey and beyond, Archbishop Khajag Barsamian, Raffi Bedrosyan, Sheri Jordan, and Naomi Shore provided inspiration. Scout Tufankjian gave me photographs and enthusiasm. Ronald Suny has been a steady source of friendship, support, and comments. Also Tavitian's contribution has been enormous.

Three research assistants were especially invaluable, and the book would not have been completed without them: Julie Leighton, Ola McLees, and, especially, Matthew Kupfer.

Finally, my daughter Zoe de Waal was a star throughout, and my wife Georgina Wilson was the rock on which everything was possible, a source of love, amazing support, and superb editorial advice. This book is lovingly dedicated to my mother, the first historian in my family.

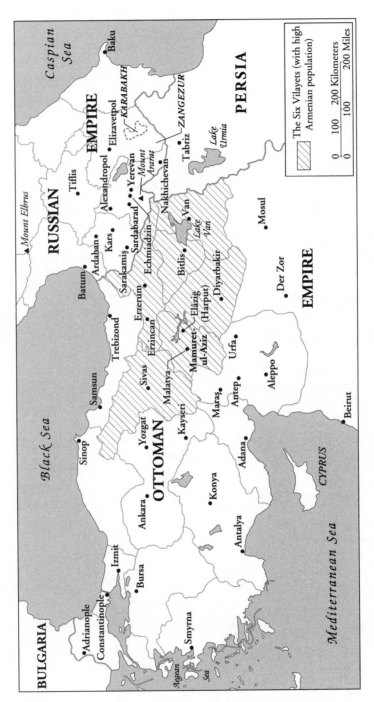

Map 1. The Ottoman Empire in 1914.

Source: Christopher Robinson.

Map 2. Turkey in 2014.

Source: Christopher Robinson.

# Introduction

## Requiem in Diyarbakir

ONE HOT NIGHT IN September 2012, a group of around 70 middle-aged American citizens walked in a crowd through a labyrinth of narrow alleys in Diyarbakir in southeastern Turkey. The women were dressed elegantly, in pearls, earrings, and big sunglasses; the men were more casual, in sweatshirts and tan or beige slacks, their sneakers and sandals clacking on the uneven bricks of the street. They exchanged curious glances with Kurdish men in baggy white shirts looking out from tea shops and small barber's parlors. The three letters of the Kurdish guerrilla movement, the PKK, and the image of its mustachioed leader, known as Apo, were stenciled on storefronts. The group paused to let an old man pulling a washing machine on a two-wheeled wooden cart go by. Then they stopped outside a gate set in an old stone wall, next to an inscription, "Diyarbakir, Armenian Church of St. Giragos, 1376."

As they entered the courtyard, a small man with a glistening forehead, dressed in a dark suit and waistcoat, stepped forward. "Welcome, my brothers and sisters! We are very glad to see you in your own country, your own city!" said Osman Baydemir, the Kurdish mayor of Diyarbakir. He grasped the hand of the equally smiling bearded Armenian bishop from New York.

Inside the tall church, 300 people were squashed onto wooden benches. The mayor again welcomed the visitors from America. "The first question is where are the real owners of this place now? Where are the sisters and brothers, Armenians, Syrians, where are they now?" he asked. The time was coming, he said, when everyone—Kurds, Armenians, and Turks—would live together.

"Come back! Come back again!" he concluded stirringly in English. A ripple went through the crowd of Armenians. Of course, there was a political subtext in the mayor's words—by inviting the Armenians back, he was also advancing the cause of Kurdish autonomy in Turkey. Nevertheless, only a few years earlier, it would have been impossible to utter these words in Turkey. In the seemingly intractable issue of Armenian-Turkish relations, this was a gesture of reconciliation. For one night at least, a group of Armenians had come home.

THE CENTURY-OLD QUESTION OF the killing and deportation of the Armenians of the Ottoman Empire in 1915—the events that have come to be known as the Armenian Genocide—ranks as the longest and most bitter historical dispute still alive. It helps keep the Armenia-Turkey border closed, parliaments discuss it, and ambassadors are recalled. It largely defines the identity of the worldwide Armenian diaspora.

The place of the Armenian question in the world's consciousness has grown and diminished. The atrocities against the Armenians were extensively reported at the time in the newspapers and drew condemnation from leaders such as Winston Churchill and Woodrow Wilson. During World War I, the average American knew about the sufferings of the "starving Armenians" who were recipients of US food aid. In May 1918, Theodore Roosevelt wrote, "We should go to war because not to do so is really to show bad faith towards our allies, and to help Germany, because the Armenian massacre was the greatest crime of the war, and failure to act against Turkey is to condone it."[1]

The central facts of the story are straightforward. The Armenians were an ancient people, whose homeland was centered in what is now eastern Turkey. In 1913, there were up to 2 million of them in the Ottoman Empire. When World War I broke out, the Ottoman government ordered their mass deportation. A few years later, there was barely one-tenth of that number in Turkey, the rest having been exiled or killed. The survivors scattered either to eastern Armenia in the Caucasus or around the world.

The story of what happened around the tragedy and afterward is more complex and has cascaded down the generations. It draws in Kurds, Azerbaijanis, Russians, the Soviet Union, and the Western Great Powers and their successors. A bitter feud dominated Armenian Diaspora politics for three generations. Since the 1960s, a political quarrel around the word "genocide" has all but taken on a life of its own. Often, hard-line Armenians and Turks still seem trapped in the politics of the early twentieth century, while the rest of the world has moved on around them.

For many outsiders, the contemporary politics of the Armenian Genocide has obscured the real history behind it, throwing up a barrier against those who otherwise would have been more ready to understand its flesh-and-blood realities. Certainly, many in the United States come up against the issue first as an irritating duel in Congress, before they have a chance to learn what lies behind it.

I confess I used to belong to that category. From 1996, in my work, I made many visits to the Republic of Armenia, the state that became independent in 1991. The Genocide lurked in the background of my visits to Armenia. On April 24, 2000, I joined the crowds walking up to the Genocide Memorial on a hill above Yerevan to commemorate the deaths of their ancestors. Around half of the current population of Armenia derives from Ottoman Armenians who fled their homeland in 1915–1920. But that day was atypical. The Genocide is not an organizing principle of identity for citizens of the Republic of Armenia. Two other national ideas are more important—building a new state and the struggle with neighboring Azerbaijan over the disputed territory of Nagorny Karabakh. The main impact of the continuing dispute with Turkey is the closed border that blocks Armenian access to Europe and the West.

So I never paid sufficient attention to the tragedy of 1915. Later, in my encounters with politicized Diaspora Armenians, I was put off by those who adopted an angry and often dogmatic tone when they talked about Turkey and the Genocide. Many of these Armenians came across as single-issue zealots. As W. B. Yeats had observed about the Irish (and his young self):

> Nothing said or done can reach
> My fanatic heart.
>
> Out of Ireland have we come.
> Great hatred, little room,
> Maimed us at the start.
> I carry from my mother's womb
> A fanatic heart.

Armenians find their own kind difficult, too. In his 1975 memoir *Passage to Ararat*, Michael J. Arlen writes about rediscovering his Armenian identity. His father, also Michael Arlen, had suppressed his Armenianness and aggressively made himself into a newly minted man of Western high society; the son writes of his father's persistent "care that I become English, American—anything but Armenian."[2]

Arlen's book records his ordeals as he shrugs off his father's advice to embrace his Armenian legacy. He observes that Turkish denial and Armenian powerlessness had inflicted a curse of "self-hatred" on some of his kin: "One thought of the wailing or hand-wringing quality of many Armenians—especially the older men, but also the sons—whose physical gestures seemed directed more against themselves than against the alleged object, the Turks. The diatribes against the Turks—tantrums, as it were, carried down now through three generations. Wasn't the surest way of tormenting an angry child as follows: to leave it alone, ignored in its rage?"[3]

For many individual Armenians, and for Diaspora Armenians collectively, the problem is that the unresolved legacy of the Genocide is a prison, and it is the Turks, and not they themselves, who have the key to release them. Many of them feel that they are honor-bound not to let go because, as one Diyarbakir Armenian told me, "We still cannot bury our grandparents."

WHAT IRRITATION I MAY HAVE harbored melted into humility on the trip to eastern Turkey I made in 2012, led by the bishop of New York.

We formed a convoy of two buses. The bishop, born in Turkey, was the quiet center, the leader and pastor of the group, while also taking time to talk to every Turkish official or tea shop owner we met on the road. Many of his flock had been afraid to come to Turkey, but the bishop had persuaded them it would be worth it. Now that they were here, they all experienced moments of recognition. "This smells just like my mother's kitchen!" exclaimed one middle-aged man over lunch one day. "I find something here in my DNA I didn't find in Armenia," observed a younger woman. Many of them discovered that they could speak more Turkish than they knew: it had been the second and sometimes the first language of their parents.

The warmth of the reception for the Armenians from ordinary Kurds and Turks surprised me. Looking for the town museum in the back-streets of Van, I stopped to ask directions and was asked in a friendly tone, "Can we help you? Are you Armenian?" When our bus stopped at a wayside teahouse, the owner stood the Armenian group 70 glasses of tea. On a visit to a mosque that had been formerly been an Armenian church in the town of Antep (now Gaziantep), the current custodian, the imam, happened to be inside. The imam suggested to the bishop that this holy space belonged to both of them and they prayed together. If politicians in Ankara warned that the ordinary population of Eastern Anatolia was still hostile toward Armenians, this was not the impression our group received. On the contrary, many people not only remembered Armenians but seemed to think that their return was a good omen.

As we went, I asked the Armenians to share their stories with me. I soon noticed two things. The first was that although the older generation did use the term "Armenian Genocide," they were more inclined to talk of "the deportations" or "the massacres." The use of this more human language, rather than the politicized term "genocide," brought the reality of the experience closer home to me. I also learned that when I asked my fellow travelers the question "Where are you from?" I would get two or sometimes three answers: Urfa-Beirut-Manhattan, for example, or Sivas-Jerusalem-Queens.

All of my Armenian traveling companions had a family story with the same triple pattern. By definition, their parents or grandparents, who came from these parts of Turkey, had been the lucky ones and had survived the desert marches of 1915. But in the process they had lost almost everything and began anew in cities of the Middle East. The parents of very many in the group, I learned, were orphans. Many of them had been matched together in marriage in orphanages in Aleppo, Beirut, or Jerusalem.

Maria was diminutive and cheerful, and her red and orange tops stood out in the crowd. Her triple-decker identity was Diyarbakir, where her family came from, Egypt, where she was born, and New Jersey, where she now lived. Between the first and second stages came the hell of the Syrian desert in 1915. "My great-grandmother was a desert-walker," Maria told me. "Before she used to go to bed she would attach all her jewelry to her underwear. I would ask her, 'Grandma, Why?' and she would say 'You never know when you have to leave in a hurry.'"

Standing near the tall steeple of St. Giragos Church in Diyarbakir, which now filled the skyline above the town again, Maria said that in the early 1900s her father-in-law had been instructed to lower the height of the bell tower because the Ottoman authorities did not want to see a church rising higher than the minarets.

Another sad story began in the town. Maria's husband's aunt was an Armenian girl who escaped deportation in 1915 by being married off, at the age of 12, to the son of a Turkish dignitary. Years later, the girl and her Turkish husband had a baby son. Then her father came back to Turkey and tracked his daughter down in her new home. "One day, they brought horses. They told her, 'Come away but don't bring your son, otherwise they will try to catch us.'" So the Armenian girl fled with her father to Egypt, leaving her baby boy behind.

In Egypt, now a young woman, she married a wealthy man, but had no more children. One day at a Mediterranean resort, someone came and sat next to her and said, "Your son is looking for you." Mother and son met at her brother's house. "But the tragic thing was that they never lived together." The boy went back to Diyarbakir, the mother to Patterson, New Jersey, where she found work in a silk factory. "So this American woman would go to Turkey, to Diyarbakir to her son's house and sit in the corner wearing black in the 1960s and 70s, frustrated because she was not allowed to cook or do anything."

THE COLORS WERE STRONG and primal. It looked as though a child had dragged a crayon across the horizon. The waters of Lake Van were turquoise like the Mediterranean nearer the shore, then they deepened into blue further out. In the middle of the lake rose a rocky island, above which fluttered a bright red Turkish flag. As our boat got closer, we could make out the dome of a church made of burnt orange sienna (see Figure I.1).

I had joined the pilgrimage two days earlier in the eastern Turkish town of Van. The island of Aghtamar on the inland sea of Lake Van is home to one of the most famous of all Armenian churches, a tenth-century cathedral that was the seat of the princes of Vaspurakan. The outer walls of the church were an unfolding tapestry in stone. The stylized images looked as though they were embossed on the stone: large grapes, endearing lions, eagles, and sheep, David reaching for his sling to strike the hulk of Goliath towering above him. The cathedral had been restored two years before. In the 1950s, it was inside a military exercise zone and was being slowly destroyed, but the writer Yasar Kemal and others preserved it from extinction.

Figure I.1 Approaching the island of Aghtamar on Lake Van and its famous cathedral, September 9, 2012.
Photograph by Naomi Shore.

A large crowd was pressing into the church, and we had to fight for a passage to get into the small inner space beneath the dome. For only the third time since 1915, by permission of the Turkish government, an Armenian service was being held at Aghtamar. A forest of cameras met us inside. Turkish security officials with dark suits and grave faces lined the walls. As if in a medieval picture, a shaft of light descended diagonally and struck the blue, silver, and gold vestments of the choir. Bishop Barsamian came out in a red miter etched with gold and began singing the liturgy in a deep voice. The choir, from the Armenian Patriarchate in Istanbul, joined in. Censers rattled and the muscular syllables of the Armenian language echoed off the walls.

The bishop preached a sermon in Armenian, looking up expansively at the dome, and said a few words in Turkish. The Armenian pilgrims passed the kiss of peace from person to person through the crowd. They made a path past the cameramen to receive communion, wafers of bread placed in their mouths. It was both a jostling bruising media event and a moving ceremony. "It was overwhelming," said one of our party afterward. "Everyone who was dead came back to me."

Outside, in the church courtyard, the Armenians relaxed and the Turks got tense. A dance group from Yerevan formed a circle, the dancers linking their arms around each other's shoulders and stepped forward and back—the same dance you see everywhere from Greece to India. Then someone unfurled the orange-blue-and-red tricolor of the Republic of Armenia and waved it above the dancers. That was not on the agenda on what was still official Turkish state property. This meant trouble, muttered a perspiring plainclothes security official with a Turkish flag badge pinned to his suit. Pointing first at the church and then the dancers with the Armenian flag, he said to me, "That is good, but this is bad. " But just as the official was tensed to intervene, the dancing subsided and the tricolor flag was put away.

That evening, in the foyer of the Elite Palace Hotel in the town of Van, I caught up with one of the Turkish officials who had organized the liturgy. He said he was pleased with the way things had gone. Van, he told me, was a complicated city, where it was not so easy to hold an Armenian event. While the Armenians of Van remembered the deportations of April 1915, the Muslims remembered the capture of the city by Russian and Armenian forces a few months later, when their ancestors were massacred. When the first Armenian liturgy had been held at Aghtamar two years before, the imam in the local mosque had denounced the event and said prayers for Turks killed by the Armenians in 1915.

It was a sign of how far Turkey had changed in the previous 10 years that the official was working with Armenians to organize events like the service at Aghtamar. From our conversation I got the impression that almost any initiative with Armenians was now acceptable to the Turkish government, but they still resisted the "genocide" word with everything they could muster. "Anatolia has a plural memory," he argued, while "Armenian memory is too singular. The fact that [what happened in 1915] wasn't a genocide doesn't minimize the suffering."

Bishop Khajag Barsamian had a glow about him after the liturgy. The bishop was so soft-spoken as to appear shy. But this concealed a determination to press ahead with trips to Turkey, despite the disapproval of nationalist sections of the Armenian Diaspora community.

On one of the long bus journeys, it was my turn to ask the bishop to tell me his own story. It had as many twists and turns as all the others I heard. He was born in the central Turkish town of Arapgir in 1951. His grandmother was a powerful influence on him as a child. In 1915, her husband had been taken away when she was three months pregnant, but "I never felt hatred in her, only pain." Although all the churches were destroyed, she taught her family to pray and read to them from the Bible. "I became a priest because of her."

The young Khajag Barsamian left Arapgir at the age of six and began a peripatetic life in search of an education. First he went to Istanbul to be schooled in the Armenian language; then, when the Armenian seminary in Istanbul closed, to Jerusalem; then to New York, Minnesota, Oxford, and Rome to study theology. In 1990, at the age of 39, "it was the end of scholarly endeavor," when he was elected bishop of the Eastern Diocese of the United States, based in New York.

The bishop's childhood in Turkey and his fluent Turkish equipped him to understand Turks as well as Armenians. On our journey, we constantly had a police escort, looking after our security. At each local boundary, responsibility would pass to a new local police force. I noticed that at each handover the bishop, with unhurried courtesy, would take time to thank the departing blue-shirted police officers and to greet the new ones. What was the best way to bridge the Armenian-Turkish gap? I asked the bishop. "The best approach is creating relations. Even this group is meeting with people. They see lots of similarities. They feel connections in music, food, even the faces are the same." But the psychological gap was still very big. "On one side there is a feeling of pride, on the other is pain."

What had he said in his sermon at Aghtamar? He had begun by thanking the Turkish government for giving permission for this service, he said. Then he quoted St. John, saying that "God so loved the world that he gave his only begotten Son" and talked about the meaning of the cross as a symbol of life. Then he talked about pilgrimage, about how pilgrims from near and far were united by this liturgy.

How had it been to sing the liturgy in Aghtamar for almost the first time in a century? "Very emotional and very inspiring. In the sanctuary I felt the unity of people, the past and the future." "Saying the liturgy is like climbing a mountain. Even if you feel tired at the beginning, you get energy."

LIKE THE LONG LITURGY, the Armenian bus pilgrimage found its rhythm. There were solemn moments in old Armenian churches when the bishop would say prayers; songs and laughter on the long journeys down dry and dusty Turkish highways; loud dinners in the evening when music played and elderly Armenians remembered their dance steps.

By the time the Armenian group reached Diyarbakir, the group seemed to be old friends. This ancient city had charged associations for many of them. Its black basalt city walls dated back to Roman times. The Armenians called it Dikranakert, or "Tigran's city." Thanks to its governor, the doctor Mehmed Reshid, it was one of the bloodiest locations for Armenians in 1915. Reshid murdered with such zeal that he received a telegram from Istanbul telling him to rein back his killing spree. Tourist landmarks had gruesome associations. As we strolled across the broad flagstones of the majestic 10-eyed bridge that spans the River Tigris, someone said that in those fateful days Armenian women had jumped off the side and had thrown their children into the water rather than face abduction and rape.

From the 1920s, the city became Turkey's main Kurdish center and the unofficial capital of what the locals call "Kurdistan." In the 1990s, it was a center under military siege at the height of the war between the Turkish state and the Kurdish militant group, the PKK. More recently, Diyarbakir had been at the forefront of reconciliation efforts with Armenians.

The two mayors of Diyarbakir—of both the inner city and the wider municipality—had warmly endorsed the plan to rebuild the big ruined Armenian church in the city. Armenians from the city had long wanted to rebuild St. Giragos, the largest Armenian church in the Middle East. It had been maintained by a small dogged Armenian community until the 1990s, but thereafter it gradually collapsed into decay, and the roof fell in. By the turn of the millennium, sheep were grazing in long grass in its ruins.

The Turkish government agreed to restore the church building, as they had at Aghtamar, but only on condition that they took over ownership. But the Kurdish municipal authorities made a much better offer, agreeing that it should be restored as a working church. So the reconstruction of the church was a joint initiative by a group of Turkish Armenians and the local authorities of Diyarbakir. That it was possible came down to two things. The first change was the more permissive environment in Turkey toward the country's minorities and its multi-ethnic past, ushered in by the moderately Islamist AK Party government. Although the old state narrative on what happened to the Armenians in 1915 was not formally rejected, officials mainly kept silent on the issue, and other dissenting views could now be expressed.

Second, Turkey's Kurdish leaders and their political party, the BDP, were at the forefront of reconciliation efforts with Armenians. In 1915 in Diyarbakir and elsewhere, marauding Kurdish tribesmen had been some of the chief culprits of the killings of Armenians. But a new narrative emerged in which the Kurds came to regard themselves as victims of Turkish nationalism, as the Armenians had been before them. They recalled a story that in 1915 an Armenian bishop who was about to be killed had supposedly warned his Kurdish neighbors, "We are the breakfast and you will be the lunch."

The Diyarbakir municipal authorities provided $500,000 for restoration, around 20 percent of the total cost. The remainder came from wealthy Armenians, mainly in Turkey. They did not say so openly, but the Diyarbakir Armenians were disappointed at how little money they had raised from Diaspora Armenians in the United States, many of whom could not be persuaded to invest money in an Armenian project in Turkey.

Now we too had come into the serene courtyard of St. Giragos Church, paved in the local black basalt stone, welcomed by mayor Baydemir. Tonight there would be a fundraising concert. It was like a typical Gothic medieval church: three aisles, a high airy space held up by tall pillars cut in thick blocks of the sturdy Diyarbakir stone, which here were a faded violet, the color of cooked eggplant. Five curtains of deep plum red embroidered with gold crosses had been drawn across the sanctuary of the church, and behind them we could see a gilded iconostasis. In front was a grand piano.

Once the mayor had finished speaking, Raffi Bedrossian came forward. His thick black hair was appropriately brushed to the side in a style reminiscent of Chopin. He sat down at the piano and played Beethoven's Moonlight Sonata. The chords found a natural home within these walls, soaring up and resounding powerfully from the stone. Bedrossian went on to play Chopin, Rachmaninov, and the Armenian composers Komitas and Alan Hovanhess.

On an evening of remarkable episodes, the story of how Raffi came to be playing the Moonlight Sonata in this church in Diyarbakir provided one more extraordinary tale. Raffi was from the small stock of surviving Istanbul Armenians, he told me later. He had studied at the prestigious English-language Robert College. His family did not talk about the deportations. "I didn't know anything about the 1915 events," he said. "It was a case of 'If the kids don't know they will be more like their Turkish friends, won't have any difficulties.'"

That changed in 1971 when, at the age of 18, Raffi went to study in Canada and started reading books about the Genocide. Returning home the next summer, he opened up the subject with his grandmother and heard her own terrible history. She told him how in 1915 she had walked in a caravan from Bursa, not far from Istanbul, the full length of Turkey to Damascus. She began the journey pregnant, gave birth to a baby boy in central Anatolia, and buried him under a rock six or seven days later. She had resettled in Istanbul after the war.

Raffi emigrated to Canada. A man of many talents, he built a double career in Toronto as civil engineer and pianist—"that complemented both sides of my brain." But he kept up his contacts in Istanbul both with Turks and with Armenians of Istanbul, like the journalist Hrant Dink, who were beginning to break the old habits of silence. "Ten years ago I realized Turkey was changing," he said. "I became more active in finding solutions instead of adopting the extremist attitudes of no contact with Turks, like the Dashnaks do."

Raffi's brother-in-law was head of the church council in Diyarbakir and asked for his help in restoring the church. Raffi put all his talents to use. He helped raise funds for the church, he did the structural engineering design for its new roof—and was now playing Beethoven for us inside the new building.

The next morning, the Armenian group went back to the church. The curtains were pulled back to reveal a golden screen set in the central alcove with an icon of the Virgin Mary lit by a full glister of 14 candles (see Figure I.2). The bishop was cowled in black, his five assistants decked out in red and gold vestments. A choir was formed from the tour party. Everyone in the group wrote down the names of departed ones and passed them to the clergy. The bishop sang a service of requiem. Appropriately enough for a service to remember the dead, the day was September 11.

I noticed our Turkish guide, Meltem, quietly lighting a candle, and stood at the back, reflecting how this trip had also changed my perspectives. In English the bishop said, "Thank God for this wonderful day," and then began the service in Armenian, a ritual of low chanting and repetitive patterns. Raffi Bedrossian whispered to me, "Two years ago there were sheep grazing here, grass up to here, birds everywhere." He gestured to the height of his waist and pointed upward. Arthur (New York, Romania, and Izmit) told me, "When we came here in 1997, there was no roof, vegetation up to here, one of the bishops got in through a broken window." He added, "The bad people are dead. They're gone. We can't hate anybody."

The choir lifted its unearthly singing. Their song was occasionally interrupted by the hammering of construction workers outside, and

Figure I.2 Bishop Khajag Barsamian sings the Requiem service in the restored Armenian church in Diyarbakir, September 11, 2012.
Photograph Naomi Shore.

once by the bass whoosh of a military jet flying over. I could not follow the service but I did hear a long list of Armenian names—the souls of the departed. "May the lord bless the souls of our departed. We also remember those who died on 9/11," the bishop concluded in English for those of us who did not know Armenian. The congregation lined up to kiss the ring.

OUR PARTY TRAVELED WESTWARD through Urfa and Antep, cities that Xenophon or Saint Paul would have recognized. Although the Kurdish city of Diyarbakir was finding a way to remember the Armenians, it could not be so straightforward in other parts of Eastern Anatolia. In towns like Van and Bitlis, the local Armenians were deported en masse and killed in 1915, only for the local Muslims to flee the depredations of the Russian army and its Armenian allies in 1916 and 1917.

No other region suffered as much in World War I. The Turkish scholar Cengiz Aktar, one of the pioneers of efforts for dialogue between

Turks and Armenians, says that the term "Great Catastrophe," or *Medz Yeghern*, which Armenians use to describe the destruction of 1915, could be applied to this region as a whole: "The 'Great Catastrophe' is very very powerful because it means a general catastrophe. Of course those who suffered the most were the Armenians but those who stayed behind suffered by all means."

I joined a small group traveling to another ancient town, Maraş. Turkey now calls it Kahramanmaraş, or Heroic Maraş, in honor of the battle that Atatürk's forces fought, driving out the French invaders and their Armenian allies in the Turkish War of Independence in 1920. That battle of 1920 spelled the end to centuries of Armenian life in Maraş. After that it turned into a provincial and conservative Turkish-Kurdish city, known in Turkey, if for anything, for its ice cream. Here the Armenians were remembered as both victims and aggressors.

On a previous trip, one of the women in our group went to the mosque in Maraş, where Armenians had their throats cut in 1915—and again when the French abandoned them in 1920. She wanted to go in, but a woman in front of the building made a gesture of slashing her throat and said, "If you try, we will do it again."

I went with a smaller party of seven, six of them Armenians with roots in the city. We hired a minibus and a Kurdish driver, Cemal, a man of few words who had taken dozens of Marashtsi Armenians back to their roots. We drove across a sun-scorched plain dotted with small domed pistachio trees, turning off the highway next to a big cement factory. I photographed my companions standing in front of the big signpost for "Kahramanmaraş, Population 428,724."

We climbed the citadel and looked down over a typical traffic-clogged Turkish town of concrete and red roofs. There was no sign of the famous "Lions of Marash" that European travelers had written about. Cathy (slim and short, from Maraş, Casablanca, and Long Island) was impressed by the bustle of the town. "Until I came here, I thought they were leaving a backwater, that my family changed a small village in the middle of nowhere for Long Island."

At last we came into the old Armenian quarter, with winding old Ottoman streets and red-tiled houses. Sheri (Maraş and New York) had never been here, but she already had an amazing sense of direction, formed by years of research of her family's history. She directed Cemal to find the house of an eye doctor, the uncle of her grandfather. And we found it still standing, a tall burnt-red building ringed by a high masonry wall. This was the house where her grandfather had stayed for nine months as a child. With war raging around him, he stepped out every day without shoes to walk to the town prison to visit his father and another illustrious local, a Mr. Kherlakian.

There was silence when we rattled the green metal gate. No luck. But then in the house opposite, two women in headscarves leaned out of the window and beckoned to us. One of them came out and pulled us into her little courtyard. Two little girls sat on the stairs. Before anyone arrived who could interpret, it was obvious who we were and what we represented. The elder woman, Salme, was eager to tell us something. She disappeared upstairs and re-emerged with a creased black-and-white photograph.

The photograph was perhaps 30 years old. There were 11 figures in it, and she pointed her finger at the oldest of them, an old lady in a white headscarf, looking straight and unflinching at the camera. "Veronica," she said. The full group had arrived now in this little courtyard, including the fluent Turkish-speaker John Vaniskhian, wearing a baseball cap and long mulberry shorts. Cameras were produced, the two women posed smilingly with their American-Armenian guests, as if they were talismans of good luck. Veronica had been the mother-in-law of Salme, our hostess. That was pretty much all Salme told us, that Veronica was Armenian, had lived in their house, and had died some years ago—and was warmly remembered. Salme's daughter got on the telephone and called her cousin. He would tell us more.

An hour later, we were squeezed into a tiny insurance office in downtown Maraş drinking glasses of tea. Kadir Besen looked like a jolly Turkish insurance clerk, but evidently large parts of him were Armenian. He had a drawer full of black-and-white photographs. Names flew back and forth and snapped Maraş threads wove back together. One of Kadir's pictures was of five men in Syria in the 1950s or 1960s. The man in the middle, he explained, was Setrak Kherlakian, his father. Several conversations broke out at once. Sheri commented, "His great-grandfather saved the life of my grandfather's father and brother." John Vaniskhian volunteered, "One of the wealthiest men in São Paulo is a Kherlakian."

"I'm not one of the 'rosy picture' school at all but today was *real* for me," said Chris, another Maraş New Yorker. She gestured around us. "For me it's about how the pieces are still there, the threads of it all are still there. There was an annihilation, now there's a coming together again." Throughout it all, our Kurdish driver impassively read his newspaper. He had done this before and had done his job well again today.

This was another episode of unexpected inspiration and clarity that I had not expected in the busy Turkish town of Maraş. I was amazed that these memories had been preserved, that a small insurance broker's office in a medium-sized Anatolian Turkish town could, despite everything, reconnect people from halfway across the world.

The optimist in me saw this as the beginning of something, the Armenian and Turkish worlds beginning to come back together. The pessimist in me saw how much had been irrevocably lost. At the very least, in places like Maraş, long overdue conversations had begun about the history of Armenians and Turks, both shared and different.

# I

---

# The Catastrophe

ON JULY 10, 1915, Henry Morgenthau, the US ambassador to the Ottoman Empire, sent a cable to Secretary of State Robert Lansing in Washington:

> Persecution of Armenians assuming unprecedented proportions. Reports from widely scattered districts indicate systematic attempts to uproot peaceful Armenian populations and through arbitrary arrests, terrible tortures, wholesale expulsions and deportations from one end of the Empire to the other accompanied by frequent instances of rape, pillage, and murder, turning into massacre, to bring destruction and destitution on them. These measures are not in response to popular or fanatical demand but are purely arbitrary and directed from Constantinople in the name of military necessity, often in districts where no military operations are likely to take place. The Moslem and Armenian populations have been living in harmony but because Armenian volunteers, many of them Russian subjects, have joined Russian army in the Caucasus and because some have been implicated in armed revolutionary movements and others have been helpful to Russians in their invasion of Van district terrible vengeance is being taken. Most of the sufferers are innocent

and have been loyal to Ottoman Government. Nearly all are old men, women, all the men from twenty to forty-five are in Turkish army. The victims find themselves dispossessed from their homes and sent on foot to be dispersed in districts where they are unknown and no provisions have been made to lodge or feed them. We have in several places been refused permission to relieve their misery or to have access to them. In some few instances where they opposed these measures and took refuge in the mountains and some arms or bombs were found it provoked the authorities to further cruelties which they attempt to justify by their opposition. Untold misery, disease, starvation and loss of life will go on unchecked.[1]

In this telegram, even as it is happening, Morgenthau encapsulates the main points of the story of the deportation and destruction of the Ottoman Armenians during World War I. These basic facts were reported at the time by diplomats, missionaries, journalists, and other witnesses on the ground. In 1915, shortly after the Ottoman Empire entered World War I, the Young Turk government ordered the mass deportation of the Ottoman Armenians from their homes to the deserts of Syria; many were massacred; great numbers died on the marches; their culture was erased; a few years later, in the Republic of Turkey, barely 10 percent of them remained. Morgenthau also alludes to the political context of this story: that the Young Turk Ottoman authorities believed or claimed to believe that they were acting out of "military necessity," to punish Armenians collectively for alleged or potential collaboration with Russian forces during World War I.

The evidence of this is so voluminous that even to say that there is a "dispute" is to stray into dubious moral relativism. Even Turkish foreign minister Ahmet Davutoğlu in December 2013 called the Armenian deportations "totally wrong" and "inhumane."[2] Only those who have not bothered to study the evidence or those with a Turkish nationalist agenda deny that in these years the Ottoman Armenians suffered a cruel destruction.

Why then is this issue still the subject of controversy? This is because of events that accumulated on top of it: several years of warfare in which both Armenians and Ottoman Muslims suffered grievously; the collapse of an Armenian state in 1920 and the formation of a new Turkish republic in defiance of the Great Powers in 1923; after 1945, a continuing confrontation shaped by Cold War politics and disputes over the application of the word "genocide"; and a wave of terrorism in the 1970s that reframed Armenians as mortal enemies of the Turkish state.

What follows in this chapter is not another history of the bloody events of 1915–1916, an issue to which serious academic historians have devoted decades of research. It is an attempt at a brief summary, intended for the non-specialist, of what occurred. This is followed in the next chapter by a discussion of the state of current historical scholarship on the issue; and in Chapter 3 by a study of the events that ended in 1923 with the founding of the Turkish Republic, to help frame the broader themes of this book: the memory and forgetting of an atrocity, Armenian-Turkish relations since 1923, and recent efforts to bridge the gap between the two peoples.

Almost every element of this has become highly politicized, even before we get to the use and abuse of the word "genocide," invented in the 1940s. Inevitably, a gruesome game of numbers looms over the issue of the Genocide. Politicized historians inflate and diminish the casualty figures, count and discount corpses, seeking to prove that greater or smaller numbers of Armenians died. Again, there are no big secrets here. During World War I, observers estimated that one million Armenians had been killed. The postwar Allied-backed Ottoman government of 1919 put the figure at 800,000, a number that Kemal Atatürk apparently accepted.[3] At the same time, hundreds of thousands of Ottoman Muslims died during World War I and the War of Independence—a number even harder to count because they were more often the victims of disease and hunger rather than targeted killing.

Where there is still scholarly debate about the Armenian Catastrophe, it is now, for the most part, over secondary issues: who in the government of the Committee of Union and Progress gave the orders and with what motive; whether this was a long-planned operation or one decided only in the context of war; whether all parts of the government approved of this action; what role the Kurds played in the destruction; how to characterize the Armenian uprising in Van in 1915; and how real was the Russian military threat.

The historical time frame and geographical limits also shape the perspective. There is disagreement as to when the story is determined to have begun and ended. Many Armenian historians write about a sequence of bloody events that begins in 1893 and ends in 1923 as one long continuum of genocide. More recent scholarship has contextualized the killings of 1915–1916 within a sequence of events in World War I. The story also comes out differently depending on whether you regard the events in the Caucasus and in Eastern Anatolia as being closely related or two separate zones of conflict.

This should not detract from—indeed it should only highlight—the fact that the mass destruction of the Ottoman Armenians by the Young Turk regime in 1915–1916 was probably the greatest mass atrocity of World War I. Ambassador Morgenthau (Figure 1.1) said in a cable in November 1915, "I am firmly convinced that this is the greatest crime of the ages."[4] Other contemporaries called it "the blackest page in modern history" or "the greatest crime of the war." But it is helpful to break down the historical narrative into two rough phases: one of 1915 into the middle of 1916, when most of the violence was committed against Armenians; and a second phase in which the Armenians had much greater agency in events.

Figure 1.1 Henry Morgenthau, Sr., US ambassador to the Ottoman Empire, 1913–1916.

Source: Library of Congress.

## The Armenians

Armenians had an ancient presence across an area that now spans eastern Turkey and the southern Caucasus. The central area of this is a highland region bounded by Lake Sevan in the east, Lake Van in the south, and the Black Sea in the north, where the Rivers Tigris and Euphrates begin their flow. It was often called the "Armenian Plateau" or "Western Armenia." To the east was an Armenian-populated territory that—with shifting borders—was incorporated into the Russian Empire in 1828, then became part of the Soviet Union, and now constitutes the independent Republic of Armenia. In the south, on the Mediterranean coast, numerous Armenians lived in the province they still call by its ancient name of Cilicia. From the eleventh to the fourteenth centuries, Armenians ruled over a kingdom of Cilicia with the support of European Crusaders.

Two features have distinguished the Armenians from earliest times. The first is their own Christian church. Armenians proudly declare that they are the "first Christian nation," the Armenian Apostolic Church having been founded in the year 301 or soon afterward. Thereafter, the Church, headed by the Catholicos of Echmiadzin, became the central focus of identity for scattered Armenians. A second defining moment was the creation of an Armenian alphabet in the year 406 by the monk Mesrop Mashtots. This gave the Armenians a strong written culture, which connected disparate communities and produced high rates of literacy. Armenian publishing houses in Venice and India were printing books and newspapers from the early seventeenth century.

Even in ancient times, the Armenian story was one of coexistence with other peoples. Armenian kings and princes generally ruled over satellite kingdoms under the higher protection of Byzantine, Ottoman, Persian, or Seljuk masters. The city of Ani exemplifies Armenians' high status in the early Middle Ages and their mingling with other nations. It is now a vast and gloomily atmospheric ruin on the Turkish side of the Turkey-Armenia border. At its zenith it had a population which rivaled that of Constantinople. Its kings belonged to the Bagratid dynasty, which had both an Armenian and Georgian identity. Byzantine kings and Seljuk princes also came here, and the oldest mosque in Anatolia is located inside the ruins.

First two, then three empires clashed in these borderlands. The Persians were the first imperial overlords of what is now the South Caucasus. From around the tenth century, the Turkic peoples who originally came from Central Asia became a dominant force in the region, establishing themselves as the Ottoman Empire in the thirteenth century. The Persians and Ottomans first drew an east-west line that divided Armenians in 1514.

In the early nineteenth century, the Russians defeated Persia, conquered the lands south of the Caucasus, and incorporated them into the tsarist empire. "Russian Armenians," living under a Christian empire, still suffered the indignities of colonial rule but had opportunities to prosper. In the nineteenth century, an Armenian mercantile class of traders and craftsmen ran the economy of the two main cities of the region, Baku and Tiflis (Tbilisi). However, in the tsarist province of Yerevan, which is now Armenia, Muslim Shiite Turks (Azerbaijanis) constituted a majority until the twentieth century, and the Armenians were more of a rural population.

Reflecting on life under Ottoman rule, many Armenian narratives now project back the tragic end of the Armenians in the empire onto the entire Ottoman period, depicting their experience as one of ceaseless oppression. A nationalist Turkish narrative, by contrast, portrays the Armenians as patriotic subjects (the Armenians were frequently termed "the loyal nation") until the work of a small group of traitors abruptly condemned them in the late nineteenth century.

A more nuanced picture suggests that for most of the Ottoman era, Armenians formed a distinct community that mostly lived in peace with its Muslim neighbors. Identity in the Ottoman Empire was defined by religious affiliation. Christians and Jews did not serve in the army or hold public office and had to pay special taxes. Yet Christians enjoyed more religious freedom under Ottoman rule than did Jews or Muslims in Christian Europe of the time. The Armenian religious community, or *millet*, had a high degree of self-rule and administered its own civil legal system.

As in the Russian Empire, Ottoman Armenians formed a skilled mercantile class. They were prominent craftsmen: blacksmiths, silversmiths, stonemasons, tailors, and cobblers—skills that were badly missed after 1915. A seventeenth-century Armenian alchemist, Avedis

Zildjian, won the favor of Sultan Osman II for devising a new alloy that gave a new bright sound to the percussion instrument, the cymbals. In the imperial capital, an upper class of Armenians (known in Armenian as *Bolsetsi*, the people of the *polis*, or the city) were close to the Ottoman elite. In the eighteenth and early nineteenth centuries, the Balian family were the chief palace architects of the Supreme Porte, the Dadians ran the Sultan's gunpowder factories, and the Duzians were keepers of the Sultan's jewels and superintendents of the imperial mint.[5]

Recent scholarship has highlighted ways in which Armenian and Ottoman culture blended together. For example, the Turkish scholar Murat Cankara has researched the forgotten phenomenon of the written language of Armeno-Turkish, or the Ottoman language written in the Armenian script. By the mid-nineteenth century, Bibles, newspapers, books, and the first Ottoman novel, *Akabi Hikayesi* (1851), were all being published in this curious language.

In the latter half of the nineteenth century, Armenian-Muslim tensions grew, as the Ottoman Empire modernized and, as in the Caucasus, some Armenians acquired economic capital, education, and the resentment of Muslims. Christian Europeans and Americans accentuated the divisions. Western Protestant missionaries were allowed to proselytize among Ottoman Christians, but not among Muslims. As a result, Armenians (as well as Greeks and Christian Arabs) enrolled in foreign elite Protestant schools and colleges, and many of them went on to take jobs as interpreters or business intermediaries.

This process fueled the stereotype of Armenians as devious traders, just as Jews were stereotyped in Eastern Europe. According to a late nineteenth-century American, "The Armenians are the Yankees of the Orient. They are the brightest, brainiest and smartest of all the people of Asia Minor. They are superior to the Jews or Greeks in business. The Turks say, "twist a Yankee and you make a Jew, twist a Jew and you make an Armenian."[6]

Throughout all these upheavals, the bulk of the Armenian population lived as they had always done in the old Armenian heartland in the east. These six *vilayets* of Bitlis, Diyarbakir, Erzerum, Mamuret-ul-Aziz (Harput), Sivas, and Van were the center of Armenian life, as well as Ottoman fears and Great Power interference. Most of the Armenians here were rural peasants and had little in common with their metro-politan cousins. The lives of these Armenian peasants became more precarious as they were caught in land disputes with their Muslim neighbors and refugees from lost Ottoman provinces. These were the people on behalf of whom European politicians and Armenian revo-lutionaries claimed to speak, but whose own voices were rarely heard.

## Great Power Games

From the last quarter of the nineteenth century, the machinations of the European "Great Powers," the six Christian powers of Austria-Hungary, France, Germany, Great Britain, Italy, and Russia, become central to Armenian-Muslim relations. Russia was the nearest and most force-ful power. From the late eighteenth century until 1918, Russians and Ottomans fought around a dozen wars in the Black Sea region. Each time, both empires deported thousands of Christians and Muslims to the territory of the other. Russia's wholesale deportation and massacre of the Circassians in the northwest Caucasus in the 1860s and 1870s prefigures the Armenian deportations 50 years later and has also, with good reason, been termed a "genocide." The Circassians and refugees who fled the Balkans were called *muhajirs* and later became another deadly factor in the Armenian Genocide.

At the Congress of Berlin of 1878, the Great Powers acquired new leverage over the Ottoman Empire, on paper at least. Russia took over the Ottoman provinces of Ardahan, Batum, and Kars. Article 61 of the Treaty of Berlin obligated the Ottoman authorities to undertake reforms in the eastern provinces to protect Armenians on pain of Great Power intervention. This emboldened the Armenians, while keeping them dangerously dependent on the whims of the outside powers and their rivalries.

The Armenians were promised a lot and believed too much. Some Europeans, such as British prime minister William Gladstone, sup-ported them out of Christian solidarity. Others merely used them as an instrument of control against the Ottoman Empire. Some nineteenth-century European travelers' accounts harbor prejudices against Armenians and Greeks, saying that they are in fact "not like us"—or are even worse than their Muslim neighbors! Here is the

British traveler Robert Curzon writing in the 1850s: "The superiority of the Mahometan over the Christian cannot fail to strike the mind of an intelligent person who has lived among these races . . . the Turk does not drink, the Christian gets drunk; the Turk is honest; the Christian is a liar and a cheat; his religion is so overgrown with the rank weeds of superstition that it no longer serves to guide his mind."[7]

### Revolutionaries and Massacres

At the end of the nineteenth century, Armenians began to mobilize. In 1890, eastern Armenians in Tiflis founded the Armenian Revolutionary Federation party, or ARF, also known by the Armenian name Dashnaktsutiun (Federation), or as the Dashnaks. The new party was secular in outlook and had no respect for the Armenian Apostolic Church. It operated in both the Russian and Ottoman empires. The ARF was actually the second Armenian revolutionary party, the socialist Hunchakian (Bell) Party having been formed three years earlier, but it soon eclipsed its rival. In the eastern Ottoman provinces, the ARF formed armed units known as *fedayee* to fight back against violence from Muslims. On the Russian side of the border, they armed Armenians in Baku and Tiflis. Fairly soon, the party would lay claim to being the sole representative of Armenian national politics—a contention that would split the Armenian community for the entire twentieth century.

In 1876, Sultan Abdülhamid II came to the Ottoman throne. His main obsession was with holding the empire together. As the Christian nations of the Balkans broke away, he accused the Armenians of plotting to truncate his state even further. The sultan commented, "By taking away Greece and Rumania, Europe has cut of the feet of the Turkish state. The loss of Bulgaria, Serbia and Egypt has deprived us of our hands, and now by means of this Armenian agitation they want to get at our most vital places and tear out our very guts. This would be the beginning of totally annihilating us, and we must fight against it with all the strength we possess."[8]

In 1891, Abdülhamid co-opted lawless Kurdish chieftains to form cavalry regiments, named Hamidiye after himself, to secure the borders and suppress Armenian revolutionaries. In 1894, these paramilitary forces massacred Armenians, in a much more savage version of Cossack pogroms against Jews in the Russian Empire during the same period.

The killings continued for two years. In one notorious episode, Armenians took refuge in a church in the town of Urfa, and 1,500 of them were burned alive in it.[9] The American missionary Caleb Gates—whose memoirs tell an extraordinary story of 50 years in Turkey—was the head of the American Euphrates College in the town of Harput. In 1895, he and his colleagues sheltered hundreds of Armenians from what looked like an organized mob of Kurds and Turks, summoned at the sound of a bugle to burn, loot, and kill. Gates writes, "We could not resist the conviction that the massacres were intended to nullify the reforms in the six provinces by destroying those in whose behalf they were projected, especially as these massacres were perpetrated under orders coming from Constantinople."[10]

The American also accused the new Armenian revolutionaries of helping to instigate the bloodshed. Gates relates that Armenian militants demanded the keys to his college printing press in Harput on the threat of violence.

> It was this element which constituted the greatest danger to the Armenians. They were few in number but they had no scruples, counting as lawful all means by which they might attain their ends. They terrorized the better part of the community into silence when they could not secure their support. These acts enraged the Turkish population and increased the danger of massacre.[11]

The German pastor Johannes Lepsius estimated that, over the two years of the "Hamidian massacres," 88,000 Armenians were killed and 546,000 were left destitute.[12] Mass forced conversions to Islam were also carried out. Some Armenian historians have drawn a direct line of connection between these killings and the 1915 Genocide and clearly they set a precedent of both massacre and impunity. More recently, however, scholars have pointed up the differences between the two, portraying the killings of 1890s as a campaign with very different objectives: to subjugate the Armenians within the empire, rather than get rid of them altogether.

As in 1915, the massacres stirred up angry denunciations in Europe—but also underlined how little the outside powers would actually do. In November 1895, Gladstone, spokesman for oppressed Christians in Ottoman lands, complained that the Great Powers of

Europe "lie prostrate at the feet of the impotent Sultan of Turkey who, with their cognizance, appears to prosecute massacres at his will from day to day."[13]

The violence also widened divisions between the revolutionaries of the Dashnaktsutiun and the old Armenian establishment. The clergy, the Constantinople upper class, and much of the merchant classes were still invested in the maintenance and reform of the Ottoman system. The revolutionaries, whose leadership predominantly came from Russian Armenia, believed that the only strategy was to copy the tactics of Russian and Balkan militants and to force change by violent action. The revolutionaries targeted and killed Armenian "traitors" as well as imperial officials. ARF Dashnak assassins even twice attempted to assassinate the Armenian Patriarch of Constantinople, in 1894 and 1903.

In August 1896, the ARF staged its most famous operation. Twenty-four young radicals seized the grand building of the Imperial Ottoman Bank near the Galata Bridge in Constantinople at gunpoint. After a gun battle, they took 150 hostages and demanded autonomy for the six eastern provinces. After European diplomatic intervention, the 14 surviving hostage-takers were allowed safe passage out of the city on the yacht of the British director of the bank. Thousands of ordinary Armenians in the imperial capital were not so lucky and died in pogroms at the hands of local Muslims.

A song reputedly composed by one of the Ottoman Bank raiders celebrates their daredevil heroism—and explains why the Ottoman authorities had reason to feel paranoid about the *gavurs* (Christians). Each verse is sung in Turkish until the last lines, here rendered in parentheses, when the singer switches into Armenian to admit his rebel sympathies in his own language:

> "Hey, *gavur*, tell the truth!
> Did you attack the Bank?"
> "No, sir, it's a slander,
> I don't know, I haven't seen,
> I don't know, I haven't seen."
> (We did that, I won't tell,
> I won't betray the Armenian nation).[14]

## The Deportations

For most of the Ottoman period, the name "Turk" had a somewhat derogatory meaning in comparison to the more cultivated term
"Ottoman." This began to change in the last quarter of the nineteenth
century. A group of Muslim intellectuals, reacting to the Christian
nationalism all around them, outlined a different ideology, which for
the first time took pride in a definition of "Turkishness." They despaired
of the moribund Ottoman state and espoused instead a modernizing
nationalism through which the Turks could gain equality with Europe
while maintaining their distinct culture. A generation of junior officers, mostly in the Ottoman Third Army in the Balkans, was inspired
by this new nationalist movement. They formed the Committee of
Union and Progress (*İttihat ve Terakki Cemiyeti*), often referred to as
the Unionists, or Ittihadists.

In 1908, the junior Ottoman officers seized power in the Young
Turk Revolution, forcing Sultan Abdülhamid to renounce autocracy.
Different ethnic groups rejoiced in the constitutional coup, among
them the Armenian revolutionaries of the Dashnaktsutiun. Six
Armenian deputies were elected to the new multi-ethnic parliament.
The new Young Turk authorities allowed their Armenian allies to
invite Armenian revolutionaries from Russia to base themselves in
Constantinople and organize their plots against the tsarist regime
from there.[15]

Gradually, the nationalist coloring of the revolution submerged
notions of multi-ethnic parliamentarism. In March 1909, an attempted
counter-coup on behalf of the sultan failed. The factional fighting was probably the proximate cause of another outbreak of mass
anti-Armenian bloodshed in the Cilician town of Adana a few days later.
No one took responsibility as local Muslims went on the rampage, looting and killing as many as 20,000 local Armenians. A smaller number
of Muslims was also killed. A cover-up and a few token prosecutions
followed.

Crucially, the new Young Turk regime failed to halt the disintegra-
tion of the empire. The two Balkan wars of 1912 and 1913 delivered both
a psychological and a physical shock to the new authorities as they lost
regions that had been core parts of the empire for 500 years. Hundreds

of thousands of more Muslim *muhajirs* fled and were resettled in the Anatolian heartlands.

In the midst of this turmoil, in January 1913, the three most radical Young Turks seized power in another coup d'état. The empire came under the control of a triumvirate, who would come to be known as "the Three Pashas," Enver, Cemal, and Talat. All of them were young, came from Ottoman European lands, and shared the ambition to reshape and modernize the empire by any means possible. On October 28, 1914, the three Young Turk pashas took the Ottoman Empire into World War I, in alliance with Germany and against the age-old enemy, the Russian Empire. This was the final fateful trigger for both the end of the empire and the destruction of the Armenians.

Eastern Anatolia and the six "Armenian provinces" were now a front line. Armenians there formed a plurality in many areas, but nowhere a clear majority. The French historian Raymond Kévorkian, drawing on a census taken by the Armenian Patriarchate in 1913, estimates the number of Ottoman Armenians as 1,914,620, about half of whom—just under one million—were living in the six eastern provinces.[16] Further east in Hakkari and around Lake Urmia in Iran lived about 150,000 Christian Assyrians who belonged to several ancient churches.

In these eastern provinces, tensions were strong between the two main national groups, Armenians and Kurds, who lived at the opposite poles of the socioeconomic scale. Kurds suffered from appalling levels of poverty and child mortality, and the eye disease trachoma was so widespread that it was rare to meet adult Kurds with healthy eyes. Many Kurds were still nomadic pastoralists, who felt closer to Assyrians than Armenians. A proverb said, "Between us [Kurds and Assyrians], there is but a hair's breadth, but between us and the Armenians a mountain."[17]

As war broke out in 1914, tens of thousands of Armenian men were fighting in the Ottoman army, but many Ottoman Armenians were not so secretly supportive of "Uncle Christian" (Russia). More than 150,000 eastern Armenians were fighting for the imperial Russian army. In late 1914, the departing Russian consul in Erzerum, A. A. Adamov, reported on a tour he had made of surrounding towns and villages, which had convinced him of Armenian support for a coming Russian invasion:

The Armenian population . . . is waiting impatiently for the arrival of Russian forces and their liberation from the Turkish yoke. They will hardly risk to stage an uprising before Russian forces arrive on their doorstep, fearing that the smallest delay of Russian assistance will lead to their complete destruction, because, even though they still have weapons hidden in various secret locations, they will not dare to take it because of the state of war proclaimed in the country and the threat of imminent massacres.[18]

At the end of 1914, Minister of War Enver Pasha led a big military push into the Caucasus and encountered immediate and near total disaster. Perhaps half of his entire Third Army, comprising 90,000 men, was wiped out by the Russians and the extreme winter weather at the Battle of Sarikamiş. In the wake of the Russian military success, in February 1915, Enver ordered that non-Muslims in the army (numbering over 200,000) should be disarmed and re-drafted into labor battalions. (Those Armenian men who did not manage to desert were later killed en masse.)

The Ottoman regime faced collapse in both the east and the west. In April 1915, an allied force from the countries of the British Empire and France attacked the Dardanelles and landed at Gallipoli, threatening the Ottoman regime and its capital city. In the third week of April, Dashnak Armenian revolutionaries, anticipating a Russian invasion, seized control of the town of Van. There was heavy destruction in the city and massacres on both sides. The Armenians held the town until the end of May, when the Russians arrived, driving the Muslim population into flight. Many Muslim villages were destroyed. When the Ottoman army recaptured the city in August, it meted out savage reprisals against the remaining Armenians. The April 1915 battle was a pivotal episode, which is interpreted very differently in Armenian and Turkish histories. It is called both a "rebellion" by Armenian insurgents against the Ottoman state order and a heroic act of "resistance" by desperate Armenians against a repressive government that intended to kill them. Clearly, it had elements of both.

Armenians were now subjected to collective punishment. Minister of the Interior Talat Pasha (Figure 1.2) had issued the first orders to deport Anatolian Armenians in February 1915. With the Gallipoli landings and

Figure 1.2 Talat Pasha, Ottoman Unionist leader and main author of the Armenian deportations, in exile in Germany.
Source: Library of Congress.

the battle over Van, the policy became more radical. On April 24—a day later commemorated as a day of Armenian mourning—250 Armenian leaders in the imperial capital were arrested. They included writers, churchmen, members of parliament, and the composer Komitas. The men were then exiled to the Anatolian interior, and most were later murdered. On the same day came the first explicit orders for deportation of Armenians to the most arid and wild part of the Ottoman Empire—the Syrian desert around the town of Der Zor.

Repeating a depressingly familiar pattern, Great Power rhetorical interventions only made matters worse. In what has been called a "legendary diplomatic démarche," on May 24, 1915, Great Britain, France, and Russia denounced the crimes against the Armenians, using for the first time the formulation "crimes against humanity." The three powers warned, "[i]n view of these new crimes of Turkey against humanity and civilization, the allied Governments announce publicly to the Supreme Porte that they will hold personally responsible [for] these crimes all members of the Ottoman Government and those of their agents who are implicated in such massacres."[19]

Following this statement, the deportations of Armenians escalated in both scale and brutality. On June 9, the interior ministry told the governor of Erzerum to put the property of the deported Erzerum Armenians up for auction—they would not return. On June 21, Talat Pasha ordered the deportation of "all Armenians without exception" from the ten eastern Ottoman provinces.[20]

The orders nominally exempted Protestants and Catholics, single women, and orphaned children, but most of them were in fact also expelled.[21] Few Armenians were deported from the three western cities of Constantinople, Izmir, and Edirne, perhaps because they were directly under the gaze of European observers and because of disagreements within the Unionist leadership.[22]

In the summer of 1915, the vast majority of the remaining Armenian population was ordered from their homes with only what they could carry. Large numbers of the men did not get far. Armed men from the Special Organization (*Teşkilatı Mahsusa*) paramilitary unit carried out most of the summary executions. The elderly, women, and children were sent in convoys, mostly on foot, toward the Syrian desert. On July 13, Talat Pasha declared that the deportations had achieved "the definitive solution to the Armenian Question."[23]

The Christian Assyrians of the Ottoman-Iranian borderlands suffered a similar fate in a lesser-known tragedy. In the spring of 1915, Halil Pasha, the uncle of war minister Enver Pasha, led a military force into these highlands. Like the Armenians, the Assyrians were accused of collaboration with the Russian army. In March 1915, a Russian consul saw evidence in the village of Haftevan of the "first planned mass execution of noncombatants committed by the Ottoman army."[24] David Gaunt, the historian of this campaign, writes that "the expulsion of the Assyrians from Hakkari took the form of genocide under the guise of counterinsurgency."[25] Perhaps 300,000 Assyrians were killed. Their terrible story, which they commemorate as the Seyfo, has been much less recorded than that of the Armenian Genocide. In part this is because the operation was all too successful and the survivors struggled to rebuild a community; in part it is because the term "Assyrian" covers several different ethnic groups, who belonged to small ancient Christian churches.

The last phase of the murderous campaign against the Armenians occurred in the Syrian desert. In September 1916, Jesse Jackson, US consul in Aleppo, wrote in a cable:

> The impression which this immense and dismal plain of Meskene leaves is sad and pitiable. Information obtained on the spot permits me to state that nearly 60,000 Armenians are buried there, carried off by hunger, by privations of all sorts, by intestinal diseases and typhus which is the result. As far as the eye can reach mounds are seen containing 200 to 300 corpses buried in the ground pele mele, women, children and old people belonging to different families.
>
> At present nearly 4,500 Armenians are kept between the town of Meskene and the Euphrates. These are but living fantoms. Their superintendents distribute to them sparingly and very irregularly a piece of bread. Sometimes three or four days pass when these famished people who have nothing to eat but this piece of bread, receive absolutely nothing.
>
> A dreadful dysentery makes numerous victims among them, especially among the children.[26]

The flotsam of the marches, mostly women and children, barely survived in rudimentary camps. Many were simply "mopped up" and killed by the brutal local commander, Zeki-Bey. Perhaps 150,000 Armenians died at two points in a triangle in Syria between Der Zor, Ras ul-Ain, and Mosul.[27]

Even before it was all over, observers were counting the dead. Serious estimates of the number of Armenians killed in this period begin at around 600,000. One of the three Unionist leaders, Cemal Pasha, wrote in his memoirs, published in 1922, "Let us assume that the Ottoman Government deported a million and a half Armenians from the East Anatolian Provinces, and that 600,000 of them died, some murdered, some collapsing on the way from hunger and distress."[28] As noted above, the Ottoman government of 1919 said that 800,000 had died. In 1920, Sebuh Aguni, a former Armenian newspaper editor published a substantial book, *Documented History of the*

*Massacre of One Million Armenians*, whose title gives his estimate of casualties. This figure of around one million dead is used by many historians. Armenians officially cite the number of 1.5 million—a figure that includes Armenian deaths up until 1923. This seems to be a high number, unless one includes all Armenian deaths from all causes, such as disease and malnutrition, during this period. Michael Mann concludes that "only about 10 per cent of the Armenians living in Turkey in 1914 remained in the country in 1922—the most successful murderous cleansing achieved in the 20th century."[29]

## Armenians' Experience

What did Ottoman Armenians experience in 1915? We have plenty of firsthand accounts.

First of all, there are hundreds of oral histories and memoirs of those who knew more than anyone—those who actually endured the Genocide. It goes without saying that oral histories are subjectively framed, but they all share essential details, which confirm their basic authenticity. Second, we have diplomatic reports from the time of the many consuls stationed in Anatolia and the Middle East, from neutral countries not involved in the war at that time, such as the United States, Denmark, and Sweden, as well as the main Ottoman ally, Germany. Third, we have the accounts of contemporary witnesses. Many of them are by Protestant missionaries, who had lived in the towns of Anatolia for years and knew the locals extremely well. While many display certain anti-Muslim prejudices (leading them to be dismissed by some Turkish scholars), they are mostly very scrupulous, containing names, dates, and local details. A vivid *sui generis* account comes from Rafael de Nogales, a Venezuelan soldier of fortune who was serving as a high-ranking officer in the Ottoman Army in the crucial months of the Armenian deportations.

These sources tell us that almost all Armenians shared one universal experience—deportation—but in different ways. As noted above, most Armenians in the cities of Constantinople (with the exception of the intellectual elite), Edirne (Adrianople), and Smyrna survived the war. All Armenians east of here, beginning with the town of Izmit, not far from the capital, were either killed or deported east on the long trek to

Syria. Many of the Armenians in western towns were allowed to travel initially by train—although they were forced to pay for the privilege and then were made to walk. All the deportees in the eastern provinces were forced to walk.

First, livelihoods and fortunes built up over years had to be abandoned in a few hours. In his memoir, Hagop Arsenian, a pharmacist from Izmit writes, "On Saturday, July 25, all the goods and furniture of the Armenians were displayed on the sidewalks for sale. But who was going to buy? All of them knew that they would be able to lay their hands on these items for free the next day, without paying a piaster. Some of the Turks, out of pity, offered to buy some items for one tenth of the price of the object. Poor Armenians, our lifetime achievements and investments were in one day left to the full enjoyment of the Turks."[30]

Arsenian survived. Most Armenian men did not. The Venezuelan officer, Rafael de Nogales, recounts meeting one local official outside Van in April 1915 who "astounded me by replying that he was doing nothing more than carry out an unequivocal order emanating from the Governor-General of the province . . . to exterminate all Armenian males of twelve years of age and over."[31]

Harput, in the highlands right in the center of Eastern Anatolia, was dubbed "the slaughterhouse province." Henry Riggs, the Protestant pastor in the town, writes in his memoir that the local governor put to death thousands of Armenian men who had arrived in convoys from elsewhere: "Some of the convoys from Erzroum and Erzingian arrived in Harpoot in comparative safety, a large percentage of men being among them. But the most reliable information that we could gather showed that the men very seldom left the province alive. Once inside of [Governor or Vali] Sabit Bey's jurisdiction, the Armenian men were marked for violent death."[32]

Two other Americans in Harput, the US consul Leslie Davis and Dr. Herbert Atkinson, went in October 1915 to investigate reports of massacres committed by the shores of Lake Goeljuk [or Golcuk, today Lake Hazar], southeast of the town. They photographed what they saw and estimated that they saw the bodies of 10,000 Armenians, including women and children, around the lake. Two thousand of the dead were in one spot right on the lakeshore. Davis later wrote:

The valley was large and bodies were strewn all over it. Most of them had been buried, but the sand that covered them had since blown away leaving them partially exposed to view. There were also the remains of camp fires and of the personal effects of the exiles, such as they had,—a few broken jugs, a few earthen bowls, some wooden spoons, and quite a number of passports. The latter upon examination showed that the people were from Erzerum and other places. There was no clothing except an occasional sock, and nothing of any value. Everything of value had, of course, been taken by the gendarmes and Kurds. The bodies were all naked, the people having been made to remove their clothing before they were killed.[33]

Grigoris Balakian, a senior priest, had been arrested in the imperial capital on April 24. While many of his comrades were later killed, he was ordered to join the deportations in Syria, meaning that in the spring of 1916, he traveled under escort through Anatolia in regions already depopulated of Armenians. There he saw the aftermath of massacres:

On all the roads we traversed between Yozgat and Kayseri, about 80 per cent of the Muslims we encountered (there were no Christians left in these parts) were wearing European clothes, bearing on their persons proof of the crimes they had committed. Indeed, it was an absurd sight: overcoats, frock coats, jackets—various men's and women's European garments of the finest materials—on villagers who were also wearing sandals and traditional baggy pants [shalvars]. Barefoot Turkish peasant boys wore formal clothes; men sported gold chains and watches. It was reported that the women had confiscated many pieces of diamond jewelry, but [as they were sequestered] we had no way of encountering them.[34]

### The Deportation Convoys

The majority of those on the Armenian deportation convoys were women and children. Their journeys could end fatally in numerous ways. There was almost no provision to feed or resettle them. Hunger, thirst, and disease claimed many victims. The "gendarmes" who escorted the convoys had the power of life and death over the deportees.

Some could be kind, but most of the oral histories describe gendarmes who prohibited their charges from drinking at water sources or who harassed and killed them.

One American missionary, Mary Graffam, walked with some of her Protestant flock from the town of Sivas and later described her experience.

> As far as the eye could see over the plain was this slow-moving line of ox-carts. For hours there was not a drop of water on the road, and the sun poured down its very hottest. As we went on we began to see the dead from yesterday's company, and the weak began to fall by the way. The Kurds working in the fields made attacks continually, and we were half-distracted. I piled as many as I could on our wagons, and our pupils, both boys and girls, worked like heroes. One girl took a baby from its dead mother and carried it until evening. Another carried a dying woman until she died. We bought water from the Kurds, not minding the beating that the boys were sure to get with it. I counted forty-nine deaths, but there must have been many more.[35]

Women faced the perpetual threat of rape. Henry Riggs writes of a convoy of women from his town:

> Left with absolutely no protection, at the mercy of those brutal gendarmes, many of them criminals of the worst type, the women and children were driven along with such rigor that many perished from sheer exhaustion within the first few days. Of the treatment received by the younger and more vigorous women at the hands of men whose unbridled lust was no longer restrained by any fear of justice, no detailed account need be attempted. The fact of so many suicides at the [Euphrates] River is perhaps sufficient comment, though the women who escaped from other convoys and came to us for relief told of their own experiences of those nightly orgies in shocking detail.[36]

All the eyewitnesses also tell stories of women and children being selected by local Muslims, taken into their households and converted to Islam. The abductors had different motives: some wanted to save lives, others were seeking sexual enslavement. Henry Riggs notes: "Some of the girls who thus entered Turkish families were treated fairly kindly and seemed to adapt themselves to the unnatural life. But others suffered indescribably, and some lost their minds."[37] Some of these young women and children were reclaimed after the Ottoman defeat in the war; others stayed with their Muslim families. Thereafter their story again disappeared from the records, only to resurface in very recent times.

Many of those who survived stressed that they did so due to Muslim families like these, or else to the bravery of ordinary "good Turks," and also Kurds, who protected Armenians. For example, a survivor from Adana said, "We were like brothers. Our Turks said later, 'Whoever was the cause of this genocide, may God blind his eyes.' They did not wish our death. In fact if it weren't for these good Turks, we would all have been killed, too. All the orders came from Istanbul."[38]

Henry Riggs praises "the real generosity and courage of the Turks who did, first and last, save the lives of quite a number of Armenian men,"[39] and tells the story of a Turkish businessman in Harput who saved his business partner at great risk to his own safety.

Survival often came at an unbelievably high price. Some of the most painful sections of the deportation stories are those that describe the moment when parents and children were separated, usually forever. One child survivor relates:

> About this time, Turkish or Kurdish women would come and take children away. They approached my mother, too. Realizing that there was nothing but death facing us at that point, she gave me to them. . . . She said to me that we will come later and join you. So these two women held my hand and took me away. . . . I kept look- ing back and wondering how I could let go of their hands and run back. So I kept walking—with my eyes and heart behind me.[40]

## Der Zor

The final part of the deportation story occurs in the Syrian desert. Here there were almost no foreign observers. The narratives get sketchier, although the ones we do have are among the most awful. Hagop Arsenian, who had the small advantage of having traveled the first part of the journey by train and having kept some of his money, reached this stage of the journey in December 1915. He writes:

> Alongside the long and narrow paths, we sometimes came across poor old people who, unable to *carry their own crosses* anymore, sat and waited for salvation. But each one of us had their own personal cross to himself and his immediate family. I saw children abandoned by their parents who could no longer carry the additional weights. I saw very sick people lying along the sides of the road, waiting for the salvation of death.[41]

Many who made it to the desert are described as being barefoot, with few clothes, parched from heat and thirst and covered in lice. One survivor recalls seeing desperate children trying to eat the carcass of a dead camel.[42]

The end of the road was the arid province of Der Zor. There are few histories of the reported mass killings here in the summer of 1916. In the documentary *The River Ran Red*, the filmmaker J. Michael Hagopian tracked down three elderly Arabs, all of whom said they were originally abandoned Armenian children taken in by local families. One of them describes surviving a massacre in an underground cave in the Sheddeh desert, which was set on fire and in which hundreds of women and children were burned or asphyxiated.[43] This episode, or one very similar, is described in a Turkish-language lament of Der Zor in dozens of verses recorded in the 1950s in Soviet Armenia by Verjine Svazlian:

> They dismantled the tents on Zatik-Kiraki [Easter Sunday],
> They drove all the Armenians into the desert,
> They slaughtered the Armenians like goats,
> Armenians dying for the sake of faith!
>
> Green grass did not grow in the desert of Der-Zor,
> My hair grew white, my teeth fell down,
> Oh mother! Oh mother! Our state was terrible,
> When we were in the desert of Der-Zor.

Green grass did not grow in the desert of Der-Zor,
Fifty thousand people were shot down,
The people's teeth fell down from affliction,
Armenians dying for the sake of faith!

Green grass did not grow in the desert of Der-Zor,
My pretty sister fell into the fire,
Fathers and mothers were taken prisoner,
They drove the Armenian nation to the mountains.

They gathered the Armenians in a cave,
They covered them with lime, set fire and burned them,
Oh mother! Oh mother! Our state was terrible,
When we were in the desert of Der-Zor![44]

For Armenians, the name Der Zor represents a nadir of their experience, a kind of black hole in which one life ended and—only if you
were a lucky survivor—another barely began.

# 2

——◦◦◦◦◦——

# The History

THE *WHAT* OF THE Armenian deportations and massacres of 1915–1916 should be clear from the preceding stories. The *why*—the historical analysis of the causes of the tragedy and the intentions of the perpetrators—is more open to interpretation.

English-language accounts of what had happened to the Armenians were published almost contemporaneously. The facts were well established, but the wartime context and Turcophobic prejudices of the era often make for awkward reading.

This context colored the famous "Blue Book" of Viscount Bryce and Arnold Toynbee, officially entitled *The Treatment of Armenians in the Ottoman Empire*, which was published in 1916 by the British Parliament. It is an exhaustive collection of eyewitness accounts of atrocities against Armenians and Assyrians in Anatolia, compiled soon after the events. Its most recent editor, Ara Sarafian, has filled in the names of many of the anonymous sources, many of them American consuls and missionaries, in the book. As such, it is a collection of detailed eyewitness reports published very soon after the events.

The main author, Arnold Toynbee himself, later identified the problem with the book as being its publisher, rather than its contents, since as an official publication of a wartime foe of the Ottoman Empire, it was "distributed as war-propaganda." Toynbee saw that the Great Powers were eager to use the Armenians' suffering to pursue their own imperial interests.[1]

Much of the literature of the time seeks a crude narrative of Christian martyrdom or the cheap thrill of barbaric atrocities. Western press articles of 1915 and 1916 wallowed in stories of "blood-curdling horrors" and "unparalleled savagery" committed against Christians. On December 19, 1915, for example, the *Washington Herald* published the story "The Massacre of a Nation," subtitled "All of the Horrors, Tortures and Barbarities of History Surpassed in List of Cruelties Practiced by Turks on Defenseless Armenians," which describes how "[w]omen have suffered all the degradations that barbaric man could heap upon them."[2]

This early literature also groups together World War I atrocities by Germans and Turks to make them doubly complicit. A 1918 polemic by the well-known British writer E. F. Benson, *Crescent and Iron Cross*, contains a chapter entitled "Deutschland über Allah," in which the author writes, "So, in support of the Pan-Turkish ideal, and in the name of the Turkish Allah, the God of Love, Germany stood by and let the infamous tale of lust and rapine and murder be told to its end."[3]

A 71-page pamphlet entitled *The Blackest Page of Modern History*, by the American author Herbert Adams Gibbons, written at the end of 1915, is more reasoned. While also pointing the finger at Germany, Gibbons chiefly blames the Unionist leadership, rather than ordinary Turks: "The extermination of a million and a half innocent, loyal to a fault, Christian subjects of the Sultan of Turkey was planned at, and ordered from, Constantinople."[4]

The first substantial analysis of the Armenian deportations came with the publication in 1918 of the memoirs of the US ambassador to the Ottoman Empire from 1913 to 1916, Henry Morgenthau. As the ambassador of a neutral nation, who moreover was Jewish rather than Christian, Morgenthau is less open to the charge of having a political agenda. Although he shares with the reader some old-fashioned prejudices about "the Turk," he mainly represents himself as the voice of American diplomacy dealing with a difficult revolutionary government. The most revealing passages are his records of many meetings with the Unionist leaders, Talat Pasha and Enver Pasha. He writes, "When the Turkish authorities gave the orders for these deportations,

they were merely giving the death warrant to a whole race; they understood this well, and in their conversations with me, they made no particular attempt to conceal the fact."[5]

As for their motives, Morgenthau gives us an explanation straight
from the horse's mouth. In August 1915, the ambassador called on Talat
Pasha for a frank discussion of the Armenian question. Importantly, it
was translated by Talat's own interpreter, not, as before, by Morgenthau's
Armenian assistant.

> "I have asked you to come to-day," began Talat, "so that I can explain
> our position on the whole Armenian subject. We base our objections
> to the Armenians on three distinct grounds. In the first place, they
> have enriched themselves at the expense of the Turks. In the second
> place, they are determined to domineer over us and to establish a
> separate state. In the third place, they have openly encouraged our
> enemies. They have assisted the Russians in the Caucasus and our
> failure there is largely explained by their actions. We have therefore
> come to the irrevocable decision that we shall make them powerless
> before this war is ended."

Morgenthau writes that he "had plenty of arguments in rebuttal" to
these claims, but was cut short.

> "It is no use for you to argue," Talat answered, "we have already dis-
> posed of three quarters of the Armenians; there are none at all left
> in Bitlis, Van, and Erzeroum. The hatred between the Turks and the
> Armenians is now so intense that we have got to finish with them. If
> we don't, they will plan their revenge."[6]

In Morgenthau's telling, Talat, in his own words, identifies the
Armenians both as a troublesome economic class and as a fifth column
of the Russians, and says he has decided to solve the "Armenian question" by eliminating the Armenians altogether.

The evidence the ambassador's memoir gives is so damning that in
1990—at the height of the propaganda battles over genocide resolutions in the United States—Heath Lowry, then head of the Institute
of the Turkish Studies in Washington, published a book alleging that

Morgenthau was a biased witness who had exaggerated his level of access to Talat and Enver. On his return to the United States, Morgenthau certainly became a passionate advocate for the Armenian cause. But it is more logical to conclude that this flowed from his experiences as ambassador than that he approached the issue with a preformed bias. It is also true that his book, which was written in collaboration with a Pulitzer Prize–winning journalist, contains long passages of verbatim conversation, which it is hard to believe are fully accurate. These apparent journalistic embellishments aside, most of what Morgenthau writes is corroborated by his official cables of the time, as well as those of his consuls, and by his own private papers.

Contemporaries confirm that Morgenthau did have privileged access to the Young Turk leadership. Caleb Gates, who had become president of Robert College in Constantinople in 1903, writes that Morgenthau's "decision to retire was particularly regrettable because he had gained the confidence of the Turkish government and had a prestige which no new man could at once command." Gates describes going riding with Morgenthau, Talat, and Enver in the Belgrade Forest outside the city, and he relates how Enver showed off his marksmanship by shooting at a visiting card that one of his men had pinned on a tree.[7] Morgenthau's papers also contain a letter written in French by Talat, gracefully accepting an invitation to dinner that evening and offering compliments to "Madame Morgenthau" (Figure 2.1). The date is a fateful one—the day of the Armenian arrests in Constantinople, April 24, 1915.

### Early Histories

In the 1920s, when interest in the story of the Armenians was still strong, a spate of memoirs came out by eye-witnesses and actors in the drama. Thereafter, the Armenian question fell into a kind of historical abyss in which the earlier collective knowledge was mostly forgotten. For 40 years, apart from small-edition memoirs by Armenian survivors, there was a big gap in the mainstream Western literature until 1977, when French historian Yves Ternon published a full-length book.

In the 1970s, the "Armenian question" revived as a political topic with the outbreak of Armenian terrorism and became, if anything, even more politicized than before. Two oversimplified narratives became

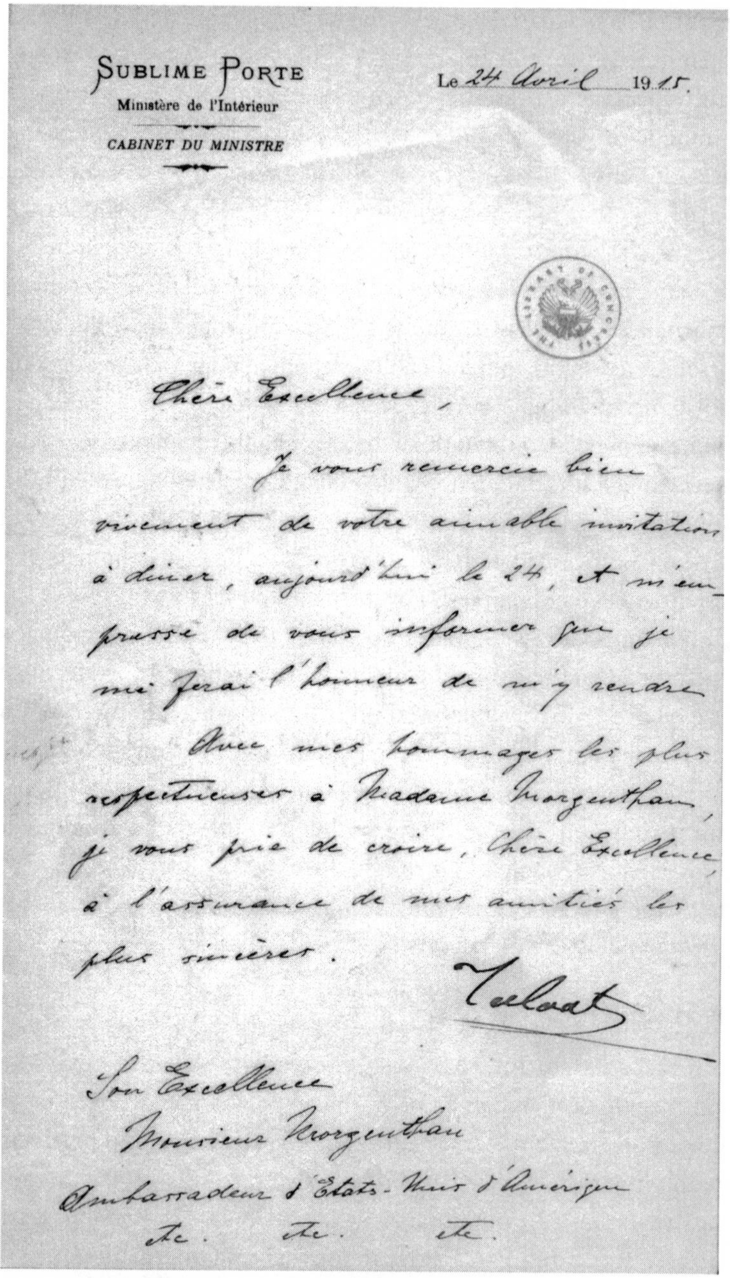

SUBLIME PORTE

Ministère de l'Intérieur

CABINET DU MINISTRE

Le 24 Avril 19 15.

Chère Excellence,

Je vous remercie bien vivement de votre aimable invitation à dîner, aujourd'hui le 24, et m'empresse de vous informer que je me ferai l'honneur de m'y rendre

Avec mes hommages les plus respectueuses à Madame Morgenthau, je vous prie de croire, Chère Excellence à l'assurance de mes amitiés les plus sincères.

Talaat

Son Excellence
Monsieur Morgenthau
Ambassadeur d'États-Unis d'Amérique
&c. &c. &c.

Figure 2.1 Talat accepts Ambassador Morgenthau's invitation to dinner, April 24, 1915.

Source: Morgenthau Papers, Library of Congress.

dominant. An Armenian one, apparently modeling the Genocide on the Holocaust, took root, containing Turkish perpetrators, passive Armenian victims, and indifferent Great Power bystanders. A crude Turkish counter-narrative was revived that portrayed the events of 1915 as a conflict with two "sides," provoked by Armenian revolutionaries, who had plotted to break up the Ottoman Empire with the assistance of their foreign patrons.

The biggest hitter in this debate was Armenian historian Vahakn Dadrian. Dadrian was born in Turkey in 1926, much of his family having been killed in the deportations. He studied in Germany and then moved to the United States, where he taught for 20 years at the State University of New York. In that position, he established himself as the most dogged and prolific chronicler of the Armenian Genocide. Dadrian described himself as "a detective" searching out evidence. He deliberately drew on foreign archival sources, especially those of Germany, the Ottoman Empire's wartime ally, to better establish the credentials of his findings. Dadrian made no secret of the political agenda behind his work. In August 1964, he wrote a letter to the *New York Times*, asking, "on what conceivable grounds can the Armenians be denied the right to reclaim their ancestral territories which Turkey absorbed after massacring their inhabitants?"[8] His work, written at a time when public knowledge about the Armenian Genocide was extremely small, now reads more like a massive and detailed dossier in a criminal case than analytical history.[9]

The analysis that Dadrian presents comes across today as rather Orientalist, a more sophisticated version of the postwar Allied Turcophobic literature. Dadrian suggests that the Genocide was an almost inevitable culmination of Ottoman policies toward the Armenians: "The wartime destruction of the Armenian population of the Ottoman Empire emerges from that perspective as the cataclysmic culmination of a historical process involving the progressive decimation of the Armenians through intermittent and incremental massacres." The killings, he writes, were driven by Islam and "the repressive and sanguinary aspects of Ottoman culture."[10]

Dadrian also reads the Armenian Genocide through the later Nazi Holocaust of the Jews, both by repeating the Entente arguments of 1916–1918 that German officers collaborated in the Genocide and by arguing that the Nazis were inspired to kill the Jews by the successful experience of the Young Turks. Central to this case is the remark that Adolf Hitler is reported to have made in a speech to his generals in 1939, on the eve of the invasion of Poland—"Who still talks nowadays about the extermination of the Armenians?" The authenticity of the phrase is disputed: It was reported by an Associated Press journalist, quoting a member of the German resistance. If we accept it as true, it should be noted that Hitler was, at this historical moment, threatening Poles, not Jews.[11] But Dadrian goes further. He argues that both the Nazis and Young Turks were inspired by the same primal genocidal ideology represented by Genghis Khan: "[t]here can be no doubt that the example of Genghis had a foremost impact upon the organization and implementation of not only the Armenian genocide but also the Nazi-engineered cataclysm of World War II in which the Jewish Holocaust occupies the center stage."[12]

## Modern Scholarship

Since the turn of the millennium, the scholarship on the Armenian Genocide has made great strides forward. New scholars have entered the field, and a vast amount of archival evidence has been published. The AKP government in Turkey, in power since 2002, while not officially abandoning its predecessors' denialist approach to the issue, has taken a more permissive attitude, allowing alternative histories to be written and read in Turkey itself. This means that, first, the Turkish nationalist (or "denialist") version of the Armenian Genocide that took root in the 1950s has crumbled in the face of the new scholarship: None of these Turkish nationalist historians has managed to write a full-length book that sets out a coherent "Turkish version" of what happened to the Armenians. At the same time, modern scholars are writing histories of 1915–1916, which, even as they emphasize again its horrors, restore agency to Armenians in the story and fill out the context of the time.

Reading the work of Taner Akçam, Donald Bloxham, Fuat Dündar, Hilmar Kaiser, Hans-Lukas Kieser, Raymond Kévorkian, Ronald Suny, and Erik Zürcher is like seeing a mountain from different angles: The perspectives are different, but the thing being described is recognizably the same. At the same time, scholars of Ottoman and Russian history, such as Peter Holquist, Donald Quataert, and Michael Reynolds, add valuable context to other parts of the picture.

The publication of Kévorkian's monumental *The Armenian Genocide, A Complete History* in 2006 (in French, and in 2011 in English) was a milestone. Based on many years' study of 10,000 pages of Armenian archives in Jerusalem and Paris, Kévorkian constructs a detailed and gruesome narrative of the events of 1915–1920, week by week and region by region. Taner Akçam also broke new ground, as the result of his work in the Ottoman archives, as the first Turkish historian to write a full-length book that supported what had hitherto in Turkey been regarded as the "Armenian version" of events. In 2002 three scholars, Fatma Müge Göçek, Gerard Libaridian, and Ronald Suny, pioneered a collaboration among scholars, entitled the Workshop for Armenian/Turkish Scholarship, which eventually established a remarkable degree of consensus among a range of historians and resulted in a book of essays, *A Question of Genocide*, published in 2011.

These historians share a consensus that has supplanted the old-fashioned view of the killings as the work of primitive atavistic Turks and instead stresses the Unionist leaders' self-conscious aspiration to modernity. Erik Zürcher writes that "many Young Turks had come under the influence of biological materialism and social Darwinism and saw the world in terms of a struggle for survival between different nations."[13] In an illuminating study that compares acts of "ethnic cleansing" in the twentieth century, *The Dark Side of Democracy*, Michael Mann makes the theme of modernization the center of his thesis. At the heart of each of these mass atrocities, he argues, was a state-building project in which traitorous inconvenient minorities were perceived as a threat and ultimately were destroyed. Mann warns us, "To blame 'primitive' peoples offers us psychological comfort, since we can view murderous Serbs or Hutus (and other African tribal hatreds) as far removed from we civilized moderns. Yet such primitives would have to include groups from all the continents, and people as modern in their time, and as culturally close to us, as 19th-century Americans and Australians and 20th-century Germans."[14]

In the Ottoman Armenian case, Mann writes, "The perpetrators were not 'the Turks' (as nationalist theories would have it). Rather, some Turks (and others) were embroiled in a decidedly top-down process of murderous cleansing."[15] Other sources confirm that the leading Young Turk officials were among the most Europeanized and best-educated members of society. In his memoir of 1915, Leon Surmelian writes of his father, "to him the Europeanized Turks were far more sinister than the conservative, old-school Turks."[16]

This insight casts a different light on the roles of ordinary Kurdish and Turkish civilians in the killings of 1915. If in the "Hamidian massacres" of 1894–1896 many ordinary Muslim civilians were directly complicit in violence against their Armenian neighbors, this time around their role was likely to be secondary to that of the state killers of the Special Organization paramilitary. This is especially true of the Kurds, who had often been demonized as collective murderers. Kévorkian writes, "The major role played by 'the' Kurds, which is stressed by Turkish historiography and also by many Western scholars, turns out, upon examination, to be much less clear-cut than has been affirmed. Indeed, it comes down to the active participation of nomadic Kurdish tribes and only rarely involves sedentary villagers, who were encouraged by the Special Organization to take what they could from deportees already stripped of their most valuable assets."[17]

In other words, the central government in Constantinople made a calculated decision to target Armenians for deportation and destruction, using the hired killers of the Special Organization to do the dirty work. Once that process had begun, many Kurds and Turks took the opportunity to raid and kill the Armenians with impunity, generally out of sheer economic greed. These people opportunistically joined in a process that had already started, but they did not begin it themselves. A courageous minority tried to protect their Armenian neighbors, while the majority—sadly and surely like most of us in a situation like this—simply did nothing.

This is an important information for latter-day Armenians as they seek to understand what "the Turks" did to their grandparents. Again, it fits with contemporary accounts. Henry Riggs, for example, said that local Kurds did "vastly more in the way of the rescue and relief of Armenians than the American missionaries."[18] Riggs also writes, "There were plenty of Turks, of course, who gladly took advantage of this opportunity to clear up old scores with their Armenian rivals, or of enriching themselves at their expense. But there was no outbreak of popular fanaticism on the part of the Turks. In fact, we who had lived all our lives among the Turks and knew something of their ways said again and again at the time, 'This is no Turkish outbreak.' It was altogether too cold, too calculating, and too efficient. The common people liked it not."[19]

What, if anything, was the end-goal of the Young Turk leaders in their genocidal campaign? Recent scholars have pinpointed the Unionists' desire for the "demographic re-engineering" of Anatolia, driven by the conviction that the security of the region and the economic development of its Muslim inhabitants would be achieved by the near-elimination of its Armenian community. Kévorkian writes of "this geographer's logic, the basis for the conception of the liquidation plan."[20] The term *near-elimination* is important. Taner Akçam, Fuat Dündar, and Raymond Kévorkian have written that the Unionist leaders set a maximum number of Armenians in the eastern provinces at 5 or 10 percent (a target that was sometimes over-fulfilled and reduced to almost zero).[21] To achieve that end, the forced assimilation and Islamicization of Armenian women and children was an acceptable part of the plan.

The Armenians were the biggest group to be deported and suffered the most violence, but Dündar has written about how others—Lazes, Arabs, Jews—were also forcibly moved during this period. Another goal of the government's "geographer's logic" was to re-settle hundreds of thousands of *muhajirs* from the Balkans and Caucasus in these former Armenian territories. (Kévorkian writes that Circassians and Chechens, many with grievances against Christian Russia, were among the active killers in 1915–1916. One of the bloodiest figures of the period, Mehmed Reshid, the governor of Diyarbakir, was also a Circassian, born in the Caucasus and deported to the Ottoman Empire as a young child.) Much of the Unionist leadership, including Talat, came from the Balkans, and the experience of the ethnic cleansing of Muslims in the Balkan Wars of 1912 and 1913 was fresh to them.

This portrait of Talat Pasha as macabre geographer and statistician was fleshed out with the publication in Turkey in 2008 of his handwritten 77-page private notebook, or so-called "Black Book," dating to 1917. The book contains Talat's own detailed estimates of the Armenian population (he puts it at 1.5 million, excluding Protestant Armenians) and his calculations on the number of Armenians whose deportation he ordered. Analyzing the notebooks, Ara Sarafian notes the massive and chilling discrepancy between Talat's record of the number of Armenians "re-located" in 1915 and the far smaller number still alive two years later:

> As his 1917 report shows, although over a million Armenians were deported, around 60,000 were counted in the resettlement zone outlined by the Ottoman government, another 50,000 were found dispersed along deportation routes, and around 100,000 were within their home provinces. Practically all of these survivors in the provinces were treated as captives and pressured to assimilate as Muslim-Turks.[22]

In other words by Talat's own reckoning, by 1917 Eastern Anatolia had been all but cleansed of Armenians and his "demographic engineering" project had worked.

## Courtroom History

There are several disputes about what happened in 1915, located both within and to the side of the broader historical discussion, which are so intense as to have greater political resonance than analytical value. One is on the issues of premeditation and intent of the perpetrators; another is on the role of Armenian revolutionaries in precipitating events.

The first issue has diverted much of the writing on the Armenian Genocide into the legalistic byways of weighing evidence as if for a trial. Briefly put, in the political and legal debate on "Genocide recognition," Armenian lobbyists and their supporters have deemed it important to attribute clear premeditation to the Unionist leaders in 1915, so as to convict them retroactively by the terms of the 1948 UN Genocide Convention, which defines genocide as "acts committed *with intent* to destroy in whole or in part, a national, ethnical, racial or religious group" (emphasis added). Conversely, Turkish political lobbyists have strained their sinews to discredit the evidence and witnesses of the other side and make the most of all anomalies in the planning and implementation of the killings in order to prove a lack of intent—and therefore a lack of genocide under its UN definition.

The more extreme Turkish polemicists engage in a game in which they cast doubt on every eyewitness report from 1915 for lack of proof of deliberate killing. For example, the prolific blogger who calls himself Holdwater and runs the website *Tall Armenian Tale* even dismisses consul Leslie Davis's report of having seen ten thousand Armenians bodies in a valley near Lake Goeljuk (see Chapter 1), because the consul did not actually see the victims die: "Yes, there were massacred bodies. Were they victimized by marauding Muslim gangs, most out for revenge for what Armenians had done to their families . . . or were they killed by the gendarmes, as part of a government sponsored policy of extermination? We don't know. We don't know, because Leslie Davis was not an eyewitness as to how these people lost their lives."[23]

Engaging with history rather than with a virtual Armenian-Turkish courtroom, contemporary historians spend less time on the issue of intent—after all, even if there is no single archival document which dots the *i*'s and crosses the *t*'s, there was demonstrably both a murderous *disposition* in the actions of the Young Turk leaders in 1915 and a genocidal *outcome* for the Armenians. Most (but not all) historians who write about the Armenians and 1915 use the word "genocide," while acknowledging that it is more a legal-political term than a historical one.

But the "intent" issue colors many of the Armenian historical publications from the 1970s to the 1990s, including that of Vahakn Dadrian. In a sense, these historians were picking up where the Allies had left off in 1919, at the height of the postwar trials of perpetrators. In the 1980s, an old debate was revived about the status of a controversial document known as the "Ten Commandments," bought by British intelligence in 1919 from an Ottoman security official. The document purports to be a Unionist government order listing the ten measures to be taken to destroy the Armenian population. Most scholars now believe that the document is a forgery—although Raymond Kévorkian speculates that it was an "authentic fake" fabricated by someone who knew the thinking of the Unionist leadership and manufactured it in order to escape prosecution by the British.[24]

The controversy highlights the fact that, although we have the eyewitness testimony of Morgenthau and other diplomats, if we discount the Ten Commandments, there is no "smoking gun," no archival paper trail that directly incriminates Talat Pasha and others with a clear order to exterminate the Armenians, rather than merely "relocate" them to Syria, as Turkish nationalist historiography claims.

For what it is worth, it is probably naïve to expect that there would be such a "smoking gun." There may or may not have been such an incriminating document, but it is unlikely that it survived the several spring cleanings carried out in the Ottoman archives of material on the Armenian issue, first performed in 1918 and repeated on subsequent occasions. Whether out of official indifference to the Ottoman past or a deliberate intent to suppress it, in the Republican era truckloads of thousands of archival documents were simply handed over to a paper-making enterprise to be pulped.[25] Moreover, the historian Taner Akçam says that the official archives may be the wrong place to look anyway. He makes the case that Talat Pasha, a former telegraph official himself, used a "dual track" system of communicating with the eastern provinces, sending out the more sensitive telegrams from a private post office he set up inside his home.

Contemporary eyewitnesses say they saw telegrams ordering the killing of Armenians. The Venezuelan officer serving with the Ottoman army, Rafael de Nogales, says that in a village near Lake Van, "I caught sight of the military commander of the place dictating orders to his officers, while a group of *kiatihs* or secretaries deciphered an enormous heap of telegrams. That unaccustomed activity made me suspect that the storm was about to break . . . . Next morning, which was the twentieth of April, 1915, we stumbled, near El-Aghlat, upon mutilated Armenian corpses strewing the length of the road."[26]

Nogales also recounts a later conversation with Mehmed Reshid, the notorious Circassian-born governor of Diyarbakir, "a man of some fifty years, of distinguished bearing, educated in Paris and belonging to a very aristocratic family of Stamboul."

[T]hrough some exceedingly prudent but very explicit remarks, [Reshid] gave me to understand also that, in regard to the extermination of the Armenians of his vilayet, he had merely obeyed superior orders; so that the responsibility for the massacres perpetrated there should rest not with him, but with his chief, the then Minister of the Interior, Talaat Bey—one year later the Grand Vizier, Talaat

Pasha. Talaat had ordered the slaughter by a circular telegram, if my memory is correct, containing a scant three words: "*Yak—Vur—Oldur*," meaning "Burn, demolish, kill."[27]

There is no surviving record of such a telegram. However, one highly incriminating telegram from Talat to Reshid did survive intact in the archives. In August 1915, Talat Pasha telegraphed Reshid in Diyarbakir the instruction, "Do not destroy the other Christians." The meaning is clear: The bloodthirsty governor was massacring other Christians as well as Armenians and was being ordered to confine his campaign of murder to Armenians alone.[28]

Other telegrams, recently uncovered by Taner Akçam, convey a murderous intent by implication. A series of them sent by Talat and Enver in early 1916, for example, ban foreigners from visiting the zones of Armenian deportation and order that any government officials found to be helping Americans or Germans give aid to the deportees be "severely punished." In other words, the Young Turk government did not want Armenian deportees to be fed and looked after—to be kept alive—even if it incurred none of the costs of doing so.[29]

## Agents and Victims

A second politicized issue in the history of the Armenian Genocide revolves around how much importance should be ascribed to the role of the Armenian revolutionaries. The key event in this debate is the seizure of the town of Van in April 1915 by Armenians, who hoped to join forces with the Russian army.

The fighting over Van has a similar status in history to that of the Easter Uprising in Dublin one year later. Traditional Armenian historiography has presented the Armenians' fighting as "resistance," a heroic effort to fight back against a preplanned genocidal program that was already underway. Turkish nationalist historiography, by contrast, identifies the "Armenian rebellion at Van" as a stab in the back by Armenians, in the league with the Russians, which necessitated a crackdown in order to preserve the state (the scholar of genocides Robert Melson calls this argument "the provocation thesis"). Both of these approaches look to be overly schematic, retrospectively projecting all the responsibility for the Van events onto the other "side." Implausibly, in one version, the Van Armenian revolutionaries are ascribed all the agency for everything that happened in 1915, while in the other they are given no role at all.

To read contemporary accounts of Van in April 1915 is to be reminded that this was a wartime situation in which actors based their decisions not on the fuller information we now have but on real-time perceptions of what was happening. It is logical that the Van Armenian revolutionaries of 1915 chose to strike rather than wait to see how events unfolded: When they had been more passive in 1896, they had been massacred. In his self-critical manifesto sent to the ARF Congress in 1923, the prominent Dashnak politician Hovhaness Kachaznuni writes that in 1914–1915 many Armenians pinned hopes on liberation by the Entente, only to be disappointed: "The Winter of 1914 and the Spring of 1915 were the periods of greatest enthusiasm and hope for all the Armenians in the Caucasus, including, of course, the Dashnagtzoutiun. We had no doubt the war would end with the complete victory of the Allies; Turkey would be defeated and dismembered, and its Armenian population would at last be liberated."[30]

The operation to capture Van on April 19 was masterminded by the ARF leader Aram Manukian, who subsequently became one of the most divisive Armenian figures of this period—he would later serve as governor of Van under Russian rule at the end of 1915 and would be called the "dictator of Armenia" when he ran eastern Armenia in the first months of 1918. Manukian's operation was a notorious cause of intra-Armenian debate both at the time and in émigré quarrels for two generations afterward, with the Van rebels portrayed either as heroic liberators or reckless provocateurs who had put their brethren at risk.

The canonic text for the heroic narrative was the memoir of one of the Armenian defenders, Onnig Mukhitarian, *The Defense of Van: An Account of the Glorious Struggle of Van-Vasbouragan*. The contrary view caused a backlash even 50 years later. In 1966, the Van-born writer Gurgen Mahari tried to publish his novel *Burning Orchards* in Soviet Armenia. Mahari was so vilified for his warts-and-all narrative that he withdrew the manuscript from the publishers and resubmitted a self-censored version. In the original novel the author savagely satirizes Manukian ("Aram Pasha") and his Dashnak comrades for being "hard fratricidal Cains" who intimidated and assassinated local Armenians and provoked a fight with the Turks they could not win. Mahari's alter ego, the businessman Ohannes, accuses one of the revolutionaries:

> Under the very nose of the Government, you bring in guns and convert churches and houses into armament dumps; you print clandestine newspapers and books criticizing the government; you send terrorists to train in the hills; you kill officials and district governors; you sing songs day and night; and you shout, "call me, oh my little sea." And after all this, you want me to pat you on the head and applaud you! Finish with it, for God's sake, and don't make me have to speak again.[31]

After the battle for Van, British journalist Morgan Philips Price witnessed the perpetual controversy between those Armenians who sought accommodation and those who wanted radical action:

> [On] January 9th, 1916, Professor Minassian took the Dashnaktsution party to task for having entered into negociations with the Russian authorities without consulting its kindred societies in Turkish Armenia. . . . The Orizon, the organ of the Dashnaktsution in Tiflis, defended itself by saying that the massacre would have happened in any case. . . . This political split between the Russian and Turkish Armenians is nothing new. Being constantly in touch with Khurds and Turks, the Van and Bitlis Armenians have understood better how to deal with them and have more than once developed a policy of their own.[32]

The global context of World War I and conflict with Russia was crucial. In *Shattering Empires*, a book that draws on research in both the Ottoman and Russian diplomatic archives, Michael Reynolds sees the destruction of the Armenians and the collapse of the Ottoman Empire through the same lens of war, state-collapse, and state-building. He makes the case that defense of the state and interstate competition with the Russian Empire was paramount for the Unionist leaders, rather than a pan-Turkic or pan-Islamic cause—an argument he encapsulates in the phrase "Buffers, not Brethren."

Reynolds quotes Charles Tilly's aphorism, "War made the state and the state made war" to define the regime run by the Young Turks. It was their view, he writes, that by getting rid of the Armenians they believed they were making a "last stand" to preserve Eastern Anatolia and therefore the empire as a whole:

> Experience had taught them that the global community of states accorded no legitimacy to pluralistic but weak empires. As long as Anatolia remained ethnically pluralistic it would be vulnerable to subversion and partition. The homogenization of Anatolia was the surest solution to the dilemma they faced. If the Gordion Knot that was Eastern Anatolia had to be cut, they were willing to do it.[33]

Reynolds therefore argues that the Van fighting was a case of the celebrated "security dilemma" in which one "side" in a conflict attacks first, out of the perceived need for self-defense, beginning a cycle of destruction in which everyone loses.[34] Donald Bloxham concurs: "In light of the Russian advance and the events at Van, the distinction between innocent and guilty Armenians was rendered meaningless both ideologically and practically in CUP [Unionist] eyes."[35] Both Reynolds and Sean McMeekin (neither of whom use the word "genocide" in their narratives of 1915) make the case that the Ottoman regime had genuine reason to fear the Russians' plans to invade Eastern Anatolia. Reynolds provides evidence from the tsarist archives of Russia, which was agitating among both Kurds and Armenians in order to extend its influence in these border areas—an influence it sought to make into direct conquest once war broke out. McMeekin, in a polemical book entitled *The Russian Origins of the First World War*, publishes a series of Russian diplomatic documents of the time in which the tsarist government promises military support to Armenian revolutionaries in 1914 and 1915—support that was to ebb away at the crucial moment. The Armenians, he concludes, "fell victim to Russia's peculiar mixture of imperial greed and impotence, as the would-be liberatees of an army unable—or unwilling—to liberate them."[36]

In their histories, Donald Bloxham and Michael Mann also focus on the context of World War I. Both have written narratives that depict the Armenian Genocide in 1915 as a "cumulative radicalization," escalating within the context of the perceived security threats of World War I. As Bloxham reminds us, for the previous 40 years the Armenians had been a (mostly willing) pawn in European Great Power politics. The outbreak of war skewed calculations: revolutionary-minded Armenians openly showed allegiance to the Entente fighting against the Ottomans. Even those who did not—and indeed fought in the Ottoman army—were tainted by association. This ended up making the Armenians' security fatally dependent on the Allies' willingness, or unwillingness, to protect them. The result, Bloxham tells us, was that "[a]nti-Armenian policy intensified with every Entente military advance or success" and the destruction of the Armenians escalated. As the Armenian priest Grigoris Balakian acidly observed in his memoirs, "We had quickly forgotten the historic words of the British government officials who said that the English fleet could not climb Mount Ararat. But they had no problem getting their men-of-war to climb Mount Everest."[37]

At the same time, Bloxham disputes the thesis of postwar writers and Dadrian that imperial Germany was an active accomplice in the killings of 1915. He portrays the Germans of the time as rational Great Power actors rather than as proto-Nazis. He argues that the Germans can be charged with "callousness, chauvinism, bureaucratic and military tunnel vision, and above all, blind pursuit of national interest" but not a direct role in the killings.[38]

Michael Mann reminds us that the 1915 Genocide unfolded very quickly, suggesting that its implementation owed as much to improvisation as to careful planning. He reminds us that the Dashnaktsutiun Party and the Unionists had been political allies not long before. (Indeed, in a curious episode, Dashnak leader Manukian fought alongside Ottoman regular troops against Kurdish tribesmen in the summer of 1913, only two years before the Van uprising.)[39] The context of war explains, though of course does not excuse, the Young Turks' slide into mass murder, writes Mann:

That the Young Turks, rather than palace and Islamic reactionaries, should be the instrument of their doom would have surprised most Armenians in 1912, even perhaps through much of 1913. As late as August 1914 the Young Turks tried a new version of their Plan A, alliance with the Armenians. . . . [T]heir Plan B—mass but strategically confined deportations—emerged quickly and turned even more rapidly into a Plan C of more generalized and much more violent deportations. This was inherently unstable and quickly slid into a genocidal Plan D. This was not as coherent, organized, and premeditated a genocide as is usually argued.[40]

## Building a Narrative

A model of "cumulative radicalization" constructs a narrative of the Armenian Genocide that allows for the apparent anomalies in its execution. In the 1970s, state-sponsored Turkish scholars produced documents from the Ottoman archives to bolster their case that the deportations were actually peaceful "relocations." Some of the documents were instructions for the deportations to be carried out in an orderly fashion, others showed that 1,600 minor officials involved in the Armenian deportations were actually prosecuted at the time—thereby allegedly showing that Talat Pasha and his colleagues only had benign intentions toward the Armenians.

The trouble with the first set of documents, historians point out, is that thus far the Ottoman archives have not yet revealed a single document showing benign intentions for the Armenians once they *arrived*, In other words, there is no evidence of anyone taking care to compensate the deportees for lost property or to resettle them in Syria. As for the prosecutions, Taner Akçam argues that these prosecutions were almost all for economic offenses against individuals who had looted Armenian property for personal gain, rather than handing over their booty to the state.[41]

All the same, although a picture emerges of a plan hatched by Talat and others to destroy the Armenians, it was not always implemented and sometimes met with dissent. Writing in 1930, Ahmed Emin said that there were strong differences inside the Young Turk government:

> Moved by the vigorous attacks of enemy propaganda and by the action of those in the Government who opposed deportations on an unnecessarily extended scale, a commission of investigation composed of inspectors of the Ministries of the Interior and of Justice was formed in 1917 to punish those guilty of excesses. Some minor offenders were

really punished; but those favoring the deportations being very influential in the Government, the whole thing amounted more to a demonstration rather than a sincere attempt to fix complete responsibility.[42]

One of the men who dissented, at least somewhat, from the program may have been none other than "the third pasha," Cemal, the Unionist governor of Syria and commander of the Fourth Army. In Cemal's memoir, published in English in 1922 (the same year that he was killed by an Armenian assassin in Georgia), he writes that the Ottoman military played no part in the deportations and that he disapproved of their severity. His motives were obviously self-serving, but there is supporting evidence for some of his assertions: The army did indeed play a minimal role in the deportations, and Cemal reportedly did not cooperate with them and tried to negotiate a separate peace with the Entente. In his memoirs Cemal writes, "I made a journey from Aleppo to Bozanti to view the situation personally, issued an order that bread was to be provided for the emigrants from the Army depots, and ordered the doctors on the lines of communication to look after the sick Armenians."[43]

This assertion actually fits with the account of the Armenian pharmacist Hagop Arsenian. He was deported through Bozanti and was amazed to be given food one day:

> Certain events were inexplicable and extraordinary. On the one hand, it was clear to all of us that the plan to eradicate the Ottoman Armenians was a definite decision and already underway. On the other hand, we could not understand why bread was distributed to the refugees who reached Tarsus. . . . To what can we attribute this clement gesture, to give some humanitarian aid to a people condemned to be sent to the slaughterhouse?[44]

The geography of atrocities was very different from place to place. Perhaps one half of the Ottoman Armenians died in 1915–1916. If you were a male Armenian from one of the six eastern provinces, your chances of living through 1915 were pitifully small. But if you came from Constantinople, Smyrna (Izmir), or Adrianople (Edirne), you stood a much better chance of survival. The governor of Smyrna reportedly asked for his Armenians to be spared to maintain the commercial life of the city.

Thus, within an overall picture of murder and deportation, Armenians did survive and on occasion were even protected by Ottoman officials. Individual regional officials acted differently toward the Armenians who came within their power. Kemal, the governor of Yozgat district, east of Ankara (and hundreds of miles from the fighting with the Russians), was so bloodthirsty that he subjected all the Armenians in his district to wholesale massacre, including women, children, Protestants, and converts to Islam. In the summer of 1915, Kévorkian writes, "Kemal organized a vast slaughterhouse in the vicinity of the village of Keller, where tens of thousands of Armenians of all ages and both sexes were slain with knives, sabers, and axes."[45] While this massacre was going on, an eyewitness said later, Kemal was "observed smoking a water-pipe amidst the moans, groans, and shrieks of the people in mortal agony."[46]

By contrast, Celal Bey, the governor first of Aleppo and then of Konya, who was later removed from his post in October 1915, saved thousands of Armenians. In his memoirs, Celal likened himself to "a person sitting beside a river, with absolutely no means of rescuing anyone from it. Blood was flowing down the river, with thousands of innocent children, irreproachable old men, and helpless women streaming down the river towards oblivion. Anyone I could save with my bare hands, I saved, and the rest went down the river, never to return."[47]

The "cumulative radicalization" model tells us that the Armenian revolutionaries were indeed agents in the story of 1915. It also suggests that looking for some kind of long-hatched evil intent in the actions of Talat Pasha and his colleagues may not be a productive line of enquiry. As Dirk Moses, a scholar of genocide, puts it:

> [f]ear and paranoia rather than hate drive the genocide along. What the evidence shows, I think is that all too often a minority group is held collectively guilty and is *collectively punished* for the actions of some of its members. Moreover, the group as a whole is seen as a potential security risk—a potential fifth column—and so it can be interned, deported or otherwise destroyed *in toto* for reasons of state. That is, genocides are generally driven by traumatic interpretations of past events in which, for various reasons, a group is constructed as

disloyal and threatening and held collectively guilty and then collectively punished, deported or destroyed *pre-emptively* to prevent the feared annihilation of the state. Despite the threatening activities of some of its members, though these communities were loyal.[48]

The Young Turk leaders did face threats to their security, but out of the options they had at their disposal, they came to choose mass murder. The evidence of collective punishment poses the biggest analytical challenge to those denialist writers who minimize or deny what happened to the Ottoman Armenians. For example, Guenter Lewy, who calls what happened a "disputed genocide," has written, "Given this context, the Armenians can hardly claim that they suffered for no reason at all. Ignoring warnings from many quarters, large numbers of them had fought the Turks openly or played the role of a fifth column; not surprisingly, with their backs against the wall, the Ottomans reacted resolutely, if not viciously." Conflating the Armenian revolutionaries who did fight against the Ottomans with "the Armenians" as a whole, Lewy repeats the Young Turks' trick of justifying collective punishment of a whole nation.[49]

As Donald Bloxham writes, the brutality of the Ottoman state against the Armenians no doubt escalated because of the Van events, but was far greater than in comparable cases of the era: "[N]owhere else during the First World War was the separatist nationalism of the few answered with the total destruction of the wider ethnic community from which the nationalists hailed. That is the crux of the issue."[50]

The London-based scholar Ara Sarafian has accumulated more eyewitness reports and archival material confirming the most gruesome facts of the Armenian Genocide than anyone else in recent years. Having collected this damning evidence, he has urged historians and, in particular, fellow Armenians to "study the Armenian Genocide with confidence." In his view, this means working to open up all available archives, abandoning the "prosecutorial" approach to history and concluding that

[t]he Armenian Genocide is not the same as the Holocaust. The Young Turks did not have the apparatus to carry out a genocide

on par with the Holocaust. It is also a fact that many Ottoman officials, including governors, sub-governors, military personnel, police chiefs, and gendarmes saved thousands of Armenians during the Genocide. Most Armenians from the province of Adana, for example, were not killed. This very basic fact is elided in the works of prominent Armenian historians. There are other examples too. The "Holocaust model" of the Armenian Genocide is fundamentally flawed.[51]

Now that the Turkish "denialist" approach to the murder of the Ottoman Armenians has been discredited and is questioned even in Turkey, the historical study of the Genocide continues and deepens, now propelled by many younger Turkish scholars, among others. This less politicized approach brings us back closer to the experiences of eye-witnesses and survivors. And it should also extend to the study of the events of 1916–1923 in Eastern Anatolia and the Caucasus, which form the next chapter in the Armenian-Turkish story.

# 3

## From Van to Lausanne, 1915–1923

IN JULY 1915 MORGAN Philips Price, a journalist for the British newspaper the *Manchester Guardian*, set out from the Georgian capital Tiflis to tour the ruined lands of Eastern Anatolia. Over the next 18 months he crisscrossed the region, covering the eastern front of World War I. Price was a Russian speaker (he would report on the October Revolution in Petrograd a year later), and he conversed freely with the Russian troops. He also helped to distribute humanitarian aid both to Christians and, on behalf of the Indian Red Crescent, to Muslims.

Price's perspective, in his book *War and Revolution in Asiatic Russia*, is different from those of the eyewitnesses in Anatolia who saw the deportation of the Armenians a few months earlier in 1915. He writes instead about the warfare that followed the "abominable massacres" of the Armenians in which Armenians, Azerbaijanis, Georgians, Greeks, Kurds, Russians, and Turks all engaged in murderous fighting.

This era of conflict in Anatolia and the Caucasus, which ended in 1921, has received less attention from historians than the Armenian Genocide. However, it saw momentous events that would shape the next century for all the peoples of the region. The Ottoman Empire collapsed and the Turkish Republic was founded from its ruins. Armenians briefly had an independent republic, run by the Dashnaktsutiun Party, whose legacy would divide diaspora Armenians for three generations. Armenians and Azerbaijanis fought a war in the Caucasus, which prefigured their disastrous conflict of the 1980s and 1990s over Nagorny Karabakh.

The human toll of these years was enormous. The story of these borderlands during this period still awaits an overarching cross-border history, such as Timothy Snyder has written for Eastern Europe in the 1930s and 1940s in his book *Bloodlands*—a word that would also be appropriate for Anatolia in this era as well. Price, who became convinced of the folly of war, sums up his experience as follows:

> I now see clearly that the guilt of war atrocities upon civil populations cannot be put down to any one combatant. The whole of war is an atrocity, and wherever it comes, hunger, disease, massacres and burnings come in its train. One side with threats forces the civil population into a course of action, and then the other side comes in and accuses them of treachery. A massacre follows with all its attendant horrors. This is the history of the war on the Caucasus front, as far as it concerns the civil population.[1]

## Russian Conquest

In September 1915, the Russian army began a long-awaited offensive in southeastern Anatolia. Morgan Philips Price accompanied them into a landscape wrecked both by fighting and the Armenian deportations. "The villages of the plain were deserted and in ruins; not a living soul was to be seen except a few black spots, that indicated a patrol of Cossacks. What was recently a paradise of richness and beauty was now a desert."[2]

The Russians captured Van and installed as governor Aram Manukian, the implacable Armenian revolutionary who had defended it earlier in the year. In early 1916 they conquered the fortress city of Erzerum and the Black Sea port of Trebizond (Trabzon) and advanced into the Anatolian heartlands. In Harput, the Reverend Henry Riggs, whose Armenian flock had been wiped out the previous year, cared for a flood of "utterly broken and hopeless" Muslim refugees. "This time the people were not being driven out from their homes by the government, but were being driven out by their fear of the Russians—and also by the terror that God was punishing them for what had been done the year before. The scene was dramatic and was taken as a clear indication of the wrath of God by the simple people of Harpoot."[3]

For almost two years, the Russian army controlled most of the six "Armenian provinces" of Eastern Anatolia. However, the tsarist authorities discouraged Armenians from settling in their former homes, not wanting to see an Armenian region formed that would be autonomous of Russia. At the same time, Armenian soldiers serving with the Russian army engaged in reprisals against the local Muslims. Price observed that the Russians (with the exception of some Cossacks) were generally fairly well-disciplined, but the Armenian volunteers attacked Kurds and Turks:

> One day I rode out from the camp and came across a little Khurdish village. The inhabitants had most of them fled with the Turks, but on riding down the street I came across the dead bodies of a Khurdish man and two women, with recent wounds in the head and body. Then two Armenians, volunteers from our camp, suddenly appeared carrying things out of a house. I stopped them and asked who these dead Khurds were. "Oh," they said, "we have just killed them." "Why?" I asked. A look of amazement came into their faces. "Why ask such a question? Why, we kill Khurds at sight. They are our enemies, and we kill them, because if we leave them here they will do us harm." This was all the reply I could get.[4]

In 1917, the pendulum swung back. Russia's tsarist regime tottered and then collapsed completely in October as the Bolsheviks seized power in Petrograd. Shouting the Bolshevik slogan "We don't want the Dardanelles!" Russian soldiers deserted en masse from the Ottoman front. In March 1918, the Bolsheviks signed the Treaty of Brest-Litovsk with the Germans and the Ottomans, surrendering most of the conquered land without a fight.

The retreat of the Russians and Armenians in 1917 and early 1918 wrought more destruction. In the summer of 1919, two American officials, Captain Emory Niles and Arthur Sutherland, reported:

> The Russians and Armenians occupied the country for a considerable time together in 1915 and 1916, and during this period there

was apparently little disorder, although doubtless there was damage committed by the Russians. In 1917 the Russian army disbanded and left the Armenians alone in control. At this period bands of Armenian irregulars roamed the country pillaging and murdering the Musulman civilian population. When the Turkish army advanced at Erzindjan, Erzerum and Van, the Armenian army broke down and all of the soldiers, regular and irregular, turned themselves to destroying Musulman property and committing atrocities upon Musulman inhabitants. The result is a country completely ruined containing about one-fourth of its former population and one-eighth of its former buildings, and a most bitter hatred [of] Musulmans for Armenians which makes it impossible for two races to live together at the present time.[5]

From this point on, outsiders traveling in this region reported that Armenians and local Muslims could not be trusted to live together peacefully, without foreign military supervision.

## The Caucasus Front

In the spring of 1918, Ottoman armies moved east again to the borders of the Transcaucasus. The three main nationalities of Armenians, Azerbaijanis, and Georgians, having rid themselves of Russian imperial rule in March 1917, were free but in turmoil. They had no common government, no agreed borders, no armed forces, and a barely functioning economy.

With the end of tsarist rule, a low-level conflict had resumed between Armenians and Azerbaijanis, the Turkic-speaking Muslims, then known by outsiders mainly as "Tatars." Armenian and Azerbaijani communities were intermingled across the entire south of the Transcaucasus. Before the twentieth century, they coexisted fairly harmoniously. However, both groups were infected by the new nationalism of the era and also came into socioeconomic competition in cities like Baku and Shusha. In 1905 they fought a brief fratricidal war.

In the spring of 1918, many Azerbaijanis saw the advancing Ottoman troops as potential liberators. There was an upsurge of Armenian-

Azerbaijani violence, especially in the highland territory of Mountainous (Nagorny) Karabakh. This was the most bitterly disputed of three regions with mixed Armenian-Azerbaijani populations, along with Zangezur and Nakhichevan. The highlands of Karabakh had a long Armenian heritage and a population that was more than 90 percent Armenian, but they were surrounded by lowland Muslim districts. Karabakh's main town, the citadel of Shusha, was also a center of Azerbaijani culture, with a large Muslim population. As in the conflict of the 1980s, both Armenians and Azerbaijanis identified Karabakh as a land vital for their national identity and survival. For the Armenians, it was the eastern outpost of Armenian culture and population; for the Azerbaijanis, it was an integral part of their economic and geographic space.

Many historians have conflated the Armenian-Azerbaijani conflict of this era with the Armenian deportations of 1915 and Armenian-Ottoman story—and it does not help that Armenians routinely call Azerbaijanis "Turks." In late 1918, the two theaters of war did indeed converge. But it is important to stress the differences between the Armenian-Turkish story and the Armenian-Azerbaijani one. Despite speaking a Turkic language that was close to Turkish, Azerbaijanis were distinct from Turks. They were mostly Shiite and had only briefly been part of the Ottoman Empire. Relations between Turks and Azerbaijanis fluctuated from era to era. As Shiites, many Azerbaijanis had willingly fought in the tsarist army in the nineteenth century against the Sunni Ottomans. In 1920, Turkish nationalist leader Mustafa Kemal had no compunction about selling out the Azerbaijani Republic to his new allies, the Russian Bolsheviks.

Unlike the Young Turks' wholesale asymmetric destruction of the Armenians, the Armenian-Azerbaijani conflict was a more or less symmetrical battle of armed groups, a grim process in which both Armenians and Azerbaijanis gave as good as they got. In Baku in 1918, for example, two horrible massacres were perpetrated, one by each side. At the end of March, when the city was under control of a Bolshevik commune, Armenian militants ran amok and killed thousands of Azerbaijanis. In September, when Ottoman forces captured the city, as many as 9,000 Armenian civilians were massacred. "When one speaks of streets of a town running with blood, one is generally employing a figure of speech," said British political officer Harry

Luke. "But if one is referring to Baku between 1917 and 1919 one is being starkly literal."[6]

In April 1918, the Ottoman army captured the Black Sea port of Batum and the fortress of Kars, two cities that they had given up in 1878. These two defeats would live on long in Armenian political memory. The anthropologist Jenny Philips found that in the 1970s the alleged "surrender" of Batum to the Turks was still a contentious topic in the émigré Armenian community of Watertown, Massachusetts.[7]

In April 1918, Armenian, Azerbaijani, and Georgian representatives declared a new independent joint state, the Transcaucasian Federation, with its capital in Tiflis. It had no working institutions, and its main purpose was to be able to negotiate with the Ottomans. The Ottoman First Caucasus Army crossed into eastern Armenia and headed for Yerevan. On May 21, it was halted by an improvised Armenian force at the Battle of Sardarapat, just outside Yerevan. "Carts drawn by oxen, water buffalo, and cows jammed the roads bringing food, provisions, ammunition, and volunteers from the vicinity" of Yerevan.[8] Armenians of the time believed they had escaped extinction by a hair's breadth.

On May 26, the Georgian Mensheviks scuttled the paper Trans-caucasian Federation, and, having struck a secret alliance with Germany, announced the creation of an independent Georgia. Two days later, the Azerbaijani delegation in Tiflis declared an independent Azerbaijan. This left the Armenians on their own. On May 30, 1918, the Armenian National Council had no option but to make a declaration of Armenian independence, retrospectively dated to two days earlier. It was possibly the most inauspicious declaration of independence in history. The first Armenian formal statement did not even mention the word "independence," saying only that in view of its' neighbors actions, "[t]he Armenian National Council declares itself to be the supreme and only administration for the Armenian provinces." Armenian leader Simon Vratsian called it the "untimely birth" of a "sick child."[9]

With the foundation of the republic, both the Turkish and Armenian elites displayed a realist live-and-let-live attitude toward one another. After the Battle of Sardarapat, Talat Pasha, the harshest of the Young Turk leaders, said that he did not want a new eastern Armenia to become a powerful "Bulgaria of the East," but he would have to tolerate some kind of Armenian entity "in an extremely weak and unviable form."[10] Talat's commanders, however, reported that they were exhausted and could not fight any more. The Armenian leadership came to the same conclusion, deciding that they had to settle for a weak, truncated state rather than nothing at all. On June 4, the Young Turk leadership signed a peace treaty with the Yerevan government, thus strangely becoming the first state to de facto recognize Armenia's independence.

One Armenian-Turkish encounter from this period has been all but expunged from the histories of both sides. But it is revealing of how Armenian and Turkish politicians dealt with one another, when desperate circumstances demanded it. In September 1918, Ottoman military commander Halil Pasha, the uncle of war minister Enver, visited Yerevan. Halil had the reputation of being one of the cruelest Unionist commanders, having personally directed massacres of Armenians and Assyrians in Van and the eastern provinces. Nonetheless, he was warmly greeted by his old foe, Dashnak leader and now Armenian interior minister, Aram Manukian. The two men had fought a battle to the death in Van in 1915, but had been political allies in the 1908 Young Turk revolution.

Descriptions of the meeting from both sides suggest that they shared a common language and willingness to do business. Halil agreed to deliver wheat to Armenia and to assist in clearing Azerbaijanis from a gorge near Yerevan.[11] According to one Armenian memoir, the two "hostile champions" Manukian and Halil "kissed each other warmly like friends." The next day Halil visited Echmiadzin and saw Ottoman Armenian refugees camped by the lake in appalling conditions. Over lunch, served on plates that were a gift from Tsar Nicholas II, the head of the Armenian church, the Catholicos, asked Halil:

"How did you like the environs of Echmiadzin, and especially the view of the lake? Did you see the countless Armenian refugees who used to be your citizens? I am thankful that this many survived."

Halil Pasha was very uneasy. To change the subject he said, "I am drinking to you, Your Holiness. It is an amazing wine."[12]

In Halil's own memoirs, published in Istanbul in 1972, he writes that his "old friend" Manukian encouraged him to give a public speech outside his hotel in Yerevan. He then quotes the speech, as assembled from the notes of his assistant at the time, with these exceptionally frank words addressed to an audience of Armenians:

> The Armenian nation, with whom I collaborated to overthrow an unjust Sultan [in 1908] and erect a free and happy homeland, the Armenian nation that I tried to destroy down to the last individual for attempting, during the most terrible and painful days of my homeland, to erase [my homeland] and enslave it to the enemy from history [Russia], the Armenian nation to which I now want to deliver peace and comfort because it has today sought refuge in the magnanimity of the Turkish nation. If you remain loyal to the Turkish homeland, I will do everything good I am capable of. Yet if you once again get entranced by a group of heedless committee members and attempt to betray the Turk and the Turkish homeland, then I shall order my armies surrounding your entire country not to leave a single breathing Armenian on the face of the earth. So, come to your senses![13]

Halil's astonishingly open confession that he "tried to destroy" the Armenians "down to the last individual" for collaboration with Russia and would do so again, though he was ready to make a deal with them, offers an amazingly clear insight into the thinking of a senior Young Turk leader. The speech and its revelations could only have been made at this brief historical moment of Ottoman-Armenian collaboration in late 1918.

## The Yerevan Republic

For two and a half years, Armenia was an independent republic, but, as its last leader Simon Vratsian said:

> The conditions were truly horrifying and independence seemed ironic in those conditions. A tiny piece of land, twelve thousand square kilometers, was left in the hands of the Armenians. A poor and semi-destroyed country squeezed between arid mountains, in a forsaken corner of the world, overloaded with migrants and orphans,

surrounded by teeth-grinding enemies, looting and ravage, tears and misery, massacre and terror.[14]

Until October 1918, the native population, plus a refugee population of up to 300,000 Ottoman Armenians, lived in an area less than one-half the size of the current Republic of Armenia. The republic then doubled in size, but was never a properly functioning state before its death at the end of 1920, caught in a pincer movement between the Bolsheviks and the Turks.

The First Republic notched up many achievements, such as Armenia's first university. It was a nominal parliamentary democracy, with universal suffrage, including votes for women, but the ARF party dominated all key offices of state, meaning that party and state were closely identified, both at the time and subsequently.

A number of strong personalities dominated the republic, including its four prime ministers and several military commanders who had legendary status both at the time and in later Armenian émigré mythology. The most famous commander was General Andranik Ozanian—known simply by his first name, Andranik—the former commander of the Armenian volunteer battalion in the tsarist army, who became a law unto himself. An imposing tall figure with a magnificent mustache and an air of natural authority, he impressed a British officer, who said, "[H]ere was a man who knew what was meant by a soldier. . . . Whatever he may, or may not, have done, instinct told me that here was a white man."[15] Andranik broke with the Dashnaktsutiun Party in 1907, disapproving of its alliance with the Young Turks. He then fought on every front, from Van to Karabakh. He accused the leaders of the First Republic of being traitors for having failed to defend western Armenian lands.

Another man who formed a category unto himself was Rouben Ter-Minassian. Also known just by his first name, Rouben, he served as both the republic's defense and interior minister. In 1915 Rouben led a partisan force fighting Ottoman troops. According to his granddaughter, the scholar Anahide Ter-Minassian, he was a hyper-realist, who was dedicated to the preservation of the Armenian Republic at all costs and dismissed the idea of a "Greater Armenia" on purely *realpolitik* grounds. She writes, "Few Armenian revolutionaries fought against the Turks with such fury, and fewer still among them were convinced of the necessity of Armeno-Turkish reconciliation. . . . Till the end of his life, Rouben followed attentively the evolution of modern Turkey, convinced that without the 'friendship' of the Turkish people, the Armenians would not be able to live 'free and secure' on their native soil."[16]

The leaders of the new republic, almost all of them natives of the Russian Empire, all agreed that maintaining the "Yerevan Republic" was their first priority. This exacerbated tensions with Ottoman Armenian refugees, who avoided taking citizenship, clustered around societies named after their native western Armenian towns, awaiting the day they could return home.[17]

On the first anniversary of independence in Yerevan, May 28, 1919, the republic's leaders declared an "act of union" in which they claimed responsibility for both Armenia's eastern and western territories. The historian of the republic Richard Hovannisian writes:

> The crowds, still bearing the grim marks of the preceding winter, were treated to an unprecedented spectacle as a band, several marching units, and, above all, two floats mounted on automobiles advanced along the thoroughfare. The first of these, strewn with flowers, carried a woman clothed and veiled in black. Above her flew black banners bearing the names of Mush, Sassun, Shabin-Karahisar, Tigranakert, Sis, and other Turkish Armenian centers—the tragedy and devastation of Armenia. Upon the second float stood the image of new Armenia, a woman in white proudly resting her hands upon a child on either side. The youths, one in the raiment of a Turkish Armenian and the other of a Russian Armenian, joined hands in the symbolic gesture of emancipation and unification.[18]

However, Ottoman Armenian leader Boghos Nubar, who was in Paris for the postwar peace conference, denounced the "act of union" as a seizure of power by the ARF, and his party boycotted the forthcoming parliamentary elections.

If "Russian" Armenians were the elite in the republic and Ottoman Armenians were poorly represented, the republic's Muslim

Azerbaijanis fell into an ever lower class. In 1897, more than 40 percent of the population of the Yerevan Governate were recorded as either "Tatar" or Kurdish. In June 1919, three Muslim "Tatar" Azerbaijanis were elected in the 80-seat parliament in Yerevan.[19] But Azerbaijanis were universally regarded as Turkish fifth columnists and bore the brunt of Armenian anger.

The military leader Rouben disparagingly referred to eastern Armenia as "Tatarstan," complaining that the Muslims occupied the most fertile territory. He waged campaigns to cleanse them from Armenia on at least three occasions. Having crushed an attempted Bolshevik coup d'état in May 1920, Rouben acquired new executive powers, which he used to expel Azerbaijanis from 20 more centers outside Yerevan and then "clean up" southern Armenia. "Rouben used, in turn, both intimidation and negotiations, but, above all, by his own admission, he used 'fire and steel,'" writes Anahide Ter-Minassian. "Utilizing all available methods, including the most violent ones, fedayee detachments 'encouraged' the Muslims of Armenia 'to leave.' In their place, Armenian refugees and peasants were immediately settled in the abandoned houses and land."[20] In this way, Azerbaijanis became the collateral victims of the Young Turks' genocidal policies of 1915.

At the same time, Armenians fled Azerbaijani attacks in the southern region of Nakhichevan and fighting continued in Karabakh. In March 1920, an Azerbaijani army sacked and burned the Armenian quarter in the city of Shusha, killing thousands and leaving it in ruins for a generation. The give-and-take of this Armenian-Azerbaijani violence of 1918–1920 suggests that it is better seen not as a continuation of 1915, but as another arena of the bloody nation-building through violence and ethnic cleansing that characterized all the lands from Trieste to Baku from 1912 to 1922 and left homogeneous or majority-dominated national entities behind it.

## Starving Armenians

Hunger was a constant in the short life of the First Armenian Republic. Overwhelmed by refugees and cut off from most of the world, it could not feed itself. In 1919, a *Time* correspondent called Armenia "the land of stalking death."

The humanitarian crisis gave birth to the world's first international charitable relief campaign, with posters of suffering women and children that tugged at the heartstrings of Americans to urge them to raise $30 million. In the spring of 1919, the first American food shipments reached Armenia amidst reports of cannibalism, people eating grass, and as many as 200,000 people dead from hunger. For a generation afterward, American children were told to remember "the starving Armenians" when they did not finish their plates.

Relief was channeled through the American Committee for Relief in the Near East, operating in Armenia, Greece, Syria, and Persia. Others also received aid, but Armenians were the primary recipients. Future president Herbert Hoover, who as head of the US Food Administration was in overall charge of the operation, recalled in his memoirs, "Probably Armenia was known to the American school child in 1919 only a little less than England. The association of Mount Ararat and Noah, the staunch Christians who were massacred periodically by the Mohammedan Turks, and the Sunday School collections over fifty years for alleviating their miseries—all cumulate to impress the name Armenia on the front of the American mind."[21]

Near East Relief managed Armenia's orphanages well into the 1920s, even after the Bolsheviks took charge. In Alexandropol they ran "Orphan City," home to 25,000 children and the largest orphanage in the world. The American nurse Mabel Elliott writes, "It was a bit of modern America inserted between the two chapters of the Old Testament—the wandering refugees led by Moses, the wars between Israelites and Philistines, the Lost Tribes in their dispersion, coming suddenly upon a gigantic American business organization which handled food and shelter and education and hospital care."[22]

The humanitarian needs were dramatic and real, but the Armenians were also used for propaganda purposes. The operation was imbued with a heavy element of Christian piety. Although Anatolian Muslims also received aid from Near East Relief, the pitch made to the American public was to save a Christian race in peril. The front page of the organization's journal of April 1922 carried three biblical quotations and the appeal in capital letters, "LEND YOUR AID TO THE RESURRECTION OF THE OLDEST CHRISTIAN RACE BY HELPING TO SUPPORT ITS ORPHANED CHILDREN."[23]

Humanitarian campaign blurred with Christian crusade when Near East Relief used a sensational movie as a fundraising tool. *Ravished Armenia: The Story of Aurora Mardiganian*, started out as a book. Aurora Mardiganian was a young girl from a town near Harput who was 14 years old when her family was killed in the deportations. She was abducted and—she implies but does not say explicitly—raped in several Muslim households. She eventually escaped and made her way

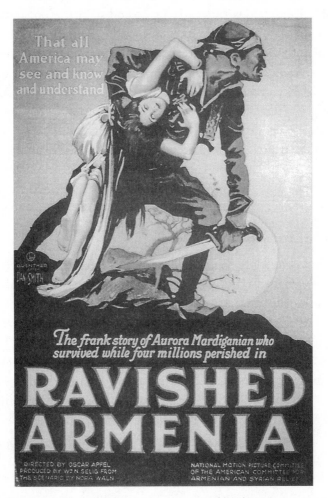

Figure 3.1 The movie *Ravished Armenia*, as advertised by the US organization Near East Relief.

Source: Near East Relief.

to Erzerum, as it came under Russian occupation. She eventually made her way to the United States, where her story was turned into a book.

After her terrible ordeals, Mardiganian herself was allowed to live out a quiet life in California, until her death in 1994—but not before her story was crudely sensationalized. Mardiganian seems to have been a woman of great courage, and the memoir, even with all its horrific details, is believable—not so the movie, entitled both *Ravished Armenia* and *Auction of Souls*, which the American Committee used as a fundraiser. One poster showed a white-skinned girl being plucked from the ground by a murderous Turk carrying a blood-stained sword and claimed that "four million perished" (see Figure 3.1).

Aurora Mardiganian played herself in the movie, of which only fragments survive. Former ambassador Henry Morgenthau, an eager fundraiser for Near East Relief, also played himself. The movie played on stereotypes of the "Terrible Turk," culminating in a scene of pornographic violence, depicting a line of young nude girls being crucified. This was the material behind posters with messages such as "How Little Aurora Mardiganian Who Escaped from the Cruel Turks is Helping to Raise $30,000,000 to Save What Is Left of These Persecuted Christians."

## An Empire Defeated

At the end of 1918, the Ottoman Empire was defeated and faced extinction. A British-led occupation force moved into the imperial capital, Constantinople. On the Bosphorus witnesses saw the smoke of docked Allied warships blackening the walls of the Sultan's palace.[24] A French force, accompanied by an "Armenian Legion" of several hundred soldiers, moved into the Mediterranean provinces. A new compliant Ottoman government was formed. The "three pashas" were sentenced to death in absentia—they had already slipped away secretly, spirited across the Black Sea into exile on a German torpedo boat named *Lorelei*.

In Turkish national memory this defeat is recalled as a historical nadir. Speaking in Washington, DC in May 2013, 95 years later, Turkish Prime Minister Recep Tayip Erdoğan chose to begin his presentation by recalling this historical moment: "The First World War was, indeed, a war which ended up having major consequences for

Turkey, for our people. What I can tell you is that, as an example of what happened after the First World War, is that the geography of Turkey changed a lot. If you look at the Ottoman past, at one time, the Ottomans covered an area of 20 million square kilometers. But after the First World War, the new Republic of Turkey found life in an area of 780,000 square kilometers."[25]

For Turkey's surviving Armenians, by contrast, it was a time of regathering. Surviving Armenians arrived in Constantinople from the provinces. The Armenian Patriarch returned from exile and led a campaign of "gathering of orphans"—*vorpahavak* in Armenian—to reclaim thousands of women and children abducted into Muslim households. In a few cases, the returnees did not want to leave the only homes they knew, but they were given no choice: there was an imperative to boost Armenian demographic ranks decimated by slaughter.[26] For the first time, the story of the destruction of the Anatolian Armenians was told in public. In 1919, a first "Mourning Ceremony" was held on April 24, the fourth anniversary of the arrest of the Armenian intellectuals. Armenians also demanded revenge from their patrons in the Entente. The Armenian women's newspaper *Hay Gin* published an advertisement for an Armenian-language version of Ambassador Morgenthau's memoirs, exhorting its readers, "In order for the fire of national revenge to be forever alive in your and your children's hearts, read this book to your children."[27]

The new Ottoman government agreed to collaborate with the Allies in investigating and prosecuting men accused of crimes against the Armenians. By April, more than 100 suspects had been arrested, many of them former officials. In February 1919, four trials were scheduled.[28] In the end, only one was heard in full. This was of Mehmed Kemal, the notorious former governor of Yozgat, who had directed the massacre of tens of thousands of Armenians in his province. Kemal was found guilty and was hanged on April 10.

The trial has been called a landmark in international justice. A postwar generation of Armenians would constantly lament the fact that there was "no Armenian Nuremberg," sometimes forgetting that a tribunal was begun but then abandoned. Had the whole judicial process been allowed to continue to the end, it might have given Armenians a collective sense of justice that would have mitigated their subsequent bitterness. However, the process quickly disintegrated. Ordinary Turks in the city resented the heavy-handed Allied occupation, and the trials were perceived as being victor's justice. Kemal's funeral, held in the afternoon so as to avoid trouble, still attracted a crowd of angry protestors.[29] The British took over the prosecutions themselves. They increased resentment by sentencing Mustafa Kemal (Atatürk) and several of his comrades-in-arms to death in absentia for their rebellion. Britain then abandoned the whole exercise in 1920, exchanging all the prisoners it held for a group of captured British officers. What had begun as a noble campaign to prosecute "crimes against humanity" fizzled out.

In 1919, the Ottoman Empire, along with its German ally, faced a own formal death sentence at the postwar Paris Peace Conference, with the Armenians and others seeking to carve out new national territories from its carcass.

The Armenians did not have a seat at the table, but sent two delegations, which represented the divergent priorities of eastern and western Armenians. The first delegation was led by the cosmopolitan Boghos Nubar, son of a former finance and foreign minister of Egypt, "a polished Levantine gentleman, fluent in French, wealthy and conservative, and well known to the European diplomatic corps."[30] During the war, Nubar had received promises from the Allies about the formation of an Armenian homeland.[31] In that spirit, he made extravagant demands for a new great Armenian state, stretching from the Black Sea to the Mediterranean.

The rougher-cut Avetis Aharonian, a poet and politician, led the second delegation from the new Republic of Armenia. Aharonian was under instructions to ask for a smaller (but still large) Armenia and not to endorse Nubar's demands. "[O]ur Delegation had carried with it from Erevan very moderate demands, commensurate with our very modest ability," wrote Aharonian's prime minister later.[32] However, in Paris, under pressure as the junior partner, Aharonian "succumbed to the euphoria that had settled over the Armenophile world" and agreed to underwrite the demands of Boghos Nubar.

On February 12, 1919, the two Armenian delegations submitted a joint memorandum. It outlined the Armenian case for liberation from the Turks and their contribution to the Allies' war effort. It laid claim to a big new Armenian state stretching "from sea to sea," including disputed territories in the Caucasus. The English version of the memorandum calls on the new mandate power to remove Muslim authorities from power, disarm the population, "expel the namadic [*sic*] tribes" and "send away the mouhadjirs." It ends with the capitalized declaration, "THE VOICE OF ALL ARMENIANS LIVING AND DEAD MUST BE HEARD."

Allied leaders, who had earlier encouraged the Armenians during the war, were non-commital. Some were irritated by the Armenians' claims, and David Lloyd George would later say, "I do know that some of the Armenian, I will not say ambitions, but aspirations, have been rather of a colossal character." Only President Wilson gave reassuring words.[33]

Delegations representing Azerbaijan, Georgia, the rump Ottoman government, and Persia lodged competing claims to some of the territories the Armenians wanted. But the main problem was how a new settlement would be enforced on the ground. Given that the map of the old Ottoman Empire would have to be redrawn, nothing would happen without agreement on a foreign mandate power. War-weary and cash-strapped Britain and France wanted to hand over this responsibility to the United States. At the start of the conference, Wilson admitted that the American public would be "most disinclined" to accept a mandate, but said "he himself had succeeded in getting the people of America to do many things, and he might succeed in getting them to accept this burden also."[34]

The Treaty of Versailles of June 28, 1919, imposed punitive terms on Germany, but the Paris conference broke up, agreeing only that a final settlement for the Ottoman Empire would be deferred until the mandate issue could be resolved. Wilson sailed back to the United States to fight the battle on this issue with isolationists and his own Congress.

## Turkish Revival

As the Paris Peace Conference met, the situation in Turkey itself was changing. Two crucial events occurred in May 1919. On May 15, encouraged by the British, the Greek army landed on the Aegean coast and occupied the city of Smyrna (Izmir). The same night, a senior

Ottoman officer, Mustafa Kemal, the future Atatürk and founder of the Turkish Republic, defied his government and slipped away from Constantinople. On May 19, he landed an expeditionary force at the Black Sea port of Samsun, initiating what became known as the Turkish War of Independence. Kemal issued a call to repel the claims of both Greeks and Armenians.

In the east in early 1919, the British agreed to hand over the eastern province of Kars to the Armenian Republic, a decision that would allow tens of thousands of destitute refugees to go home. However, the British did so just as they were downscaling their military commitment to the region. Colonel Alfred Rawlinson, a British intelligence officer entrusted with ensuring a peaceful transfer of power in Kars, believed he had been handed an impossible task, because it "could only have been carried into effect by the permanent occupation of the districts dealt with by considerable forces of European troops."[35]

In the summer of 1919, Rawlinson toured the Kars region and heard reports of atrocities by incoming Armenian soldiers against local Muslims. He confronted three Armenian generals about this:

> As I expected, many of the facts they found it impossible to deny, and confined themselves to making counter-charges against the Turks, doubtless equally well founded. Their main argument, which they insisted on all through, was that the Allies had authorized them to take possession of the country, and in order to obtain control it was an absolute necessity that they should disarm the Tartar Moslem population; as this could only be done by force, it obviously led to fighting; and fighting, as between Moslem and Armenian, of necessity led to massacre and atrocities of all kinds.[36]

Rawlinson later telegraphed his bosses in Tiflis with the advice that "in the interests of humanity" the Armenians could not be left in control of a Muslim population.[37]

At the same time, US President Woodrow Wilson sent a special envoy, General James Harbord, to the region to report how an American mandate could be established in Anatolia. Harbord sent back a depressing report of devastation and interethnic hostility. Everywhere he went he saw orphans, Turkish as well as Armenian, whom he described as "these pathetic little survivors of the unhappy years of the war (see Figure 3.2).[38] He was shocked by the sight of empty Armenian towns and villages, estimating that between half a million and more than one million of them had died in a "definite system" of destruction. Now, Harbord wrote, "[m]utilation, violation, torture, and death have left their haunting memories in a hundred beautiful Armenian valleys, and the traveler in that region is seldom free from the evidence of this most colossal crime of all the ages."[39]

The general also noted, "In the territory untouched by war from which Armenians were deported the ruined villages are undoubtedly due to Turkish devilry, but where Armenians advanced and retired with the Russians their retaliatory cruelties unquestionably rivaled the Turks in their inhumanity."[40] Harbord concluded that any mandated territory would need a strong foreign military force to oversee it and that the US mandate should extend not only to Armenia but to most of Turkey as well—a logical but unworkable suggestion. In any event, Wilson's request to the US Senate for an American mandate for the region was rejected in June 1920.

The scale of the task, a lack of resources, and general war-weariness all played into the hands of the two rising players in the region, Mustafa Kemal and the Bolsheviks. In early 1920, Kemal's forces drove the French army out of Cilicia, along with tens of thousands of Armenians who had resettled in the region. When the French retreated from Maraş on February 10, 1920, the Armenians of the city fled on foot in a snowstorm, resulting in the loss of thousands of lives. By 1922, all of this area of southern Turkey was under the control of the Nationalists.

Meanwhile, the Bolsheviks moved south. In the summer of 1920, the Turkish and Bolshevik revolutionary movements spectacularly threw aside two centuries of Russian-Ottoman history and signed an alliance to share money, weapons, and spheres of influence. As Michael Reynolds comments, "The reversal of the geopolitical dynamic could not have been any more stunning. In less than two years' time, Russia had metamorphosed from the greatest threat to the Ottoman empire to the best hope for Muslim sovereignty in Anatolia."[41] The first victim of the alliance was the Republic of Azerbaijan. In April 1920, Kemal assisted the Bolsheviks in conquering Baku and its all-important oil fields and occupying Azerbaijan.

In August 1920, the Allies and the tiny Ottoman government still in charge of Constantinople finally signed the Treaty of Sèvres. It formally ordained the breakup of the Ottoman Empire and declared not just a new independent Armenia but an autonomous Kurdistan as well. Article 89 of the treaty entrusted President Wilson with the task of drawing the frontiers between the new Armenia and the new Turkey. But the treaty was a stillborn document designed for a situation that no longer obtained on the ground. It presupposed the active intervention of the Great Powers, and offered so little to the Turks that it provided an extra boost to Mustafa Kemal's insurgency. "The Sèvres treaty constituted the final resolution of the Eastern Question as it had been interpreted by the European powers during the nineteenth century. It was a nineteenth-century imperialistic solution to a nineteenth-century imperial problem," comments the historian Paul Helmreich.[42]

Figure 3.2 Turkish Orphans turn out to meet US General James Harbord, Erzerum, 1919.

Source: Harbord Collection, Library of Congress.

## Armenian Defeat

In September 1920 a Turkish army surged east for the third time in six years. Kemal recruited the talented general Kazim Karabekir to reconquer the eastern provinces of Ardahan, Batum, and Kars. On October 30, Karabekir conquered the fortress of Kars, which was supposed to be impregnable. At least one of the Armenian generals charged with defending the city committed suicide, and thousands of officers were taken prisoner. The surrender occasioned much Armenian shame—both at the time and for generations afterward. The governor of the city said, "Kars fell, but it was not defeated; it became the victim of our criminal negligence."[43] Had they held on to it, as the Georgians did to the Black Sea city of Batum (Batumi) a few months later, Kars might have been incorporated into Soviet Armenia.

As Turkish troops approached the Armenian Republic, the US president finally unveiled his map of "Wilsonian Armenia." It drew the borders of a vast entity, comprising most of Bitlis, Erzerum, and Van provinces and including an outlet to the Black Sea at Trebizond—but of course it bore no relation to the military situation on the ground. Mustafa Kemal later commented, "Poor Wilson did not understand that a frontier which is not defended with bayonets, force and honor cannot be secured by another principle."[44]

Simultaneously, the Bolshevik Eleventh Army was advancing from the east. Simon Vratsian, who formed a new government on November 24, later described the Armenian Republic as being caught between "the Bolshevik hammer and the Turkish anvil." The realist line—seek an accommodation with the Turks, do not rely on Great Power or Russian protection—came to the fore once more. Vratsian published a proclamation saying, "Armenia's state structure will be anchored not on the empty and dangerous encouragement of foreigners, but on Armenia's true abilities. Our operational motto will be sincere reconciliation with Turkey and harmony and peaceful existence with all our neighbors."[45] On the same day, the Dashnak newspaper *Haraj* editorialized, "If the Armenian people had not had Russian orientation during the recent pan-European war, but had been with Turkey, most probably it would have avoided the massacres. We must understand that it is not by leaning on outsiders that we can achieve peace, but that only by relying on our own strengths that will we decide our fate with our strong neighbors, the Turks."[46]

On November 27, under Vratsian's instructions, Armenian negotiators renounced the Treaty of Sèvres, just five days after the declaration of Wilsonian Armenia. They then reluctantly signed a treaty with the Turks, which confirmed the loss of many territories. "We had long debates about Ani, Nakhichevan and Surmalu [the area around Mount Ararat], but the Turks made no compromises," the chief Armenian negotiator said later.[47] They then asked the Bolsheviks for terms. On December 2, Vratsian and his government resigned. Two days later, they handed over power to a new Soviet Armenian government. The First Armenian Republic was dead. Many Armenians welcomed the Bolshevik takeover. In Vratsian's words, "Only the Turkish-Armenians, who were grieving the destruction of independence, were extremely sad. Because of communication difficulties, the majority of the districts were surprised, but there again did not seem to be any particular regret. Some were even happy, saying, 'Finally the Russians will come and save us. We will be safe from the Turks, we will have bread, we will also have fuel, and life will become easier.' This was the general feeling."[48]

The treaties of Moscow and Kars of 1921 between Kemalist Turkey and the Bolsheviks confirmed the new borders and the Armenians' loss of Kars and the region around Mount Ararat. A brief counter-revolution in Yerevan lasted for six weeks. An insurgency continued in Zangezur against both the new authorities in Yerevan and the Azerbaijani population, until the Bolshevik government offered an amnesty and assurances that Zangezur would be part of Soviet Armenia. Only in the summer of 1921 did the last leaders of the First Republic cross the Araxes River into Iran and exile.

## The Collapse of the Armenian Cause

In 1923, with the Treaty of Lausanne, the Armenian cause vanished from the international agenda. This was mainly because Mustafa Kemal succeeded in establishing a new Turkish state, but also because of the withdrawal of interest by the Western powers. In the United States, the Armenians had many sponsors but there was no single policy.

In 1919 the first representative emerged of what was to be a long tradition: the American-Armenian political lobbyist. Named Vahan Cardashian, he was a graduate of Yale University who had worked as a lawyer on Wall Street and had served in the Ottoman consulate in New York. Despite lack of connections with Armenians in the region itself, Cardashian was a talented political activist and succeeded in attracting major luminaries to his newly formed American Committee for the Independence of Armenia. His biggest catch was Woodrow Wilson's erstwhile rival in the 1916 presidential election, former Republican Party candidate and governor of New York, Charles Evans Hughes. At the committee's inaugural banquet at the Hotel Plaza in New York on February 8, 1919, Hughes inveighed against "the ferocity of the Turk." He told his audience, "Now we rejoice that the hour of liberation has come."[49]

President Woodrow Wilson, the man who had beaten Hughes, pressed ahead throughout 1919 and 1920 with his idea of an American mandate over either Armenia or a much larger territory, despite opposition from Congress and the lack of a promise of troops to protect this would-be entity.

In Turkey and Armenia, American officials had a different agenda: maintaining the massive humanitarian operation run by Near East Relief and its associated missionary activities; seeking a post-Ottoman territorial arrangement that would work on the ground; and dealing with the new political reality represented by Mustafa Kemal and his Nationalist forces. In 1920, James Barton, head of Near East Relief, Caleb Gates of Robert College in Constantinople, and other leading lights in the Ottoman Empire backed the idea of an Armenian "national home" to be established in the Middle East, perhaps in Cilicia or Syria, as a more workable alternative to a new Armenian state established on Turkish-inhabited lands.

An exchange of letters in this period between the relief coordinator Barton and Admiral Mark Bristol, US High Commissioner to the Ottoman Empire, reveals them both agreeing that the Armenians have over-played their hand and are demanding too much, Mustafa Kemal is on the rise, the French and Greeks have stirred up a "hornet's nest" by invading Anatolia, and that in Washington there is "no statesmanship" and no understanding of how much the situation has changed on the ground.

Barton, a Quaker-born former missionary who had lived for years in the Ottoman Empire, believed the priority was buttressing the Armenian Republic, rather than expanding it. On January 14, 1921, he told Bristol that he had almost secured a deal for a big US loan to independent Armenia, which he hoped would then be matched by a European commitment of troops. "I took the matter up with the President and he assured me some days in advance of the opening of Congress that he would make the recommendation. But almost upon the day that the message was sent to Congress, Russian Armenia went Soviet."

On March 28, 1921, Bristol wrote to Barton that although his government was "contaminated by the advocacy of Greek and Armenian claims," he still hoped an American mandate could be set up for both Armenian and Turkish territories. "The Near East is a cesspool that should be drained and cleaned out without any half-way measures. The idea of establishing an independent Armenia and placing the Greeks over a part of the territory is only creating what, with the new Turkey that would be established, three cesspools, instead of one. . . . Let us adopt a big policy and stand for it and do our best to get this policy carried out."[50]

Vahan Cardashian and his allies in the United States denounced this approach as a betrayal of the Armenian cause. In February 1921, Cardashian published a pamphlet entitled "Wilson—Wrecker of Armenia," which accused most of the American actors associated with Armenia of treachery. In the pamphlet, Cardashian excoriated the departing president, who was just leaving office, for being "mischievous." Wilson's territorial offer to the Armenians, he wrote, had given them much less than they had been promised at Paris and "resulted in the dismemberment of Armenia by 60 per cent." What Armenians needed now was active American military support.[51] Cardashian then turned his guns on the US missionaries of Near East Relief, whom he accused of conspiring to deny the Armenians a homeland because they wanted to evangelize Turks. "It is not the Armenian who interests these good people, save as a point of departure, as furnishing a background for action. It is the Turk—the Turk whom they are seeking to Christianize."[52]

Barton, writing to Admiral Bristol, was furious, describing Cardashian as an adventurer who was discrediting the Armenian cause:

> We have had many a conference with Armenian leaders as to what can be done to stop this vicious propaganda carried on by Cardashian. He is constantly reporting atrocities which never occurred and giving endless misinformation with regard to the situation in Armenia and in Turkey. We do not like to come out and attack him in public. That would injure the whole cause we are all trying to serve, because people would say that we are quarreling among ourselves and would lose confidence in the whole concern.[53]

Very soon these debates were irrelevant as Mustafa Kemal established his full authority in Turkey. The new US president, Warren Harding, made non-intervention the default policy, spurning the League of Nations and working to remove the United States from European entanglements.

The Armenian political cause finally crumbled in 1923. The Great Powers made their peace with Kemal at the Lausanne conference and focused on their last remaining interests in the Middle East. Proceedings were directed by the veteran British Foreign Secretary Lord Curzon, who succeeded brilliantly in fulfilling Britain's two main aims: to keep a claim on the oil-rich province of Mosul and to have the Straits to the Black Sea demilitarized and open to passage for international vessels.

The Treaty of Lausanne was a stunning victory for Kemal, who proclaimed the Turkish Republic three months later. Turkey agreed to the surrender of the Middle Eastern provinces it had lost in World War I, but would keep the territory it controlled. A massive exchange of populations was confirmed that had in fact almost been completed: almost 1.5 million Greek Christians were deported from their age-old homeland in Turkey in an exchange with half a million Turkish Muslims from Greece. Armenians were not mentioned by name, receiving only minimal guarantees as Christian "minorities," with special rights in Istanbul. Kurds received no guarantees at all.

In Washington, Cardashian used his considerable lobbying skills and his Armenian Committee to try to block ratification of the treaty. He won the battle but lost the war. The US Senate declined to ratify Lausanne, but Western governments all successively recognized the new Turkish Republic. In 1927, the United States simply set up diplomatic relations and exchanged ambassadors with Ankara, a move the Senate retrospectively approved a year later.

The push for the new US rapprochement with Kemalist Turkey was led by none other than Charles Hughes, the former leading light of Cardashian's committee, who had become secretary of state. In January 1924, making a pitch for ratification, Hughes spelled out an apologia for recent US policy and a rationale for its strategic withdrawal from the region:

> It should also be remembered that a large part of the distress in the Near East has been caused by encouraging action which failed of adequate support. *At various times the Armenians and Greeks have been encouraged to take up arms*, later to be left to their own devices. This Government, however, would not be justified in promoting such a policy on the part of others which it was not prepared adequately to sustain. It has no mandate from the people to intervene by arms and thus to impose by force a solution of the problems of the Near East. And, for this very reason, it could not essay the role of a dictator in order to determine how others should solve these problems.[54]

In effect, five years after he had declared "the hour of liberation" to an Armenian audience, Hughes was drawing a line under the Armenian question as a lost cause.

# 4

## Aspects of Forgetting

### Buried Sorrows

AMIDST THE TOWERING APARTMENT blocks of the Armenian district of Bourj Hamoud in eastern Beirut, the space flattens out to reveal an older type of habitation: a labyrinth of low square houses, narrow alleys, with a thicket of electricity cables and telephone wires swarming above. This is Sanjak, the world's last surviving Armenian refugee camp. By some miracle, this settlement has continued to function on the same spot since the 1930s, and the visitor gets a reflected impression of what post-1915 existence was like for hundreds of thousands of Armenians.

"First the roofs were bamboo, then they were wood, then corrugated iron," one old lady said. Nowadays, the structures are more like houses, but still extremely cramped. In one house, a family of seven was squashed into three tiny rooms. In their front room, everything was crammed into one big wall cabinet: a television set, books and CDs, stuffed animals, icons, a statue of the Virgin Mary. The grandmother said she was born here in 1937, her parents having fled the town of Dörtyol on a French ship.

Sarkis, the head of the household, was proud to stress that they were working citizens: he had a job in a jeweler's shop, and his family did not accept welfare. Nonetheless, their miniature house—like those of millions of people across the Middle East—still had the feeling of impermanence, of being a ship in the storm. Sanjak had been burned down once in the Lebanese Civil War in 1978. It was now threatened with demolition once again as the municipal authorities threatened to raze the camp, making its inhabitants offers of compensation and rehousing that they were wary of accepting. This group of refugees was bracing itself to move again some time soon.

In the early 1920s, most Armenians were in exile. Alongside Soviet Armenia, Syria and Lebanon were the main new homes of the refugees, and Beirut gradually turned into the capital of the new Armenian diaspora. In Lebanon, there was no pressure for assimilation into a new assumed identity, and Armenian remained the primary spoken language. Armenians also became a political force in the country: Lebanon had de facto preserved the old Ottoman *millet* system on a more equitable basis, giving each religious community—Sunnis, Shias, Maronite Christians, Armenians, and so on—a quota of representation in local government and parliament.

Several Armenians wrote tragic accounts of the deportations in their immediate aftermath. In 1917, the poet Zabel Esayan published the story of a survivor from Syria. The writer Aram Andonian collected testimonies in Aleppo. The author Ervant Odian and the bishop Grigoris Balakian wrote memoirs. This wave of testimony ebbed around 1922. There are different explanations for this. One is that both Constantinople and Yerevan, the two main centers hitherto for Armenian publishing, had become inauspicious locations for an Armenian writer. The political environment had changed.[1]

From that point, there is much less literature on the disaster that Armenians had just endured, which they generally called *Medz Yeghern*, meaning "Great Catastrophe" or "Great Crime" in Armenian.

In public life, at least, there was little reference to the Armenian tragedy; as with many others, there were many silences. The concept of "psychological trauma" would only gain currency after World War II. Before that, survivors were not encouraged to talk about terrible experiences. This was the experience of Leon Surmelian, as he tells it in his vivid memoir of a childhood broken apart by the 1915 catastrophe.

Surmelian and his brother and two sisters were reunited in 1916, but never saw their parents again.

> Neither my brother nor sisters spoke about their most painful inner experiences, which, like mine, could not be told. In fact I could not tell them anything about myself, nor did they question me. They knew I had escaped from Jevizlik, and that was enough. By a sort of silent agreement we took care not to mention our parents, and other relatives whom we dearly loved. Their names, or anything to remind us directly of them, were barred from conversation. If one of us, for instance, had said "Mother" inadvertently, we would have bawled, all four of us. Our deepest sorrows lay buried in our hearts, wounds that would never heal, and we tried to forget them in the joy of our reunion. Onnik and I were resuming our interrupted schooling, and we looked hopefully to the future.[2]

Men, women, and children, young and old, had different roles in Armenian society and had also experienced the Catastrophe in very different ways. Well more than half of Ottoman Armenian men had died.[3] We can assume that, as with the aftermath of other mass atrocities, men harbored hidden feelings of "survivors' guilt" and of shame at having been unable to defend their women and children; an Armenian author would later write that, with the assassinations of the Unionist leaders in Operation Nemesis (see later in this chapter), "the shame of having walked like sheep to the slaughterhouse was wiped away from the face of the Armenian nation."[4]

In some of the few memoirs and diaries of 1915 from this period, there is a theme of "Golgotha," of martyrdom for the Christian faith, perhaps as a way of seeking to rationalize loss on such a scale. The Armenian literature of the 1920s dwelt more on heroic exploits or on political quarrels than on massacres and deportations—perhaps so as to combat a collective sense of shame.

The first major work of literature on the Catastrophe was written not by an Armenian but by an Austrian Jewish novelist. In 1929, Franz Werfel met a community of Armenian survivors in Damascus and decided to turn their experiences into fiction. His massive historical novel, *The Forty Days of Musa Dagh*, came out in German in 1933. A year later, its English translation was a bestseller. Werfel writes some vivid passages about the deportations, but he chose mainly to tell a rare story of resistance and heroism. He described the most famous case of Armenian armed opposition to the Ottomans in 1915, when 5,000 villagers in Cilicia, close to the current Syrian border, organized an improvised defense of a mountain citadel of Musa Dagh. They held out for 53 days (longer than Werfel's fictional 40) before eventually being rescued by a French warship. Even Werfel's heroic epic did not meet approval in all quarters. The editors of the journal *Masis* opposed translating the novel into Armenian so as not to renew "the bitter and terrible memories of the recent past among the masses of our people."[5]

With the ranks of men depleted, women played a central role in the new communities. Tatul Sonentz, who grew up in Cairo in the 1930s, says, "Armenian women really were the source of national education of their children, first of all because they did not work outside, they were at home. They gave full time to the raising of their children. They were very nationalistic."[6] Women could mourn at home. In the 1950s in Soviet Armenia, Verjine Svazlian, a researcher of oral history, taped the recollections of 300 survivors of the deportations. She heard hundreds of songs, sung by women, which preserved the folk memory of the Catastrophe and enabled them to mourn what was lost. Around 100 of the songs are in Turkish, some with Armenian words mixed in. Some are songs of praise for Armenian heroes such as Andranik or the defenders of Musa Dagh. Some curse Enver and Talat Pasha:

> I tied my horse to the hollow stone,
> May you lose your sight, Enver Pasha!
> No more Armenian youths were left.
> The rose and nightingale went away, what should I say?
> You may cry, you may laugh, what should I say?[7]

Many are dirges mourning the lost homeland and family members:

> A deer is wandering around Urfa,
> It has lost its fawn and is seeking it anxiously,

Deer, my heart is also wounded like yours,
I sought but couldn't find a cure for my grief,
Don't roam, deer, in these mountains,
They will ravish you and
Separate you from your father and mother.[8]

The song of the lost fawn mourns the broken families and in particular the tens of thousands of lost young Armenian women who were taken in by Muslims, either by force or as an act of kindness.

After the defeat of the Ottoman Empire in 1918, many of these women and children—both those adopted out of charity and the victims of abduction and sexual violence—were reclaimed from Muslim families by fellow Armenians and Christian missionaries. There were so many young women that Armenian communities usually decided to overlook the taboo of rape and accept them back as suitable candidates for marriage. In the 1920s, hundreds of single Armenian women came, no questions asked, to the United States as "picture brides" in long-distance arranged marriages.[9]

A prevalent image from this era is of the needy Armenian orphan—and Armenia itself was frequently likened metaphorically to an orphan or a sickly child. Some of them fended for themselves; others were in institutions. In December 1921, the US organization Near East Relief reported that it was looking after 114,107 children in 124 orphanages, the majority of them Armenian. A Near East Relief report of 1920 reads, "At one center, Alexandropol, we have approximately 18,000 orphan children, probably the largest single assemblage of children and almost certainly the largest assemblage of orphans that the world has ever known" (see Figure 4.1). The authors go on, "It should be noted that most of the children in the orphanages are not only without parents but have no known living relatives, while some of them, orphaned in infancy, do not even know their own names."[10]

Many children were found living with Bedouin families in the Syrian desert. One became the nanny of Herant Katchadourian, who was born in Cilicia and later in life became a professor at Stanford in California. In his autobiography, he writes about his childhood nanny and lifetime family companion, Lucine. Before she came to his family, she had been living in a Danish orphanage and before that with a

Figure 4.1 The largest orphanage in the world, Alexandropol, Armenia, 1921.
Source: Near East Relief.

Bedouin family, who tattooed her with tribal markings. Lucine cherished one memory from this Bedouin family of being given a lamb as a pet—a sign that they had been fond of her. In her orphanage, she painstakingly plucked out the tattoos from her chin with her fingernails and then scoured the wounds with ash and lemon juice. Lucine died in California in 2001. Katchadourian writes, "She was an orphan who didn't know who she was, who her parents were, when or where she was born, or even her real name."[11]

## The Turkish Republic

In 1923, the new Republic of Turkey was scarcely less traumatized. The country was emerging from 10 years of continual warfare that had begun with the First Balkan War of 1912. Almost no part of it was untouched. The historian Erik Zürcher records that an estimated 2.5 million Anatolian Muslims had lost their lives over the preceding decade. He writes:

[I]n some eastern provinces half the population was dead and another quarter had become refugees. There were 12 provinces, most of them in the west, where the number of widows among the female population exceeded 30 per cent. Anatolia's high mortality rate was due not only to warfare and atrocities. The wars had led to disruption of the infrastructure and a shortage of labor in agriculture. These in turn had led to famine and famines usually had epidemics, notably of cholera and typhoid, trailing in their wake.[12]

Traveling through southern Turkey in 1927, the British writer Harold Armstrong was appalled by the devastation of places he had last seen a decade before. He found the village of Incerlik—now the site of a US airbase—still half-ruined, several years after the end of the War of Independence. "Everywhere I met with an almost incredible poverty—the village of Injerlik, once a prosperous place, was reduced to a few mud huts." The villagers blamed the French invasion of 1920 for the destruction. "They gave me a sense of desolation and hopelessness as they sat in their broken villages."[13] Not far away, in another village, Armstrong got to know the local imam, who was full of hatred toward Armenian "traitors":

The *hodja* took me shooting many miles away into the low hills and lent me ponies. Only when we talked of Greeks and Armenians he grew stern and his eyes hard and dangerous.

"If one came back I would kill him with my own hands," he said. "I led the villagers out when we drove the *rayahs* down to the river and drowned them by the score. You are English. You work for your country. I have no quarrel with you, but these were traitors. Let us talk of other things."[14]

In these conditions, Mustafa Kemal set about building an entirely new state and drew a line under the past. At home, the central idea of the republic was Turkishness and its central slogan was Atatürk's famous phrase, "Happy is he who calls himself a Turk"—a phrase meant to turn on its head the former negative associations with the name "Turk." In foreign policy, in contrast to other authoritarian leaders of his era such as Benito Mussolini, Kemal emphasized that imperial days were over. Formally abandoning the foreign adventurism of his predecessors, he adopted the slogan "Peace at home, peace in the world."

From 1923, Kemal began a breathtaking series of top-down modernizing reforms. Turkey was declared a secular republic, the sultan and his family were exiled, and the caliphate was dissolved. A new legal system was introduced, borrowed from different countries in Western Europe. Women were emancipated. The Islamic calendar switched to a Western one. Western dress was made compulsory, as were surnames, with Kemal in 1934 assuming the special name Atatürk, or "Father of the Turks."

Atatürk was hailed around the world as a great modernizer. Many of those who had seen Ottoman Empire in its decrepitude were full of admiration. Caleb Gates, the president of Robert College in Istanbul, ends his memoir of five decades living in his adopted country with a paean of praise to the new Turkey: "Government has become the friend of the people. In the cities the intelligentsia are working in alliance with the government, and the youth have caught the contagion of hope for a well-organized and progressive nation. Such facts speak louder than words and give new ideas to minds that had become sodden with long years of hopeless struggle against oppression."[15]

The new Turkey lived by the famous formulation of Ernest Renan that a nation-state is founded on a deliberate act of forgetting. In this case, the forgetting was made even more radical by the language reform of 1928 in which the old Ottoman alphabet was replaced by a Latin one and thousands of non-Turkic words were officially expunged. That made it almost impossible for children to read the same books as their parents had. In history books, this enforced amnesia of the new Turkish history covered not just Christian elements but most of the Ottoman era and recent tragedies such as the Balkan Wars. The 606-page *Outlines of Turkish History*, published in 1930 by the new Turkish Society for Historical Research, outlined a new national history that focused primarily on the distant past, recasting the Turks as the ancient ancestors of Anatolian civilization. The entire Ottoman Empire only merited 50 pages in the history, and the Christian peoples were given a marginal supporting role in the epic story.[16]

Kemal Atatürk's personal attitude to the destruction of the Armenians was ambiguous. As an army officer, he had served at Gallipoli and in the Middle East but had had no personal involvement in the deportations of 1915. His approach toward the Armenians was contingent on political circumstances. During the War of Independence, Kemal identified Armenians and Greeks as the biggest threat to his would-be nation-state. He began his famous six-day programmatic speech of 1927, known as the *Nutuk*, with a description of Turkey in 1919 as prostrate and under the control of the Allied powers, while their local proxies, the Greeks and Armenians, were trying "to hasten the break-down of the state."[17]

At the same time, Kemal spoke disapprovingly about the Armenian massacres. Speaking to Turkey's National Assembly on April 24, 1920, Kemal referred to the deportations as "the shameful act that belongs to the past."[18] In December 1920, Kemal called them a regrettable episode provoked by the Armenians' Great Power sponsors, but, in his view, more than equaled by what the Armenians did in return: "I can decisively argue that these circumstances occupy a much lower rank than the cruelties executed with no justification in the European states."[19]

The argument that Christians and Turks had engaged in an equal struggle also served to disqualify any possible claims by Armenians or Greeks on the property and businesses they had lost. Those losses were to be treated as an accomplished fact and as the basis for the building of a new Turkish business class. Indeed, Kemal Atatürk's presidential palace and grounds in Çankaya in Ankara, subsequently used by other Turkish presidents, were formerly a vineyard and mansion of an Armenian merchant, Ohannes Kasabian, who fled to Istanbul. Vehbi Koç, the most successfully businessman in modern Turkey, got his start in Ankara in the vacuum left by departed Christians.[20]

The new Turkey lived by a universal but unspoken hierarchy of ethnic and social groups. Although the republic was formally secular—and its urban elite mostly became fully secular—Sunni Islam remained the hidden common denominator of identity for most of the country. Sunni religious clerics had a special status, although strictly subordinated to the state. The scholar Şener Aktürk describes this hybrid system as being "anti-ethnic but mono-religious."[21]

The Turkish state now directed most of its violence at Kurds, attempting to force them into its new model. Their homeland of eastern Anatolia continued to be the most violent part of Turkey throughout the twentieth century. Kurds fought against Ankara in the Sheikh Said uprising of 1925 and in the insurgency in Dersim in 1937–1938. Thousands were killed. A series of Turkifying reforms forced Kurds to abandon their language and customs, and in 1934 a new formulation stipulated that "Kurds" no longer existed and that they were now to be called "mountain Turks."

Turkey's remaining Christians were too small in number to be regarded as a political threat. When the Hatay province was re-allocated to Turkey from Syria in 1939, an Armenian village named Vakifli ended up in Turkey, and its inhabitants—the descendants of the defenders of Musa Dagh—have lived there peacefully ever since. However, Armenians and Greeks were very much second-class citizens. Bigotry against the Christian *gavur* ("infidel" or "unbeliever") was part of the everyday culture. In 1928, the Armenian Catholic diocese quit Istanbul for Beirut. In 1934, under Turkey's new surname law, Armenians and Greeks were forced to take Turkish names. In 1935, the Patriarch and his community in Istanbul felt compelled to display their loyalty by publicly burning a picture of Franz Werfel, author of *The Forty Days of Musa Dagh*.[22] Armenians steadily emigrated. According to Turkey's 1927 census, around 100,000 Armenians lived in Istanbul and around 25,000–30,000 lived in their historic eastern provinces. Over several generations, these numbers declined even in absolute terms. In 2014, there were probably fewer than 80,000 official Armenians in Turkey, mostly in Istanbul.

## Operation Nemesis

In 1921, Mustafa Kemal and the exiled Armenian Dashnaktsutiun Party briefly shared a common goal, to extinguish traces of the Young Turk Committee of Union and Progress.

In that year, Kemal viewed the exiled Ottoman Unionist leaders, especially the military adventurer Enver Pasha, as potentially the biggest threat to his rule. He was ready to co-opt Unionist officials of the second tier so long as they displayed loyalty or to destroy them if they did not. One of those he recruited was the notorious Unionist Şükrü Kaya, who had directed the Armenian deportations in 1915. He would serve as Atatürk's interior minister and oversee the forced relocation of Kurds. One of those who was destroyed was Nazim Bey, one of the leaders of the Special Organization paramilitary, who was hanged in 1926 for allegedly plotting to assassinate Kemal.

In 1919, two radical Armenians devised a plan of revenge, which they called Operation Nemesis. They were Shahin Natali, a US-educated professional revolutionary, and Armen Garo, the veteran Dashnak revolutionary, former Ottoman member of parliament and survivor of the Ottoman Bank raid of 1896. In meetings in Paris, Tbilisi, and Boston, the two recruited a team of assassins and drew up a list of targets. Besides prominent Unionist leaders, the list of men selected for assassination included three Armenian "traitors" and several prominent Azerbaijanis. The first victim, in June 1920, was Fatali Khan Khoisky, the prime minister of the Azerbaijani republic.

The number-one target was the chief nemesis of the Armenians, Talat Pasha. He had been living under an assumed name in the Charlottenburg quarter of Berlin. The young agent Soghomon Tehlirian, an Armenian from Erzincan, tracked him down and, on March 15, 1921, shot him dead in a street near the Zoological Gardens. As instructed by his masters, Tehlirian did not run away but surrendered to police.

As Natali and Garo had intended, the trial of Tehilirian, the assassin of Talat Pasha, received massive newspaper coverage across the world and turned instead into a posthumous trial of the crimes of the victim. Liman von Sanders, the former German commander in the Gallipoli campaign, was called as a prominent witness. He confirmed that the "Armenian massacres" had taken place but said that no German military officers had played any part in them.

Tehlirian did not reveal that he was a hired agent. He claimed to be an ordinary Armenian student who had witnessed the massacre of his family. (In fact, although his family members were indeed killed, he himself had been fighting with the Russians at the time.) He said that his mother had come to him in a dream asking for vengeance. On only the second day of the trial, on June 3, 1921, a sympathetic Berlin jury acquitted Tehlirian on grounds of temporary insanity. When he traveled to the United States, he was received ecstatically by the Armenian community. He is still memorialized as a hero.[23]

Over the next 16 months, the assassins of Operation Nemesis killed five more prominent Turks and Azerbaijanis. Among them was Cemal Pasha, who was gunned down in the center of Tbilisi (Tiflis) in July 1922. (Enver Pasha was killed fighting the Bolsheviks in Tajikistan August 1922.) The assassinations echoed through the generations. In the 1970s, the Armenian terrorists attacking Turkish diplomats cited Operation Nemesis as a precedent for their own campaign—despite the very different circumstances. In Turkey, Talat Pasha and his comrades were suddenly remembered as "martyrs" in World War II during a moment of Turkish nationalist revival and rapprochement with Germany. In February 1943, the Nazi government in Berlin exhumed Talat's body and repatriated it to Istanbul by train. His coffin, draped with a Turkish flag, was paraded through the streets of the city on a gun carriage with full military honors, and then was reburied next to the Monument of Liberty, a memorial hill in Şişli in central Istanbul. The bloody shirt Talat was wearing when he was killed was later put in Istanbul's Military Museum, and many streets in Turkey were given his name.[24]

## A Divided Diaspora

In the 1920s, along with other exiles from the Caucasus and Russia, the Dashnak leaders of the former Armenian Republic settled in Paris. There they engaged in cantankerous skirmishes in émigré journals about who was to blame for defeat by the Bolsheviks. In the early 1930s, their ARF party again decamped, this time to Cairo, to get away from these quarrels and to move closer to the large Armenian community of the Middle East.

In exile, the ARF partly remained a public party for émigré Armenians and partly reverted to its status as an underground revolutionary organization. Some of its members organized the Operation Nemesis assassinations; others would try to assist the Kurdish rebellions of the 1920s and 1930s. A later generation formed the terrorist group the Justice Commandos of the Armenian Genocide in Beirut in the 1970s.

The ARF was led by the "Bureau," a secretive committee of men (almost never women). On more than one occasion, an individual leader would rise and dominate the committee, leading to authoritarian imposed control and resulting in splits, defections, and expulsions from the ranks. A prominent defector was Hovhanness Katchaznouni, the first prime minister of the Armenian First Republic and one of the last Dashnak leaders to flee it in 1921. In July 1923, Kachaznuni published the iconoclastic speech he had written for the party conference in Vienna two months before. The party was no longer fit for purpose, he said:

> Is it necessary to repeat again the new conditions? Here they are: Turkish Armenia does not exist anymore; half the Armenian people have been massacred, others are dispersed in the four corners of the world, the other half is homeless and bleeding, in need of long rest and recuperation; the Armenian Republic is united with Communist Russia as an autonomous state; to separate our State from Russia we cannot, even if we wish—and we must not wish it, even if we were able to do so; the Party is beaten and has lost its authority, has been expelled from the country, cannot return home, while in the colonies it has no work.[25]

Kachaznuni recommended that the ARF should dissolve itself. By contrast, Soviet Armenia, he said, had done more for ordinary Armenians in two years than the leaders of the First Republic (including himself) had ever done. Kachaznuni himself then returned home to the Soviet Armenian republic to resume his old career as an architect. His notions of Soviet Armenia also proved entirely false. In 1937, he was arrested and executed as a foreign agent.

For two generations, the Armenian Diaspora was bitterly, sometimes murderously, divided. "It is no exaggeration to say that few, if any, communities are as completely divided or show such intense conflict as the Armenian community anywhere in the world," wrote Sarkis Atamian in a 1955 book on Armenians in the United States.[26]

From the 1920s until the 1960s, Armenian Diaspora politics was focused on the Soviet Union, not Turkey, with the consequence that the Catastrophe of 1915 barely figured as a public issue. Instead, recriminations about who had or had not defended the First Republic from the Bolsheviks bled into a perpetual bitter quarrel about whether Soviet Armenia was a legitimate Armenian entity that deserved support, or a usurper.

One pole in this conflict was the ARF. The other pole was the Apostolic Church, whose head, the Catholicos, remained in Soviet Armenia. The bourgeois Ramgavar Party was the nearest thing this community had to a secular wing. Its presiding spirit was Boghos Nubar, the Egyptian Armenian who had led the Ottoman Armenian delegation to the Paris Peace Conference. Nubar was also the founder of the world's biggest Armenian charitable organization, the Armenian General Benevolent Union, the AGBU, which funded Armenian projects across the world, including in Soviet Armenia.

In emigration, these two sides of the Armenian community led a rival parallel existence. Each had its own churches, schools, youth groups, newspapers, and lobbying organizations. In the United States, the quarrel was so intense that it resulted in the murder of an archbishop.

## American Quarrels

In the early 1920s, tens of thousands of Armenian immigrants arrived in the United States. The American-Armenian population had reached a total of about 100,000 by 1924, when the Immigration Act slowed the flow of emigration. Aside from an old Armenian community in Fresno, California, the biggest centers for Armenians were New York and the towns of Worcester and Watertown in Massachusetts.

Snapshots from this era depict Armenians working in shops and coffeehouses serving American customers, but with Armenian iconography on the wall—typically a portrait of Woodrow Wilson pointing to his never-realized map of Armenia. Like most immigrants to the United States, the newcomers aspired to fit into the New World, while still keeping up the traditions of "the old country" at home. They had a precarious status at first. In 1925, an Armenian rug merchant named Tatos Cartozian fought and won a case to prove that Armenians were Christians of "European descent" and therefore eligible for the same naturalization quotas as other white-skinned immigrants.[27]

Paradoxically, the political freedom of the United States enabled the two feuding sides of the intra-Armenian dispute to wage their conflict more aggressively than elsewhere. The quarrel can be tracked in the competing Armenian newspapers: the Dashnaks' *Hairenik Weekly* and the anti-Dashnak *Mirror* and *Spectator* (which eventually merged into one publication).

In 1933, the Armenian Diaspora was gripped by a virulent condition that the press dubbed "flag fever." The issue was the red-blue-and-orange tricolor of the First Armenian Republic. Dashnaks regarded the flag as the symbol of the lost homeland, while the other parties said that it was an outdated symbol that insulted Soviet Armenians. Neither side was prepared to compromise. In August 1933, the Dashnak Party staged a "rally for the tricolor" in New York.

In support of the flag, a veteran Dashnak general, Garegin Njdeh, founded an ARF youth movement named Tzeghagron, or "Race Worship." (Its name was later changed to the less controversial Armenian Youth Federation.) Njdeh propagated "Racial Patriotism" as "the natural and logical reaction against the foreign environment which is threatening the very existence of our race." In style and slogans, his movement echoed the fascist movements of Europe. Each chapter had to make a pledge (*ookht*). The uniform used two of the three colors of the tricolor flag, having blue shirts and orange kerchiefs. Njdeh wrote, "To deny the flag is to deny our identity. We cannot be neutral in this matter. For if we remain neutral, what is to be the identity of the Armenians outside the homeland."[28]

The lightning rod in the feud was Archbishop Levon Tourian, the prelate of the Eastern Diocese of the Apostolic Church. Tourian was a distinguished clergyman who had served in Smyrna, Istanbul, Greece, Bulgaria, and Manchester. He was also a highly divisive figure, being a vocal supporter of the Soviet Armenian government.

On July 1, 1933, the Archbishop was scheduled to speak at an Armenian exhibition being held at the World's Fair in Chicago. When he saw the tricolor above the stage, he refused to begin until the flag was taken down. There were strong objections from Dashnaks, but the crowd voted to have the flag taken down. Fighting broke out, with three thousand people "caught in a milling riot."[29] On August 13, the bishop was physically attacked at a church picnic in Worcester, Massachusetts.

The Eastern diocese split, with opponents of the bishop taking over four of the 14 churches.

The violent denouement occurred on Sunday, December 24. Bishop Tourian came to say the liturgy at the Church of the Holy Cross in Washington Heights, a district in the far north of Manhattan. He had a bodyguard, who stayed by the main door of the church. As the bishop processed up the central aisle, with a pastoral staff in one hand and carrying a cross in the other, men sprang at him from the corner seats and stabbed him with butcher's knives. Tourian sank to the floor, with his staff crumpled underneath him. Two of the assailants were seized by parishioners; the others fled. The bodyguard drew his revolver to try to keep order. The bishop died a few minutes later.[30]

The murder pushed the already boiling Armenian community into civil war. The bishop was given a big funeral service in the Cathedral of St. John the Divine on New Year's Day, 1934. The *Mirror* and *Spectator* fumed with outrage. Someone nailed placards to ARF-affiliated businesses in New York, reading "Do Not Patronize This Store! It is a member of the Dashnag—A secret order that assassinated Archbishop Leon Tourian of the Armenians of U.S.A." Three days after the killing, the ARF organ *Hairenik Weekly* made expressions of regret but more or less suggested that the bishop had brought this on himself, blaming those who "took advantage of that revolting event of Chicago and encouraged the Prelate, who had become intolerable to the great majority of the Armenian people."[31]

Nine men associated with the ARF were eventually arrested, and the Armenian activist and lawyer Vahan Cardashian was hired to represent them. The following July, all nine detained men were convicted. Two were sentenced to death, but New York Governor Herbert Lehman commuted their sentences to life imprisonment.

Men from the two Armenian factions fought public battles, generally on Sundays. In February 1934, the *New York Times* reported on a brawl outside Manhattan's Metropolitan Life Building. The *New York Times* reported, "The raiders fled when the police arrived, but re-formed their ranks and again attempted to parade around the building. They offered no resistance when the patrolmen and detectives drove them away, contenting themselves with flinging Armenian insults at the police and

Tashnags. The epithets were beyond the ken of the patrolmen and the Tashnags pretended to ignore them."[32]

On another Sunday morning two months later, the Boston police were caught unawares by two rival Armenian town-hall meetings whose supporters went to war. "Knives, icepicks, iron bars and other crude weapons were freely brandished by the shouting, rioting factions whose outbreak took police, Sunday autoists and the throng which moved leisurely about Boston Common by surprise. . . . Seeing that the police were outnumbered, the rioters paid them little attention. When struck, they would shout 'Who cares about being hurt in a just cause?' Like shouts came from the victims on either side."[33]

The violence ebbed with time, but the recriminations about the archbishop's murder cast a long shadow over the community. In the 1950s, the church split widened into a schism between "diocese" (those affiliated with the Catholicos in Soviet Armenia) and "prelacy" (those loyal to a rival church in Lebanon and the Dashnak Party). As late as 1976, a planned wedding across the political divide in Providence, Rhode Island, in the United States, turned into a "Romeo and Juliet" story. Neither of the two churches of the bride and groom's family could agree on how to hold the ceremony, and it was called off.[34]

### Soviet Armenia

The chief reason for the fratricidal Diaspora feud was the Soviet Union and the status of its new constituent part, Soviet Armenia. The Armenian Soviet Republic kept nominal features of independence for several years, including a Turkish consulate in Yerevan. Until 1936, it was part of the Transcaucasian Federative Republic, together with Azerbaijan and Georgia, before becoming the Armenian Soviet Socialist Republic.

The first period of Soviet rule equally inspired loathing among the Dashnaks and enthusiasm from their opponents. In February 1934, in the aftermath of Archbishop Tourian's murder, the columnist John Tashjian wrote in the *Armenian Spectator*, "Meanwhile, blissfully indifferent to the partisanships going on outside its borders, the people of the homeland have been working feverishly to rebuild the shattered country. While the Tashnags have been planning for the Promised Land, the Armenians have been rebuilding it."[35]

The enthusiasts spoke of reconstruction, modernization, and education. New towns such as Nor (New) Arapkir were built for Ottoman Armenian refugees. The narratives of Western travelers were remarkably similar and hopeful. Here is Louis Fischer: "Wherever one looks— tearing down, digging up, building, hauling for building purposes, painting, planting of trees and parks, etc. If ever a city had a 'boom' it is Erivan. Even persons accustomed to the usual mad Soviet construction 'tempo' are astounded. The old city, which was one big slum, is quickly disappearing. Soviet Erivan is out-Sovieting the Soviets. Erivan had a population of 13,000 a hundred years ago. It counted 13,000 inhabitants in 1913. It has 110,000 inhabitants today."[36]

The writer and journalist Arthur Koestler, visiting Yerevan in 1932, had the impression of a nation rising from the ashes:

> Erivan was then a kind of Tel Aviv, where the survivors of another martyred nation gathered to construct a new home. They were full of hope, and as grateful to the Soviet regime which had provided them with an Autonomous Republic as the Jews had been to England in the days when Balfour promised them a National Home. The new capital looked like a huge building site. At the end of the First World War it had been a dirty Asiatic village, crammed with refugees who had escaped massacre by the Turks; by now it was well on its way to becoming a modern capital.[37]

The American-Armenian writer Aghavni Yeghenian also hailed the new "security" that Armenians felt under Soviet rule during her visit in the same period:

> It is this feeling of security that has turned a veritable death house where the Armenian people were doomed to perish, into a house of resurrected people with hope written large on their faces. When I went through the chief park in Erivan I was told that eleven years ago it was littered with the dead bodies of starving people. Today the best open-air restaurant in town is located in that park and people sit around on their benches and enjoy the mellow warmth of the autumn sun.[38]

When it came to those recent memories of death and destruction, there was in the 1920s and 1930s, says historian Suren Manukian, "a period of enforced silence." During this era, says Manukian, "every mention of the genocide of Armenians was made only in the context of liberation of Russian soldiers. The Armenian Genocide was mentioned only in context of 'If it wasn't for Russian soldiers you would all have been destroyed.' "[39] In part, this was because of the Soviet doctrine of forgetting the past in order to forge a socialist future. In part, it was because the good relationship between Kemalist Turkey and the Bolshevik Soviet Union persisted for a time, with the two countries signing a Treaty of Friendship in 1925.[40]

Armenian patriotism was reframed to accommodate the coming socialist future. The most famous Armenian writer of the era, Yeghishe Charents, wrote lyric poetry about his homeland. He also wrote a novel, *The Land of Nairi*, published in 1922, that was fully in tune with the new Soviet zeitgeist. Charents's novel is set in his own hometown of Kars just as World War I is beginning. In the style of Nikolai Gogol, he evokes its provincial boredom, gossip, and poverty, and introduces a cast of eccentric fondly observed characters, such as "Telephone Seto" who runs a café. But the town is run by a "committee" (clearly the Dashnaktsutiun) who have big ambitions for Nairi (one of the historic names of Armenia) and believe that once war begins with the Turks, "wide horizons will open" for their country. Of course, those ambitions prove to be an illusion, the town is not properly defended, and the enemy Turk over-runs it, with devastating results.

Nairi, we are told, is a national illusion, while Soviet *Hayastan* (Armenia) is a normal healthy country. Marc Nichanian writes about the novel: "The satire in *Yerkir Nayiri* is aimed at precisely this illusion, to which Charents, like all his contemporaries, had himself succumbed. Charents's ferocity in this novel finds its explanation in the fact that it targets not an external enemy, but, in fact, 'ourselves,' the cherished illusion that nourished 'us' for decades."[41]

Charents's own dreams about the new era proved to be a different kind of illusion. Whatever the achievements of the 1920s, the 1930s were a period of repression and fear, as elsewhere in the Soviet Union. Charents, along with most of the intellectual elite of the republic, was arrested and executed. The First Party Secretary Aghasi Khanjian was murdered or driven to suicide in 1936 by Stalin's chief henchman in the Caucasus, Lavrenti Beria. The Apostolic Church, which had escaped persecution, was now repressed. In 1938, Catholicos Khoren I died, almost certainly at the hands of the NKVD, and was given only a perfunctory burial. His post remained empty. Soviet Armenia and the Diaspora were divided, until the politics of World War II drove Armenian politics in a new direction.[42]

# 5

# Postwar Politics

## World War II

IN 1945, JOSEPH STALIN and the Soviet Union basked in the adulation of the world as the Red Army crushed Nazi Germany. Both Armenians and Turks had ended up on the same side. Armenians fought against the Nazis in the armies of both the Western Allies and the Soviet Union, and the wartime alliance strengthened relations between the Diaspora and Soviet Armenia. A Soviet tank regiment named after the hero of a medieval Armenian epic, David of Sassun, was formed in Echmiadzin in 1943. It was funded entirely by donations from the Diaspora and the Apostolic Church.

At its congress of July 1944, the ARF also reversed its stance on the Soviet Union, now speaking of it as a potential ally, rather than merely the usurper of the First Republic. The party relaunched *Hai Dat* ("The Armenian Cause" in English), the mission to claim territories in Turkey for Soviet Armenia. In June 1943, the Dashnak newspaper *Hairenik Weekly* wrote:

> We may confidently state that, were it not for the reconstructive labor of the Armenian Revolutionary Federation during those brief two and a half years of the Republic we would not have in

Transcaucasia today a Soviet Armenia, which although unfree, is nevertheless the only concrete nucleus around which future hopes of Armenian regeneration are centered.[1]

Issues of *Hairenik Weekly* in this period are full of patriotic material: articles on the war effort and photographs of young Armenian-Americans in the services. Yet, the ARF's reputation was tarnished by the activities of some who collaborated with the Nazis.

Many Eastern European émigré politicians had collaborated with Hitler against Stalin. When Germany invaded the USSR, leaders of all the anti-Bolshevik Caucasian nations were invited to Berlin to discuss collaboration in return for ill-defined promises of power once their homelands were liberated from Soviet rule.[2] The Armenian Revolutionary Federation had been founded as a socialist party, but one wing of it looked to the Nazis. Two leading Armenian Dashnak politicians made the journey to Hitler's Berlin: Alexander Khatisian, former prime minister of the First Republic, and Vahan Papazian, former Ottoman parliamentarian and one of the leaders of the Van rebellion.

The most famous Armenian collaborators were two generals. General Dro Kanayan, a famous Armenian commander, had briefly served as "military dictator" of Yerevan in 1920. In 1943, Dro recruited both Armenian émigrés and Soviet Armenian prisoners-of-war into the 812th Battalion and marched with the Germans to Crimea and the North Caucasus.[3] The other general who fought with the Nazis was Dashnak veteran Garegin Njdeh, who had been Dro's comrade-in-arms in the tsarist army. He had genuine fascist leanings, having founded the Armenian "Race Worship" movement in the United States in the 1930s (see Chapter 4). After the war, Dro settled in Beirut. Njdeh was arrested by the Soviet regime, put on trial, and imprisoned. He died in the Russian town of Vladimir in 1955.

## Stalin and the "Turkish Crisis"

As Stalin fought World War II, he began to redraw the map of Europe and the Soviet Union. In 1943 and 1944, Stalin diverted wartime resources, including American lend-lease trucks, to engineer the mass deportation to Central Asia of ethnic groups deemed to be "enemy nations." Hundreds of thousands of people died in these mass deportations. Amongst the "punished peoples" selected for collective exile were almost all the Soviet Union's Turkic minorities. Crimean Tatars, the Kalmyks on the Caspian Sea, the Balkars and Karachais in the North Caucasus, and the Meskhetian Turks of Georgia were all deported en masse to Central Asia in 1943–1944.

Turkey had stayed neutral for most of the war. After the Yalta conference in February 1945, the Allies warned the government in Ankara that if it kept its neutrality it would not be granted a seat in the forthcoming United Nations conference. On February 23, 1945, Turkey duly declared war on Germany, but its troops played no part in World War II.

Turkey's move did not satisfy Stalin. He planned to annex parts of both Iran and Turkey and reallocate them to the three Transcaucasian republics, Azerbaijan, Armenia, and Georgia. In late 1945, a Soviet-backed Iranian Azerbaijani republic established itself in northern Iran, seeking unification with Soviet Azerbaijan. Soviet troops rolled into Tabriz in March 1946, but the project crumbled under international pressure later that year.

In March 1945, the Soviet Union began menacing Turkey. Moscow annulled the 1925 Soviet-Turkish Friendship Treaty and told the Turks that if they wanted a new treaty, they would have to make concessions. Soviet Foreign Minister Vyacheslav Molotov said that the USSR wanted to establish a Soviet military base next to the Turkish Straits (the Bosphorus and the Dardanelles). He also announced that the Soviet Union was claiming the eastern Turkish provinces of Ardahan and Kars, which had been part of the Russian Empire until 1918. Molotov said that his government considered the Treaty of Kars null and void, conveniently forgetting that Stalin, as Soviet commissar on nationalities, had been one of the authors of the treaty. Kars, including the area around Mount Ararat, should go to Soviet Armenia; Ardahan should be allocated to Stalin's homeland of Soviet Georgia.

Thus, in 1945, Stalin, for his own purposes, dramatically put the "Armenian Question" back on the international agenda. Armenian nationalist interests again aligned briefly with those of a Great Power champion, this time the Soviet Union.

The Soviet authorities coordinated the new campaign against Turkey with both Yerevan and the Diaspora. Armenian Diaspora organizations were encouraged to press their claims at the United Nations conference convened in San Francisco in April 1945, even though it had no authority to discuss territorial disputes.

Two Armenian rival delegations showed up in San Francisco, as they had done at the Paris Peace Conference of 1919. Simon Vratsian, the veteran leader of the First Republic, presented a petition on behalf of the ARF's Armenian National Committee, calling for a "just and durable peace" for the Armenians. Twenty-five years of enmity toward the USSR was forgotten, as *Hairenik Weekly* declared, "The Uncle from the North has come to the rescue. The Armenians the world over are solidly behind the Uncle from the North."[4]

The alternative Armenian group in San Francisco, the Armenian National Council of America, represented a coalition of non-Dashnak parties, which was working with the Soviet delegation. Its memorandum, *The Case of the Armenian People*, said that the council was "comprised of and supported by all the Armenian civic, social, cultural and religious organizations in the United States except a small fascist party known as the Dashnags."[5] The memorandum announced two goals: annexing Turkish territories to Soviet Armenia and organizing mass migration of Armenians. "We want no less than the joining of our historic land of our Armenia still in Turkey to the existing state of free and independent Armenia, and the repatriation there of all Armenians abroad who wish to go there."[6]

Soviet Armenia was enthused. Archbishop Gevorg Chorekchian, the de facto leader of the Armenian Apostolic Church, had spent several years virtually in hiding after the suspicious death of the last Catholicos seven years before. Now he emerged from the shadows to champion the new cause. The archbishop was invited to meet Stalin in the Kremlin on April 19, 1945. He requested the lifting of restrictions on the church and the election of a new Catholicos. The two men then discussed Stalin's proposed claims on the Turkish territories and the need for a program of Armenian repatriation to populate them. Stalin reportedly said:

The war will come to an end soon. Our government is preparing to take back from Turkey the western provinces of Armenia handed over in 1920. It is clear that Armenians must live on these lands. It would be desirable for them to be the same Armenians who were obliged to flee from Turkey and who now live in the diaspora. Because of this the immigration of about one hundred thousand Armenians must be organized. Soon there will be a government decree on this. You in your turn must help us with this.[7]

Bishop Gevorg later recalled:

When I heard this I could not contain my joy. For a moment it seemed I was dreaming all this. I promised to do everything, but expressed misgivings about taking in such a quantity of people given the difficult economic situation in the republic. They will have to be given homes, provided with food. . . . "Don't worry," Stalin reassured me, "we will do everything possible so that the repatriates won't suffer any hardship."[8]

On June 22, 1945, as promised, the Armenian Apostolic Church held an assembly in Echmiadzin to fill the vacant post of Catholicos. Bishop Gevorg was elected to the office by 110 votes out of a possible 111, having modestly declined to vote for himself. The Soviet authorities had invited a guest from Great Britain, the controversial Communist Anglican dean of Canterbury Cathedral, Hewlett Johnson, known as "the Red Dean." Johnson publicly supported the Soviet Union's claims on Kars and Ardahan and he went much further than was customary at the time in discussing the massacres of 1915: "I completely and wholeheartedly agree that the regions seized by Turkey must be returned to Armenia as quickly as possible—with unbelievable cruelty Turkey exterminated the Armenian population. The victorious powers declared after the First World War that justice demanded the return of these territories to their rightful owners."[9]

The church assembly concluded by thanking Stalin in fulsome tones and fervently anticipated the transfer of territories from Turkey to Soviet Armenia: "Great Stalin, in these glorious days of the victory of the heroic Red Army and the allied armies, a million and a half Armenians have their eyes turned, full of nostalgia, towards glorious Soviet Armenia and await impatiently the blessed day when Armenian lands still under the foreign yoke will be returned to the dear Soviet Armenian Republic."[10]

The Soviet leadership turned up the heat on Turkey at the Potsdam Conference in July 1945. Accounts of the conference suggest that Stalin's primary interest was the age-old issue of gaining control of "the Straits" connecting the Black Sea and the Mediterranean. But both Molotov and Stalin also raised the issue of "rectifying" Turkey's frontiers. In discussion with British foreign secretary Anthony Eden, Molotov made several arguments, even mentioning the Red Dean. Asked by Eden how many Armenians were living in the territories in question, Molotov mentioned the fantastical figure of "400–500,000."[11] Both Winston Churchill and Harry Truman temporized and suggested that they "defer consideration" until research had been done on the two Turkish provinces. Stalin agreed.[12]

A subsequent British Foreign Office report of April 1946 seems to be the product of the promised research. The British author revisits the history of 1915 and writes, "These massacres [of Armenians] were so atrocious and have left such a lasting mark on the memory of the world, that if the Soviet government chose to launch a propaganda campaign recalling this, it would be likely to rouse a lot of sympathy in humanitarian circles all over the world and it might put Turkey in a very awkward position as Black Sheep No. 1."[13] However, he then raises the glaring problem with Stalin's plan: How would it be possible to reallocate territories from Turkey in which there was currently no Armenian population? The report concludes that it was doubtful whether sufficient numbers of Armenians (and even more so Georgians) could be found to make the new territories viable.

A US intelligence report of the same time argues that Stalin's chief interest was in creating a new buffer zone:

[S]trategic and political considerations regarding the Middle and Near East in general weigh infinitely more than championship of Armenian irredentism in the Soviet claims regarding the Armenian (or Georgian) provinces of Turkey. As a by-product, however, the Armenian question is played up both as a good pretext for the Soviet claims and as an effective means of enlisting the sympathies and/or support of Armenians throughout the world.[14]

Stalin's territories campaign rolled on, in spite of Western suspicions. Armenian nationalism was now ideologically compatible with Soviet patriotism, and Armenian authors took advantage of the moment, publishing pamphlets about forgotten Armenian tsarist generals who had fought the Turks. Professor Alexei Dzhivilegov, an Armenian-Russian historian, had last written extensively about the "Armenian question" during World War I. He had then transferred his interests to the politically safer topic of the Italian Renaissance. Now aged 70, Dzhivilegov was suddenly brought out of retirement on February 20, 1946, to give a public lecture in Moscow, entitled "Armenia and Turkey."[15]

In the text of his lecture, Dzhivilegov takes advantage of the auspicious moment to set out a detailed narrative of Armenian history, including a frank assessment of 1915 as a period in which the Ottoman Armenians were "subjected to cruel, systematic destruction." The historian blames the Entente allies of World War I for betraying the Armenians because "the dictate of the Treaty of Sèvres turned out to be as fragile as Sèvres china." The loss of Kars and Ardahan is attributed to the deal done between Dashnaks and Kemalists, before the Bolsheviks came to the rescue of the Armenian people. Dzhivilegov concludes that historical justice will be served only when territories in Turkey are given over to Soviet Armenia. He mentions not just Kars and Ardahan, but Bitlis, Erzerum, and Van as well. "The gazes of more than a million overseas Armenian refugees, scattered across the whole world are now fixed on Soviet Armenia."

In Turkey, there was consternation at the Soviet campaign to annex its eastern territories and take control of the Straits. On July 2, 1945, Turkish Prime Minister Şükrü Saracoğlu told US ambassador Edwin Wilson, "You and the British have many problems. We have only one problem, but it is a matter of life and death for us. If the USSR tries to go against our independence, we are going to fight."[16]

In late 1945 and early 1946, Turkish public opinion rallied against the Armenians and its new imperial sponsor, the Soviet Union, in tones reminiscent of World War I. A *New York Times* correspondent reported from Istanbul, "The papers widely hold that the country presents no problem except that allegedly manufactured for it and suggests that there is an effort afoot to weaken Turkey by reporting discontent not only among the Armenians but also among the Kurds."[17] A patriotic book of verse entitled *Do Not Touch My Motherland* was published in a large print-run.[18] Kazim Karabekir, the conqueror of Kars in 1920, also re-emerged into the spotlight and famously declared, "The world must know that the Straits form the throat of the Turkish nation and the Kars Plateau its backbone."[19]

In the end, Stalin's campaign only succeeded in pushing Turkey into an alliance with the Western powers and speeding up the start of the Cold War. In March 1946, the Western powers braced themselves for a military showdown with Stalin over Turkey, which did not materialize. US ambassador Edwin Wilson wrote to the secretary of state in Washington, "The real Soviet objective toward Turkey is not a revision of the regime of the Straits, but actual domination of Turkey. In the vast security belt of the Soviet Union, which extends from the Baltic to the Black Sea, Turkey constitutes the sole gap."[20]

On April 6, 1946, the warship the USS *Missouri* sailed into the Straits, and received an ecstatic reception from the Turkish public. A year later, in March 1947, President Harry Truman announced the "Truman Doctrine," asking Congress to grant economic and military support to Greece and Turkey to stop them falling into the Soviet sphere of influence. In 1952, both Greece and Turkey joined NATO, a move that turned the Armenian-Turkish border into a Cold War front line. Shortly afterward, Turkey became a major contributor of troops in the Korean War. In 1953, after Stalin's death, the new Soviet leaders quietly dropped Soviet territorial claims on Turkey.

## Repatriation

In September 1946, an Armenian newspaper cartoon depicted a Turk in a fez smoking a hookah sitting by the Bosphorus and watching a ship crammed with Armenians sailing by. The man exclaims, "Allah! I thought I finished them off thirty years ago."[21] Thousands of Armenians were streaming across the Black Sea to the port of Batumi and onward to Soviet Armenia. They were going "home," but they had only a dim idea of what awaited them.

Even as Stalin's plan to seize territories from Turkey faltered, the project to repatriate Diaspora Armenians intended to populate those territories went ahead. The program was authorized in December

1945, with plans for up to 300,000 Armenians to emigrate. The *Mirror-Spectator* eulogized, "A glorious page of Armenian history is being written these days. A call has been issued to Armenians in exile to return to the Fatherland. Soviet Armenia is waiting with open arms to receive her distant children, dispersed all over the world, who waste their lives fruitlessly and meaninglessly in strange lands."[22]

The program was officially called one of *re*-patriation, but almost none of the immigrants had ever lived in eastern Armenia before. Diaspora organizations, especially the Armenian General Benevolent Union, the AGBU, organized the logistics and raised $1.5 million to fund it. The largest group came from Lebanon, Syria, and Iran. Only the ARF party struck a skeptical note, telling its members they could only emigrate if they gave up party membership.

A documentary film, *My Unfamiliar Fatherland*, captures the naïve enthusiasm that possessed the migrants. They sang and danced on the ships taking them to the Soviet Union (see Figure 5.1), singing a song with the refrain, "The road to Armenia is stony, stony. Stalin misses

Figure 5.1 Repatriation. A ship prepares to leave Alexandria carrying Armenian immigrants to the Soviet Union, 1947.

Source: Nubarian Archive, Paris.

us, misses us. Hey *jan* [dear] Yerevan, lovely Yerevan."[23] Wealthy Middle Eastern Armenians gave up houses and businesses in order to emigrate. They signed up because they were enthralled by the Soviet Union's victory in World War II and believed that Soviet Armenia was a socialist success story. In the documentary, a Lebanese Armenian, Martiros Vardanyan, recalls, "People would say 'Go there, Armenia is a paradise.'"

As soon as they arrived on Soviet soil in Batumi, the immigrants met a cruel reality. The arriving Armenians were required to pass through a quarantine station. Many of them were carrying baskets of fresh fruit and produce they had brought with them, but these were tossed into the sea as potential carriers of disease. "The water was covered with oranges, bananas and cookies," recalls one immigrant. It was even worse in Armenia itself. There were shortages, lines for scarce food. The immigrants, many of them wealthy Armenians who had left behind homes and cars, were housed in poorly heated cramped rooms with no running water. There were tensions between the *teghatsis* (the locals) and the *norkalogh* (the immigrants). Incoming western Armenians were called *aghper*, or "brother," a word that had a derogatory tone in the eastern Armenian dialect. Many were shunned as politically dangerous capitalists.

Tom Mooradian was a 19-year-old from Detroit and one of the few American-Armenians to migrate. In his memoir *The Repatriate*, he relates how he quickly realized he had made a mistake and sank into depression. He had renounced his US citizenship and bought a one-way ticket. Letters home were censored so as not to spoil the propaganda message. In a coded postcard, Mooradian warned his parents not to come, asking them to encourage Uncle Avak and Auntie Vartouhie (who were both deceased) to repatriate: "Our homeland needs more workers like them. They will fit in with the rest of us who are dying to see them." His family took the hint and did not follow him. Mooradian eventually made himself into a leading Soviet Armenian basketball player and 13 years later found a way back to the United States.[24]

The repatriation project became the latest hot topic in the perpetual duel between the two main Armenian-American newspapers. The Soviet-sympathizing *Mirror-Spectator* was already on the defensive for having sponsored the program. In March 1948, the paper published an article, which did not exactly deny the negative reports from Soviet Armenia, but said, "These repatriates, plain people with great pride and high hopes, had finally realized their dream to live among their own people."[25] But the Dashnak *Hairenik Weekly* was merciless. Quoting the accounts of a few escapees, it depicted Soviet Armenian as a locus not just of economic misery, but moral degradation:

> **Godlessness, Atheism, Immorality, Robbery and perpetual spying on one another!** There is not a trace of our family sanctities left there. Having repudiated the idea of the existence of a God, the Bolshevik ignores every conception of family standards, every moral principle, every social order. Aram's wife or watch equally can belong to Hagop, Ali, or Stalin. There is no conception of nationality. A Kurd, a Caucasian, a Georgian, or a Turk have the right to become your son-in-law when they wish it. They have the right to divorce the very next day.[26]

The flow of immigration to the Soviet Union slowed and eventually stopped in February 1949. A total of 90,000 Armenians had migrated from 10 countries, many fewer than had been anticipated. No return was allowed. On the contrary: more Stalinist demographic engineering was to follow. In the summer of 1949, Stalin ordered his last round of mass deportations from the Caucasus in a paranoid response to the Truman Doctrine. Greeks and Turks were exiled to Siberia or Kazakhstan. Around 13,000 alleged "Dashnaks," many of them recent immigrants, suffered the same fate and were deported to the remote Altai region of Siberia.

Again, Azerbaijanis of Armenia suffered the repercussions of the Armenian-Turkish question. Enjoying a lower status in the Soviet hierarchy of nations than Armenians, they were selected to pay the price for the logistical failures of the repatriation program. In December 1947, the two party leaders of Armenia and Azerbaijan, Grigory Harutyunov and Mir Jafa Bagirov, wrote a joint letter to Moscow proposing a mass relocation of Azerbaijanis from Armenia to the cotton-growing plains in central Azerbaijan, where the Rivers Kura and Araxes meet. Removing the Azerbaijanis would free up housing for the Armenian immigrants.

Initially, the plan was to move 100,000 Azerbaijanis. In the end, as the Armenian migration program stopped, 53,000 of them were forcibly removed. They did not want to be uprooted from their homes and suffered miserably. As an Armenian interior ministry report of May 1948 recorded, "We have detected numerous statements of Azerbaijanis about their unwillingness to go to a new place of residence and a number of them began visiting cemeteries and entreating the souls of the deceased to help them remain where they live." The report noted that others decided to leave because they feared being victims of the Turkish crisis: "The Azerbaijani population of Armenia was apprehensive that in case of war with Turkey, Armenians would massacre all of them, so it was better to go to Azerbaijan."[27]

Once the Azerbaijanis arrived in their new homes, the same story played out. The settlers mostly came from highland parts of Armenia and found life hard in the hot dusty plains of Azerbaijan. Conditions were poor, and many died of disease. Some of them tried to move back to Armenia and fought to reclaim their former homes.[28]

## Cold War Divides

With the failure of Stalin's Turkish gambit, disappointment about the Soviet Armenian emigration program, and Turkey's accession to NATO in 1952, the Armenian Diaspora quarrel split emphatically down Cold War lines.

In Lebanon, the ARF supported the pro-American Maronite president Camille Chamoun, while the other parties aligned themselves with leftist pan-Arabism and General Nasser in Egypt. This ended up splitting the Armenian Apostolic Church. In 1956, the pro-Dashnak candidate elected to be the semi-autonomous Catholicos of Cilicia, based in Antelias in Lebanon, rejected the authority of the church in Echmiadzin in Soviet Armenia. Across the world, individual Armenian churches were divided between the authority of the two sides on left-right lines. In 1958, when Lebanon was wracked by a brief civil war, the country's Armenian factions ended up on different sides, and dozens of Armenians died in fratricidal fighting in Beirut.[29]

In the United States, with the Cold War in full swing, the Dashnaktsutiun Party, which had just recently been on the defensive for alleged links with "fascism," went on the offensive against its alleged "Red" and "Communist" opponents. A 1949 *Hairenik Weekly* editorial, for example, denounced a new youth organization on the other side as Soviet stooges: "The handful of riff-raff who arrogate unto themselves the presumptuous name of Armenian Youth of America, are supposed to be Armenians, champions of enslaved peoples, and yet, they have not a word of criticism or censure of the greatest tyranny and enslavement which the Soviet has imposed on the Armenian fatherland."[30]

In 1954, *Hairenik Weekly's* editor, Reuben Darbinian, former justice minister in the Armenian First Republic, published a polemical article entitled "Our Neutrals." He warned that the activities of the "so-called neutrals" and "fifth columnists" in the American-Armenian Diaspora community were jeopardizing the fight "against the common enemy of mankind which is Soviet imperialism." His targets were parts of the church, the Ramgavar Party, and the Armenian General Benevolent Union.[31]

The United States government wholeheartedly backed the ARF as a Cold War ally. In 1957, US Secretary of State John Foster Dulles and Vice President Richard Nixon both received the new Lebanese Cilician archbishop, Khoren Paroyian, in Washington, fresh from his bruising row with the Armenian Catholicos. Nixon "praised the Armenian people for their successful struggle to keep the Armenian church free of the shackles of dark and sinister forces," and told the bishop, "It is absolutely necessary to fight spiritually and I am happy that has been done in your church."[32]

In the early 1950s, the idea was launched that the Soviet Union was holding "captive nations," non-Russian peoples imprisoned within the walls of the USSR. The third week of July was declared "Captive Nations Week" in the United States, and ceremonies were held to commemorate the "submerged nations" of the Soviet Union. Charles J. Kersten, a Republican from Milwaukee, formed what would soon be called the Committee on Communist Aggression. One of the committee's regular hearings, in October 1953 in New York, was devoted to the "Investigation of Communist Takeover and Occupation of the Non-Russian Nations of the U.S.S.R." The committee asked witnesses to describe how the Bolsheviks had overthrown their independent nations—including Armenia and Azerbaijani in 1920. In the process, the bumpy story of preceding histories or conflicts between the nations concerned was ironed out.

On October 14, 1953, the anti-Communist committee heard from New York resident Zahid Khan Khoisky a detailed account of the crushing of the First Republic of Azerbaijan by the Bolsheviks in April 1920. Khoisky was the nephew of the prime minister of the Azerbaijani First Republic of 1918, Fatali Khan Khoisky. Asked by the committee how the elder Khoisky had died in 1920, he answered, "He was murdered by the Soviet Russians." The younger Khoisky must have known that this was not true: the actual assassins were Armenians from the Dashnak-inspired Operation Nemesis. Most probably, he was taking the hint that all possible blame must be pinned on the Communist Russians, rather than intra-Caucasian violence.[33]

On the previous day, four Armenian witnesses told the Congressmen how the Bolsheviks had overthrown the Armenian First Republic in 1920. All of them were affiliated with the ARF, and two, Reuben Darbinian and General Dro Kanayan, had served in the government of the First Republic. The Armenian testimonies also appear to have been choreographed with the aim of throwing all possible blame on the Bolsheviks and suppressing the role of other culprits in the fate of the Armenians—in this case, the Turks. So Beglar Navassardian, executive secretary of the still-extant American Committee for the Independence of Armenia (and son of the ARF leader in Egypt), gave a brief excursion through the history of Armenia that surely would have caused apoplexy in his predecessors in that committee in the 1920s.

Navassardian barely mentioned the 1915 Genocide in his testimony. He managed only to say, "Finally during the First World War, the Armenian people made the final and supreme sacrifice. They firmly and squarely sided with the Allies, gave volunteer forces under the Allied Command in the Middle East, on the eastern front and elsewhere. For a people whose numbers had been decimated to less than 4 million, they gave a participation of 250,000, fighting against the Axis Powers."[34]

General Dro spoke through an interpreter. The awkward issue of his wartime collaboration with Nazi Germany was not mentioned. The general reminisced about a luncheon in 1921 hosted for him by Stalin, whom he described as an old comrade from the revolution of 1905, at which promises were made and then broken. Dro, a veteran of the Russian-Ottoman war, also conspicuously failed to mention Turkey or 1915. He only spoke about atrocities committed by the Bolsheviks, who, he said, "took over Armenia with a brutality and persecution character-istic of the Middle Ages."[35]

A certain kind of Armenia—one that had lost its independence, bravely fighting Soviet Russia—was required by the Cold War American political imagination. Concluding the hearings, the chair-man, Representative Michael Feighan, praised General Dro, saying, "Our committee appreciates very much this first-hand testimony from you who have fought so vigorously for the freedom and independence of Armenia."[36]

# 6

## Awakening, 1965

IN JUNE 1966, THE American-Armenian newspaper, the *Armenian Mirror-Spectator*, published an editorial that excoriated not only Turks for their denials but Armenians for their failure to speak out on their nation's historic tragedy. The editorial urged Armenians to follow the example of the Jews in seeking justice for the "Great Crime" committed against them. And the article used the word "genocide" to describe what had happened to the Armenians:

> Indeed, so remiss and supine have we been that the Turks are now so bold as to deny that they ever committed genocide. The question may well be asked, "Cannot Armenians ever forget? Must the tragedy of the past be forever evoked?" And the answer must be that they cannot forget or forgive until justice is done. The tragic ghosts of yesteryear can never be laid to rest until their offenders acknowledge their crimes and make some gesture of atonement.[1]

Armenians were becoming politically active again. The turnaround was visible in the stance of the newspaper, the *Mirror-Spectator*. For the previous 15 years, it had filled its pages with a social calendar of weddings, church announcements, and sports results, but it had now rediscovered politics.

The catalyst was the fiftieth anniversary of the start of the deportations on April 24, 1965. This can be dated as the moment when the Armenian Diaspora community collectively began to use the term "the Armenian Genocide." As the idea of the Holocaust postdated the actual destruction of the Jews and it took a new generation to conceptualize it, so in the 1960s the Armenian Genocide became both a collective idea and a political cause.

Each generation of Armenians dealt with the legacy of loss in different ways. In the late 1940s, talk of the losses of 1915 was still mostly a private affair. In her memoir, *Through the Wall of Fire*, American-Armenian Muriel Mirak-Weissbach recalls Sunday visits to the houses of the grandmothers in Massachusetts whom she knew as "nannies." (Strictly speaking, they were adopted grandmothers because both her parents were orphans.)

> As everything was in Armenian, I had little idea of what it was all about. The only frequently repeated phrases I could pick up were "the Turks," "the massacres," the "Old Country" and so on. The nannies had lived through the trauma in Arabkir, while their husbands had been in America. There was a large picture hanging on the wall, in both nannies' homes, which showed the figure of a woman sitting wistfully with her head resting in her right hand, in what looked like a graveyard, amid signs of waste and ruin. This picture, either as a painting or an embroidery, was prominently exhibited, there as in most Armenian homes. It was Armenia, I later learned, mourning her losses. During these Sunday dinners, the nannies, usually dressed in black, as well as my mother, would end up in tears. They looked remarkably like that figure of Mother Armenia, weeping.[2]

Sociologist Natasha May Azarian, who researched the different narratives of the Armenian Genocide among different generations in Fresno, California, concluded that it was most difficult for the children of survivors to find the language to talk about the Genocide: "There is not a collectivity pronounced beyond the family, in other words, the children of Genocide survivors do not evoke a collective 'we' as found in later generations."[3]

The next generation down, the grandchildren, tended to be much more Americanized:

> The first generation born in America were the listeners of trauma, the narrative from this vantage was the pathway to overcome the trauma itself. As a result of what the first generation born in America endured in "moral weight" some chose to raise their children with American names and to avoid incessant discourse about the Genocide. The grandparents on occasion . . . spoke about their experiences. For them, being Armenian at this juncture in history was a religious demarcation, Turks were Muslim, and Armenians were Christian. This explains why there is a predominance of a Christian evaluation with respect to the Genocide within the second generation born in America.[4]

In the mid-twentieth century, many American-Armenians, such as Mirak-Weissbach's family, were decidedly American during the working week and then tended their Armenian roots on Sundays with rituals of family, food, and church. The two worlds remained separate.

Three Armenian-American authors, all born in the first decade of the twentieth century, write about how they have an identity of two equal but very different halves. The slaughter of their parents' generation and the deep loss of 1915 are taken as a given: they are a pervasive background, not a foreground, in their writing.

Leon Surmelian, born in 1905 in Trebizond (Trabzon), finishes his 1945 memoir, *I Ask You, Ladies and Gentlemen*, as a successful man acclimatized to America—and yet melancholy and drunk on New Year's Eve, as he reflects on his lost Armenian childhood. "There are millions like me, tonight, in free happy America, haunted by their early years, which are always, everywhere, the happiest."[5]

> I voted for President Roosevelt and I repeat, I'll fight for America any time. But what can you do on New Year's Eve, when, though you are wearing a tuxedo and own an automobile, you remember the baker who kept his accounts by cutting notches on a tally stick and collected once a month? . . . When you remember the wreaths

of daphne leaves and wild flowers on May Day, framing winged cherubim, that hung from every door in a blessed street; and going to the hills with hundreds of happy school kids to gather violets, and then pressing them dry in books.[6]

For Surmelian, the "Old Country" is a lost irrevocable Eden. William Saroyan (Figure 6.1), born in Fresno in 1908, also writes about it as a lost cause. In his 1935 short story, *Antranik of Armenia*, the famous Armenian-American author dares to be irreverent about the most famous Armenian hero, General Andranik (Figure 6.2). Saroyan's child narrator and alter ego contrasts the adulation the general receives from adoring local Armenians on a visit to Fresno with his redundancy in the world at large:

In 1915 General Antranik was part of the cause of the trouble in the world, but it wasn't his fault. There was no other way out for him and he was doing only what he had to do. The Turks were killing Armenians and General Antranik and his soldiers were killing Turks. He was killing fine, simple, amiable Turks, but he wasn't

Figure 6.1 The writer William Saroyan, 1940.
Source: Library of Congress.

Figure 6.2 Legendary Armenian general Andranik Ozanian.
Source: Library of Congress.

destroying any real criminal because every real criminal was far from the scene of fighting. An eye for an eye, but always the wrong eye. And my grandmother prayed for the triumph and safety of General Antranik, although she knew Turks were good people. She herself said they were.[7]

Saroyan the narrator takes the same position in his story that Saroyan the person took in his life: intense pride in both his Armenian culture and roots and his American identity, combined with sarcastic disinterest in Armenian politics or "causes."

In 1964, Saroyan visited his ancestral town of Bitlis and was given a warm welcome by the municipal authorities. He evidently found it both a moving and melancholy experience. In a short play written in 1975, he expressed his contradictory emotions through a dialogue between different Armenian characters. "Bill" is Saroyan himself; "Bedros" an Armenian newspaper editor in Istanbul. They discuss the fact that the last Armenian in the town is leaving for Lebanon:

BEDROS: That's it for Armenians in Bitlis, then. He is the last of us, and homesick for what Bitlis was and really is, but now the very graveyard has been demolished and wildflowers are growing there among the planted wheat, and one of our most beautiful churches is the home of cattle and the belltower houses pigeons. And wherever we walk, out where the mineral waters bubble out of great stones, the water which only cows and horses drink, the Turks and Kurds watch us, for they think we have come to dig up the buried gold of our fathers. Good God. You heard them with your own ears, Ara, and I don't know about you, but it made me feel almost glad that we have all of us left here.

BILL: I am not glad. Bitlis is ours. It is mine. It is theirs, too, they are all inhabitants of Bitlis, and whoever they are, or whoever they become, they are welcome, but it is really ours, it is mine, and I wish to God I could stay. I really want to stay.

Although Saroyan says he "wants to stay," he of course heads back to America.[8]

A third writer, George Mardikian, restaurateur, columnist, and famous American personality, called his memoir of 1956 *Song of America*. Mardikian was born in 1903 in the town of Bayburt, south of Trebizond. He was so proud to be an American that he celebrated his birthday on July 24, the day of his arrival at Ellis Island in 1922. He later opened the famous Omar Khayyam's restaurant in San Francisco and was awarded the Medal of Freedom for service in feeding US troops in Europe in World War II.

Yet Mardikian resolutely maintained an Armenian identity. In the book he tells us how he yielded to the pleadings of family and friends "and all my wise ancestors who were speaking through them," in breaking off his plans to marry his *odar*—or foreigner—American girlfriend.[9] He was also active in Armenian politics. After World War II, he worked to win several thousand Armenians stranded in European refugee camps the right to emigrate to the United States. However, Mardikian worked in an era when Armenian and American politics did not mix. In these years Armenians were more likely to end up fighting fellow Armenians over Diaspora political quarrels than Turks over the legacy of 1915. In his memoir Mardikian describes how a rare Armenian-Turkish encounter played out in his restaurant at the 1945 United Nations

San Francisco conference—with comedy and frostiness, but no hint of violence:

> Almost every evening, the Turkish delegates came to Omar Khayyam's for dinner. Some of my Armenian waiters still had not forgiven the Turks for the massacres of 1915 and other years, so I instructed Bart to see that they were served by waiters of other nationalities.
>
> One night, when the restaurant was particularly crowded, Bart forgot. He assigned Hovagim, the most patriotic of all the Armenian waiters, to the Turks. Everything went well until the last course. The chief delegate called Hovagim over. "Waiter, five Turkish coffees."
>
> Hovagim stood beside their table, arms folded like an Armenian Patrick Henry, and gazed sternly at the wall above their heads. The delegates took no notice. "Waiter," repeated the chief delegate, without looking up, "we will have five Turkish coffees, please."
>
> "Sir," said Hovagim loudly, "in this restaurant we do not serve Turkish coffee. If you mean the dark, thick coffee made with powdered grains, that is cooked and served in a *jazveh* and sometimes drunk by people of your nationality, we have that. But we refer to it as 'Armenian' coffee."
>
> The Turk, a real diplomat, bowed slightly. "Thank you. Then we will have five Armenian coffees."[10]

## Lemkin's Idea

In the 1940s, as the postwar settlement dissolved into the Cold War, a new concept was being devised that would reinterpret Armenians' experience to themselves and mobilize a new generation—genocide. The word was coined in 1944 by the Polish Jewish lawyer Raphael Lemkin. Within a few years it had became a universal concept.

Even before the Nazi Holocaust of the Jews, in which most of his family perished, Lemkin was preoccupied by the paradox that the mass slaughter of a national group was not a punishable crime. Lemkin elaborated on the idea in his book of 1944, *Axis Rule in Occupied Europe*, combining the Greek word *genos*, meaning "race," and the Latin word *cide*, meaning "killing," to make a "new term and new conception for destruction of nations."

After Lemkin's coinage, the word entered the language of international rights and politics with great speed. Since then, "genocide" has acquired multiple overlapping meanings. First there was Lemkin's conception of the term. Then came an official legal definition as set out in the 1948 United Nations Convention on the Prevention and Punishment of the Crime of Genocide. Thereafter, the word also became a concept in the social sciences, the subject of hundreds of books, and the title of several dozen academic centers, such as the Genocide Studies Program at Yale University. It has also become a highly politicized term: politicians throw the word at their enemies to accuse them of evil, and nations engage in "genocide competition." The number of historical genocides claimed by nations has proliferated, even as the number of legal prosecutions remains tiny.

Lemkin revised his conception more than once. In his implacable campaign to have genocide declared an international crime, he employed different arguments with different countries. He quixotically opposed the adoption of the United Nations' Universal Declaration of Human Rights, adopted a week after the Genocide Convention, believing that it diluted the force of the convention. There are some constants in his writing, however. Running through all the historical cases of genocide that Lemkin cites, from Genghis Khan to that of Hitler, is the notion that it describes not just slaughter in large numbers but an attempt to destroy the culture or civilization of the victims as well. Indeed, he suggested that "genocide" could be effected without mass killing but through actions such as sterilization or forced mass conversion.

Lemkin also evidently regarded the slaughter of the Ottoman Armenians as a prime historical instance of genocide—and as his other main example from the twentieth century, along with the Holocaust. In February 1949, he told a CBS television interviewer, "I became interested in genocide because it happened so many times. It happened to the Armenians, and after the Armenians Hitler took action."[11] While a student in Lwow in 1921, Lemkin had puzzled over the moral challenge of the case of Soghomon Tehlirian, who had resorted to assassinating Talat Pasha in order to achieve what he regarded as justice and had only been acquitted on grounds of insanity. In his memoirs, published long after his death, Lemkin wrote, "Tehlirian, who upheld the moral order of mankind, was classified as insane, incapable of discerning the moral nature of his act. He had acted as the self-appointed legal officer for the conscience of mankind. But can a man appoint himself to mete out justice?"[12]

On December 9, 1948, the United Nations General Assembly, meeting in Paris, unanimously adopted the Convention on the Prevention and Punishment of the Crime of Genocide. Article 2 said:

> In the present Convention, genocide means any of the following acts committed with intent to destroy, in whole or in part, a national, ethnical, racial or religious group, as such:
>
> (a) Killing members of the group;
>
> (b) Causing serious bodily or mental harm to members of the group;
>
> (c) Deliberately inflicting on the group conditions of life calculated to bring about its physical destruction in whole or in part;
>
> (d) Imposing measures intended to prevent births within the group;
>
> (e) Forcibly transferring children of the group to another group.

This wording was the result of legal and political bargaining between the new UN states. The term "cultural genocide" was dropped from the final draft, despite Lemkin's advocacy. The use of the phrase "committed with intent" was designed to stop genocidal murderers when they were still planning their deeds and before they started actually implementing them. However, the requirement to prove intent on the part of a perpetrator was problematic because it required evidence of planning, which might be hard to establish—and, sure enough, the issue of the intent or otherwise of the Unionist leadership in 1915 became central in Armenian-Turkish historical, legal, and legislative battles over genocide.

Equally controversial was the phrase "a national, ethnical, racial or religious group, as such." This categorization explicitly excluded a targeted group defined by political affiliation. This was mostly on the initiative of the Soviet Union. Stalin was, of course, a mass killer of people he defined as political enemies, from Whites to Kulaks to "Trotskyites," and the USSR evidently negotiated this exemption as an insurance policy against the eventuality of a charge of genocide being leveled for these Soviet crimes.[13]

The international political bargaining continued after the signing. For the convention to become international law, 20 of the UN member states that had voted in favor of it had to ratify it. Lemkin threw himself into a ferocious round of lobbying for ratification. On October 16, 1950, it was confirmed that 22 countries had acceded, ensuring that 90 days later the convention became international law. However, the US Senate, hampered by fears about the encroachment of international law on American sovereignty, would not ratify the convention until 1988.

Though the United States did not ratify the convention, Turkey did. Lemkin describes in his memoirs how in 1950 he lobbied the Turkish delegation at the United Nations:

A bold plan was formulated in my mind: I would obtain ratification by Turkey among the first twenty founding nations. This would be atonement for genocide of the Armenians. But how could it be achieved? A longer conversation was required. I called the counselor Adnan Kural, with whom I was on friendly terms, and asked for an appointment. The previous night I kept thinking and planning how I would address the matter with him. I could not reach any decision but this: let me rely on intuition, which would guide me during the discussion. A few ideas simmered vaguely in my mind. The Turks are proud of their republican form of government and their progressive ideas, which distinguish their government from the rule of the Ottoman Empire. The Genocide Convention might well put this within the framework of social and international progress. I knew, however, that in this conversation both sides would have to avoid speaking about the other, although it would be constantly in their minds: the Armenians.

In the morning I started planning. I would like to see the name of Turkey among the first twenty nations, which would bring the Genocide Convention into force and open the way for the U.N. to proclaim social progress and advancement of international law. Modernized nations should help bring forward modern ideas. "Your country has achieved great reforms: the modern transformation of your alphabet, the liberation of your women, and the introduction of modern methods in education. The world has been watching you. But this progress must be dramatized during the next General Assembly. Otherwise, your ratification, in which I believe, would be lost in later ratifications. Why not be a teacher instead of a pupil?" And then I added: "In the light of your present progress I see you are breaking radically with the past."[14]

Turkey accepted the challenge and acceded to the genocide convention on July 31, 1950. Lemkin's successful lobbying and Turkey's ratification give us a revealing insight into the way both of them interpreted the meaning of the term "genocide" at this historical moment. The implication is that neither Lemkin nor Turkey nor other parties believed the convention had retroactive force—otherwise the Turkish government would surely have fretted about possible prosecutions of those perpetrators of massacres in 1915 still alive. At this moment the consensus was that it was all about genocide prevention, not judgments on past crimes.

### "Genocide Is Hardly the Cure"

Armenians were quick to notice Lemkin's new word. In 1947, *Hairenik Weekly* also welcomed the coining of the new term of "genocide," but more with sadness than with triumph, because of its lack of retroactive force. On January 30 of that year, the newspaper commented on the new concept: "Outlawing wholesale slaughter of peoples is welcome news to the Armenians, the Greeks, the Syrians, the Arabs and the Balkans peoples who used to be systematically decimated under the rule of the barbarous Turk, but ironically enough it comes after the mischief has been done." The newspaper concludes,"The Genocide is hardly the cure for Armenian wounds."[15]

Once the UN Convention had been adopted, *Hairenik Weekly* again regretfully called it only a "step" in the right direction:

But what shall we say of the criminals themselves who have gone scot free? What shall we say of the authors of Armenian deportations who still are at large, and who under changed names, are directing the destiny of "modern Turkey," respected by the world, and courted at the councils of the nations? If they cannot restore the countless lives they have snuffed out, what about the loot which they have confiscated, what about the territories they have seized? What about the fruits of the genocide?

To have any meaning at all, the decision to outlaw genocide must go deeper. It must also offer a remedy to the wronged parties. To outlaw genocide, but to sanction the basic aims and results of the action is only a half measure. The Turks today are in possession of the fruits of their genocide. The Turks must be dispossessed of their loot. The United Nations owes justice to the Armenian people.[16]

The same assumption, that the Genocide Convention looked forward, not back, evidently underlay thinking in Washington. In this period the US government combined the words "Armenian" and "genocide" several times. In a 1951 submissions to the International Court of Justice in the Hague on the UN Convention, US lawyers followed Lemkin's example in giving a brief history of genocide through the ages that included the elimination of the Armenians: "The practice of genocide has occurred throughout human history. The Roman persecution of the Christians, the Turkish massacres of Armenians, the extermination of millions of Jews and Poles by the Nazis are outstanding examples of the crime of genocide. This was the background when the General Assembly of the United Nations considered the problem of genocide."[17]

Nor was it controversial in 1950—as it would be later—for an official Jewish spokesman explicitly to link the killing of Armenians in 1915 with Hitler's Final Solution of the European Jews. In hearings on the Genocide Convention in the US Senate, Jacob Blaustein, president of the American Jewish Committee, again mentioned the "travesty" of the Soghomon Tehlirian case, in which a man was forced to resort to the assassination of a mass murderer "in the absence of a law against genocide." Blaustein concluded, "Yes: there was need for a convention against genocide back in 1915, just as there was such a need in the days of ancient Carthage and in the reign of Nero."[18]

After 1948, the word "genocide" was quickly politicized. It had the misfortune to have been devised in a noble moment of consensus at the end of World War II, only to be adopted as a legal term in the more cynical climate of the early Cold War. The first successful prosecution of a state under the convention would only be made decades later, in 2007.

In the 1950s, the United States and the Soviet Union each accused the other of "genocide," with little regard for the viability of the term. The Soviet Union ratified the genocide convention early, in December 1949. But in Soviet literature on "genocide" of the 1950s there is little mention of the word's historical antecedents: the Jews of World War II are barely mentioned and the Armenians not at all. Instead, the relentless focus is on genocide committed by the "imperialist" nations of the West. In a 1956 book, *The Defense of Peace and the Struggle with Crimes Against Humanity*, Anton Traynin writes, "In imperialist states and colonial countries cultural-national genocide is an organic part of the system of class exploitation and national oppression." Traynin's examples of genocide include the treatment of "Negroes" in the United States, its colonial war in Korea, apartheid in South Africa, and the plight of Bolivian miners. The oppression of the world's workers, says Traynin, is also a kind of genocide, or a "lynching in slow motion."[19]

In a rhetorical mirror image of this, *Hairenik Weekly* in 1950 applies the term "genocide" to the Soviet Union in its public polemic—but not to Turkey. An editorial states, "Let there be no mistake in the mind of anyone. What has been taking place in the Soviet Union during the past year is genocide of the first order, the very same genocide which only recently was outlawed in the United Nations."[20]

In this Cold War environment, on May 22, 1955, Senator Herbert Lehman of New York delivered a stirring speech to an Armenian gathering on the occasion of the thirty-eighth anniversary of the First Republic of 1918. Praising "[t]he unquenchable devotion of the Armenian people to freedom and nationhood," Lehman drew parallels between the foundation of Armenia and Israel.

Yet in his historical discourse, Lehman skipped over Turkey and 1915 almost entirely before coming to the core of his speech: Armenians, he said, were the victims of genocide—by the Soviet regime.

The crime of genocide has been perpetrated, persistently and brutally, in many parts of the Soviet Union. But nowhere more violently and nakedly than in Soviet Armenia. . . . Genocide, developed to a science by Nazi Germany, has been practiced on an even vaster scale by Soviet Russia. Although history is not without its long instances of genocide, never has the commission of this crime taken place on such a prodigious scale.

The senator concluded with a plea for the United States to ratify the Genocide Convention, "which has been gathering dust in a pigeon-hole of the Senate Foreign Relations Committee."[21]

### An Idea Meets an Anniversary

In their own language, Armenians had different words to describe the tragedy of 1915, ranging from *aksor* (dispossession) or *chart* (massacre) to *aghed* (catastrophe). The phrase that was used mostly commonly to sum it up was *Medz Yeghern*, meaning "Great Catastrophe" or "Great Crime." This was a kind of equivalent of the word *Shoah* as used by the European Jews.

In the late 1940s, Lemkin's word "genocide" soon acquired an Armenian translation—*tseghasbanutiun*—and entered the Armenian vocabulary. Scholar and editor Khatchig Mouradian has traced the earliest use of the word by an Armenian to December 9, 1945, in an article on the Nuremberg Trials by a French Armenian editor. In March 1947, the Armenian National Council of America used the phrase "a monstrous plan of genocide" in a memorandum.[22]

As many scholars have noted, the concept of "the Holocaust" as a term to encapsulate the destruction of Europe's Jews took root only in the 1960s, with the 1961 arrest and trial of fugitive Nazi Adolf Eichmann being a turning point. In the same period and in parallel, the concept of the Armenian Genocide mobilized Armenians. In the words of historian Richard Hovannisian, Armenians' collective awakening about 1915 took place "on the coat-tails of the Holocaust." Hovanissian argues, "Genocide was not the subject of interest to the academic community, until Holocaust scholars and Jewish communities made it one—at which point other people said 'what about us?' "[23]

The idea then met an approaching date, the fiftieth anniversary of the Genocide in 1965. Younger Armenians were awakened. They were more distant from events and less confident of their Armenian identity—and perhaps for that very reason they wanted to close the gap between themselves and their grandparents. In parallel, in the United States of the 1960s, groups that had previously felt marginalized discovered "identity politics" and asserted their right to be heard. The Civil Rights Movement was the biggest manifestation of this change, but others spoke out, too. In the words of Efraim Sicher, the status of a victim was now transformed from "humiliated degradation to moral leadership and almost heroic pride."[24]

On April 24, 1965, Armenians held commemorative events and marches in a string of cities across the world, from Teheran to Marseilles to Buenos Aires. There was no obvious coordination. In Beirut around 80,000 Armenians attended a ceremony in the city's sports stadium. All religious leaders there—Apostolic, Catholic, and Protestant—attended in a sign of partial reconciliation. No political protests were allowed.[25]

In the *Mirror-Spectator's* April 24, 1965, edition, the writer Leon Surmelian published an essay entitled "Mourning Is Not Enough," calling for Armenians to take a stand 50 years on. "The time has come for Armenians to stand up and be counted. Counted before the eyes of the world, and counted among themselves. For too long now we have been the forgotten people of the western world. And we deserve to be forgotten forever, if we take no action now." Surmelian also told his readers, "We need an 'Armenian lobby' in Washington."[26]

The United States was becoming the Armenian Diaspora's main center. But unlike in Beirut or in Marseilles, the rallies in the United States in 1965 were quite small. The biggest turnout was in a location where everyone least expected it—in Yerevan.

## Yerevan, 1965

On April 24, 1965, tens of thousands of Armenians filled the streets of Yerevan in a ceremony of commemoration that turned into a political protest.

Nationalist sentiments had been bubbling below the surface in Armenia for several years. As scholars of the Soviet Union have noted, the metaphor of "Captive Nations" was misconceived. In actual fact, in the words of Ronald Suny, from the 1950s the Soviet Union was "the incubator of nationalities." After the death of Stalin in 1953, the non-Russian Union republics of the Soviet Union all fostered an identity built around the titular nationality of the republic, from Armenia to Uzbekistan. This national identity was wrapped up in an overall ideology of Soviet socialism, and many taboos were still observed—any questioning of the leading role of Moscow and the Communist Party was strictly off-limits. But when it came to history, culture, education, and language, Armenians, Latvians, Uzbeks, and so on, were allowed to develop what might be called their own "national consciousness." This had dramatic unforeseen effects in the late 1980s, when it only remained to add politics to generate nationalist movements and, eventually, new independent nation-states.

In Armenia the process got underway in 1960 under the patronage of the republic's Communist Party boss, Yakov Zarobian. Zarobian himself was born in 1908 in the town of Ardahan. His family fled to the Caucasus, but his father and elder brother died in the evacuation.[27] As party leader, Zarobian re-authorized immigration from the Diaspora and there was a renewal of cultural contacts with Armenians abroad. He twice invited William Saroyan to visit Armenia in the 1960s, and Saroyan's plays were staged in Yerevan.

In 1960, a collection of documents under the title *The Genocide of the Armenians in the Ottoman Empire*, edited by historian Mkrtich Nersisian, was published in Yerevan. The book told the story of the Armenian deportations, while dressing it up in appropriate socialist language. In April 1962, the massive statue of Stalin overlooking Yerevan was taken down overnight from its plinth; eventually, it would be replaced by an equally huge Mother Armenia. In the same year, celebrations commemorated the 1,600th birthday of Mesrop Mashtots, the creator of the Armenian alphabet. Monuments were opened to commemorate pre-Soviet national events and figures such as General Andranik and the Battle of Sardarapat.

Armenians also benefited from an unobtrusive patron in Moscow, Politburo member and Bolshevik veteran Anastas Mikoyan. Mikoyan was excessively cautious about any manifestations of Armenian nationalism, but on a visit to Yerevan in 1963 he reportedly told the local party leadership that they should try to lead the new nationalist mood, not be led by it. After Mikoyan's visit, purged writers such as Yeghishe Charents were rehabilitated and their works were published in large editions. Contemporary writers and poets were given space to write on "national themes." Franz Werfel's *Forty Days of Musa Dagh* was published in Russian.[28]

Party leader Zarobian believed he could frame the fiftieth anniversary of the Genocide in 1965 in an ideologically appropriate manner. He went to Moscow in the spring of 1964 to make his case in the Kremlin. He encountered skepticism. Foreign Minister Andrei Gromyko had been pursuing a rapprochement with Turkey to bring relations out of a 30-year freeze. This would pay off in October that year, when the foreign minister of Turkey, Feridun Cemal Erkin, made the first high-level visit to Moscow by a leading Turkish official in 25 years. Eventually, however, Zarobian received approval for his planned fiftieth anniversary commemorations on the strict understanding that the territorial issue of the 1940s would not be revived.[29]

Later in the year, three Armenian academics wrote a formal letter urging the leadership to mark the anniversary. They recommended that April 24 be commemorated "with the aim of unmasking the politics of the imperialists and pan-Turkists and also to strengthen our contacts and influence with the Armenian workers living abroad and actively fighting for peace and democracy." They petitioned the Soviet leadership to build "a monument to the victims from the Armenian people in the First World War. The monument ought to symbolize the resurrection of the Armenian people." In February 1965, agreement was granted for the construction of the memorial.[30]

April 24, 1965, was a Saturday. An official ceremony was planned to mark the fiftieth anniversary of the Genocide in the evening in Yerevan's grand Opera House. It was to be an invitation-only event for Armenia's elite, with speeches and music. However, Yerevan's intellectuals also wanted to mark the anniversary, as did students from Diaspora families who had immigrated to Soviet Armenia.

On the morning of April 24, a large group of students and intellectuals met in the theater of Yerevan's Academy of Sciences. Everyone was abuzz with conversation about how they would mark the day. Then, the famous poet Paruir Sevak jumped onto the stage and recited a poem written for the occasion: "We are a few, but we are Armenian!" There was an awed silence.[31] A different group, including some of Armenia's best-known writers, met at the Pantheon, the burial place of illustrious Armenians, next to the tomb of the composer Komitas, who had been arrested in April 1915.

Crowds gathered throughout the day in different parts of the city. They were peaceful, and the police did not interfere. Some came to mourn, others to protest. "We had the feeling there was no one left at home," said Ophelia Injikian, a recent graduate from medical school who was the daughter of Ohanes Injikian, one of the three scholars who had written the letter to the party leadership. "All the young people had gathered, the boys in black suits with white shirts, girls in white blouses and black skirts, with banners, with photographs of all the elite of the Armenian people killed in 1915."[32]

Young protestors carried homemade placards, some with pictures of Mount Ararat, others with the phrase "Our Lands." The phrase could refer to Turkey's eastern territories, but some of the demonstrators clearly had in mind nearer-to-home claims on Soviet Azerbaijan over the territories of Nagorny Karabakh and Nakhichevan. A mass of people began moving down Yerevan's widest street, Lenin Avenue, toward the Opera House, where the official ceremony was due to begin. Ophelia Injikian recalls, "It was so packed from one edge of the pavement to the other, a needle couldn't fall between them. Such a huge crowd went along."

In the Opera House, the closed official event started as planned. An American-Armenian, Haig Sarkissian, who was visiting Yerevan, described how the evening began with a moment of silent prayer for the victims of 1915. Then speeches began. As prescribed, there was no mention of any territorial claims. The republic's most senior academic, Viktor Hambartsumian, mixed socialist and nationalist slogans as he "unfolded more comprehensively the gruesome details of the Great Massacre, castigated the planned monstrosities of the criminal Turkish leaders, extolled the heroic stands of unarmed Armenians in several sectors, and slung cursory shafts in the direction of the Armenian Revolutionary Federation."[33]

Outside, the crowds had grown rougher and resentful at being excluded from the elite ceremony. The chant "Our Lands" intensified. Protestors threw stones. "The broken glass was tumbling down the shattered windows and doors of the Opera House were being rocked under the blows of hurling rocks." The police turned water cannons on the angry crowd, but a few desperate young men, soaked to the skin, broke through the doors. Policemen immediately screened off the stage where all the Communist Party dignitaries were sitting and evacuated them from the building. "It was like an iron curtain came down," said Injikian. This enraged the interlopers even more. " 'Why are you doing a closed meeting? Do it on the square, in the stadium' they shouted."[34]

The head of the Armenian church, Catholicos Vazgen, tried to calm the intruders, but to no avail:

Before me stood one youth whose wet clothes clung so tightly to his flesh he looked like a ballet dancer. Shouts, cries, jostling one another and commotion took charge of the hall. It was bedlam. Finally was heard a clear ringing voice: "Silence, the Catholicos of the Armenians will speak."

Catholicos Vazgen of Etchmiadzin rose to his feet and waited for the tumult to subside. All eyes were fixed on him.

"My dear children," the Catholicos began in his sonorous voice. "We understand you well and your grief and anguish is also our anguish. But the demand for territories is an international question which is beyond our jurisdiction . . . "

"Is the demand for Karabagh and Nakhitchevan, too, an international question?" A youth standing on a chair shouted at the Catholicos in a ringing voice. Shouts, snarls and a general tumult in support of the youth's sentiments followed. Presently a voice shouted, "Vazgen chan, Dear Vazgen." But the Catholicos could not control the tumult. The irreverent intimacy of "Dear Vazgen" provoked general laughter. I could not help but be shocked by the tragedy which was being unfolded before my eyes. The youth who had been cut off from the Armenian church did not know that there is a proper way of addressing a Catholicos of All Armenians.[35]

The situation in the city was tumultuous for 24 hours before it stabilized. The party leadership did not call in troops to restore order, knowing that nationalist disturbances in Georgia nine years before had ended in mass bloodshed. Dozens of protestors were detained, but none for more than a few days. The local party elite tried to downplay what had happened, informing Moscow that the unrest had not been serious. However, in February 1966, Zarobian was removed from his post and transferred to a new job in Moscow, as a punishment for the April 24 unrest.

## A Genocide Memorial

The events of April 1965 in Yerevan inspired a nationalist mood, which became part of Soviet Armenian life for the last 25 years of its existence. Among the cultural and scholarly elite, new assumptions took root. The chants and placards saying "Our Lands" were as much, if not more, about territorial claims over Azerbaijan as they were about Turkey, which was now hidden behind a Cold War frontier. The topic

Figure 6.3 The architects of Armenia's Genocide Memorial: Sashur Kalashian (left) and Artur Tarhanian (right), Yerevan, 1967. The person in the middle was a stranger whose identity is unknown.
Source: Courtesy of Sashur Kalashian

of the Genocide was no longer taboo. This had an aggressive side. In 1966 the Van-born writer and Gulag survivor Gurgen Mahari tried to publish his novel *Burning Orchards*, which gave a jaundiced view of the Armenian defense of Van in 1915 (see Chapter 2). In the new nationalist environment, Mahari was vilified by many of his peers. Copies of the novel were burned, and the chastened author withdrew the first edition from the publishing house and resubmitted it in a self-censored edition.

Despite the unrest, the authorities went ahead with the project to build a memorial to "the victims of the mass destruction of the Armenians in 1915." A site was chosen on Tsitsernakaberd hill above Yerevan (see Figure 6.3).

Sashur Kalashian was a young architect from the town of Leninakan (formerly Alexandropol, now Gyumri). Tall and gregarious, he was also a born communicator. Kalashian was born in 1936. He was a product of a generation that graduated in the years of Khrushchev's "Thaw," optimistic about the Soviet Union, instinctively socialist and atheist. "I had wonderful perspectives for the future. I knew I had a happy, lucky and very full life ahead of me."[36]

Kalashian came from an educated family, and his father was a teacher of Armenian literature with an extensive book collection. And yet, even in 1965, he knew nothing about 1915 and the Catastrophe. "My family and I did not go through the Genocide. My ancestors lived here [in eastern Armenia]. Maybe my parents knew, they should have known about it . . . but in our family there was no conversation about it."

That changed in 1964. "At one of the meetings [of the Union of Architects] one of the senior architects told us, 'The 50th anniversary of the Genocide is approaching and as architects we need to mark this anniversary.' I listened and did not understand what he was talking about. Even then, I didn't know what this story was about."

He and his colleague, Artur Tarhanian, decided to enter the competition for the memorial, but first of all resolved to study what it was they would be commemorating. Remembering his father's library, Kalashian went home to Leninakan and fetched a copy of Mkrtich Nersisian's *Genocide of the Armenians in the Ottoman Empire*.

We worked together during the day and read [Nersisian's book] in the evening. It was a documentary history, it was set out in documents, we did not know anything of it, there were just documents, no photographs. We read, we looked at and we were enraged "How can this be, how could this happen?" and we learned the scale of what had happened. And we wanted to convey the scale of this tragedy in our construction. And whatever we thought of, we thought it was not enough.

To their surprise, the two young architects won the competition. Their idea was for a memorial in three parts, all to be made from basalt stone: a long memorial wall; a tall stele like a blade of corn, which fitted the demands for something to symbolize "resurrection" in Soviet Armenia; and—the central part—12 huge slabs of basalt sloping inward to make a kind of circular tomb, with a sunken section below and an eternal flame. (Figure 6.3) Kalashian says, "For us it was one collective tombstone for one and a half million people, and the souls of the departed are in the center, as no one is buried there. And we depict this by breaking it open in the middle and there is a flame." Music of lamentation would play in and around the tomb. Kalashian left his architectural institute to work on the construction site.

In 1966, Zarobian had been replaced as party leader by his deputy, Anton Kochinian. Kochinian was committed to seeing the memorial through to completion but was increasingly nervous that the Kremlin would halt the project. He did his best to make the project as inconspicuous to Moscow as possible. For example, worried that the large price tag of 600,000 rubles would look too high in Moscow, the Yerevan officials presented the accounts as if half the sum was going on the park around the memorial, which was described as a place of leisure for the citizens of Yerevan. The work proceeded at a fast pace. Every weekend, Kalashian said, volunteers would arrive in buses at the site from far-flung corners of Armenia, offering to work for free.

"Kochinian visited privately, incognito. He said, 'Try to finish it quickly, you are dragging it out. The situation is such that if someone in Moscow so much as makes a peep,'—I am quoting his words—'we will be forced to stop the construction. Go faster.'"

Eventually, the memorial was finished. The local party leadership selected November 29, 1967, the forty-seventh anniversary of the foundation of Soviet Armenia, as the date for the opening, so as to deliver the message that it was also a monument of Armenia's Soviet-era "resurrection." No visitors came from Moscow, and party leader Kochinian lit the flame. At that moment, Kalashian was so overcome with emotion and accumulated nerves that he ran into the trees and sobbed.

Only with time did Tsitsernakaberd become an official memorial. April 24 was established as an official day of mourning in Armenia in 1975 and dignitaries then officially visited the memorial. A Genocide Museum was opened next to the monument only in 1995. When the museum was expanded, with a new opening date set for 2015, Sashur Kalashian was again commissioned to be its architect.

# 7

## Assailing Turkey

### Anger

BY THE 1970S, THE generation of Armenians that had survived the 1915 deportations was beginning to die out. Diaspora Armenian newspapers bemoaned the fact that the Armenian language was being forgotten—a process that was referred to as a "White Genocide." In 1967, the *Armenian Mirror-Spectator* used a phrase that would soon become common: "The Forgotten Genocide." In the same year, the newspaper published an angry letter to President Lyndon Johnson, urging him to put off a visit by the Turkish president to the United States. The writer resorted to the technique of the desperate in trying to make himself heard—capital letters and bold font—telling the president, "You MUST postpone the Turkish president's visit to the United States in April." He went on to say that his murdered family members were crying out "from **their unmarked graves**."[1]

The angriest Armenian was a retired civil engineer named Gurgen Yanikian, born in Erzerum (today's Erzurum) in 1895 and a survivor of 1915. Two Turkish diplomats, the consul in Los Angeles Mehmet Baydar and his vice-consul, Bahadir Demit, had the misfortune to be his victims. Baydar, aged 47, was the father of two teenage girls. Demit was 30 and a graduate of Robert College. He had recently gotten married and this was his first foreign posting. In January 1973, Yanikian lured these two men to a hotel room in Santa Barbara on the pretext of giving them a painting. He shot them both dead, then surrendered to police.

Yanikian went on trial in May 1973. His defense attorneys tried to make the occasion a repeat of the trial of Soghomon Tehlirian, the assassin of Talat Pasha in 1921, and called witnesses to testify on the Armenian Genocide. Yanikian said he wanted a "Nuremberg."[2] But this was a different era and a different jurisdiction. The two victims had been born long after the events and had no connection to the killings of 1915. The judge refused the invitation for a historical debate.

Without supporting witnesses, Yanikian tried to deliver the historical verdict himself. In rambling, aggressive testimony, in often broken English, he tried to tell the history of the Armenian Genocide to a confused courtroom. Only when he started to give testimony about the tragedy of his own life, of the death of 26 family members and seeing destruction and mutilated bodies, did he become more lucid, reportedly moving jury members to tears.[3] In July 1973, Yanikian was given a life sentence. He died in 1984, shortly after being released on parole on grounds of poor health.

Many Armenians vainly hoped they could dismiss the killings of the two consuls as an isolated act of revenge by a crazed old man. One Armenian editorialist spoke of "the hope that, like a bad dream, it would go away, but that was not possible."[4] Instead, more than $50,000 was raised for a defense fund for Yanikian called American Friends of Armenian Martyrs, The trial pushed the Armenian-Turkish quarrel into a new downward spiral. The cousin of one of the two murdered men, an American-educated Turkish businessman, said he encountered an aggressive atmosphere in the Los Angeles courtroom, to which Armenian schoolchildren had been bussed to watch the proceedings. He said that Armenians had abused himself and his wife, telling her "Get out of there, this is an Armenian trial, you have no business of being here."[5]

## Terrorism

In the foyer of Turkey's ministry of foreign affairs in Ankara is a large black marble plaque etched with 39 names in gold letters. It is a memorial to "martyrs," diplomats and members of their families who have

been killed while on foreign service. Thirty-one of the names, beginning with Baydar and Demit in Santa Barbara in 1973 and ending in
Vienna in 1984, were victims of Armenian assassins. Four of the names
are wives of diplomats, and two of them are children.

In these years, Turkey was terrorized by an Armenian campaign of
violence that put its foreign ministry in a state of siege and resurrected
the World War I image of Armenians as a mortal threat to the nation.
The campaign began in Beirut, still the center of Diaspora Armenian
politics. The year 1975, when Lebanon descended into civil war, was
probably the high point for its Armenian community, before emigration severely sapped its numbers. In that year, the sixtieth anniversary
of the Genocide was marked on a much bigger scale than 10 years previously. On April 24, more than 200,000 people marched from Bourj
Hamoud to downtown Beirut. The Lebanese political elite attended
the ceremonies. The three Armenian political parties signed a truce
pledging not to get drawn into Lebanon's civil war, a stance they called
"positive neutrality." They also sent a joint memorandum to the United
Nations, calling for "the return of Turkish-held Armenian territories to
their rightful owner—the Armenian people."[6]

A group of radical Armenians who had grown up in Beirut were
unhappy with the domination of the ARF. They were young, left-wing,
and sympathetic to the Soviet Union. Some of them formed the
Armenian Secret Army for the Liberation of Armenia, or ASALA.
Following Yanikian's example, ASALA decided to target Turkish diplomats for assassination. From 1975 to 1985, it would claim more than
40 victims. Yet ASALA's reputation appears to have been bigger than
its reality. Its headquarters was a tiny seventh-floor apartment in West
Beirut, grotesquely adorned with toy skeletons. Monte Melkonian, who
later split from the group, wrote, "ASALA took credit for imaginary
operations or the operations of others. It was impossible for any alert
person not to notice the cynical and disrespectful approach of ASALA
to the patriotic feelings of our nation."[7] The founder Hagop Hagopian
was a "dictator with a serious psychological imbalance." "Several times
he has openly said that his purpose is not to liberate Armenia but only
'make noise' (tsayn hanel). All this, plus a lot of similar talk, the picture
of the skull and crossbones on the door, the plastic skeleton hanging
from the pictures of the martyred boys. . . . "[8]

Hagopian cleverly caught the wave of young radical Armenians disappointed in the Dashnak Party who wanted to wage an Armenian "armed struggle." One of them was Alec Yenikomshian, a keenly intelligent graduate in economics from the American University in Beirut, who turned 20 years old in 1975 and then joined ASALA. Yenikomshian never got to carry out an operation. On the evening of October 3, 1980, a bomb he was assembling in a hotel room in Geneva exploded, blinding him and severing his left hand.

Reflecting on ASALA 30 years later in his apartment in Yerevan, Yenikomshian was a calm and well-spoken but passionate individual. He said he had no regrets of the path he chose. He cited the decision in 1973 by the UN Human Rights Commission to delete a reference to the Armenians from its report on genocide as proof that the world was forgetting the Armenians:

> After silence for many decades, many Armenians and especially the youth said, "Enough was enough," and started talking about the Genocide, the lost homeland. In the Diaspora it was mentioned but there was a realization of the fact that 50 years have passed, and nothing has changed. . . . Then the 60th anniversary approached and the new youth in the Diaspora again realized we've done all these things, but still—nothing.[9]

The young Armenian radicals were inspired by the example of Palestinian terrorism. Yenikomshian and other Armenians trained with the revolutionary left-wing group, the Popular Front for the Liberation of Palestine, or PFLP. They also sought out other "anti-imperialists": the Kurdish guerrilla movement (the PKK), the Red Brigades in Italy, and the Irish Republican Army (IRA). What were Yenikomshian's motives? First of all, he said, he wished to remind Turkey that the Armenian issue was not dead. Second, he wanted to send the same message to international public opinion.

> So in one sense it was to put back the Armenian question on the international agenda. There was also a third objective in my opinion, to revive the Armenian Diaspora. Because of very understandable reasons, time and assimilation, the youth started to forget

about their past and get assimilated. In France, with the biggest Armenian presence in Europe, I can definitely say that the generation of that time, the '70s and '80s, revived their Armenianness. But this was a third objective. So that's why, specifically for the first two reasons, we called this phase "the phase of armed propaganda." This objective was more or less realized. The Turkish authorities became aware of the existence of this problem, they couldn't deny it just to pretend that it didn't exist, the same thing for the powers which decided the fate of the world, etc., etc. More or less, that objective was hit.[10]

Asked what was the ultimate goal, Yenikomshian answered, "The liberation of western Armenia. It might seem a fantasy, it might be a fantasy, but it doesn't cease to remain the aim of the Armenians."

In 1978, Yenikomshian teamed up with another zealous ASALA recruit, Monte Melkonian, an archaeologist and left-wing idealist, who had drifted from California to Beirut in pursuit of the Armenian cause. For Melkonian, high-minded aims clashed with the dirty reality of armed struggle, when he carried out an operation in Athens on July 31, 1980. Outside the office of Turkish Airlines, he aimed a pistol at the tinted windows of a car with Turkish diplomatic plates and killed Galip Ozmen, an attaché at the Turkish embassy. An ASALA statement called the killing "another step in our struggle against the Turkish regime, reactionary Turkish forces, NATO, American imperialism and the reactionary Armenian forces."[11] But it did not say that, besides the diplomat himself, Melkonian had also killed Ozmen's 14-year-old daughter Neslihan, who was sitting in the back seat, and wounded his wife and son.

Asked about the Athens killing, Yenikomshian says that he himself does not regret the targeting of Turkish diplomats such as Ozmen because they were "the Turkish state—and the Turkish state got what it deserved." But he calls the death of the 14-year-old girl "very sad and regrettable." Of Melkonian, he says, "[i]t was on his conscience." Melkonian slowly split away from ASALA, as its campaign of violence became more indiscriminate. In his memoir of his brother's life, Markar Melkonian writes of the Athens assassination, "As time passed, [Monte's] expressions of regret became less glib. Five years after the shooting, he described it as a counterproductivce and indefensible crime, the likes of which should never be repeated, and for the next thirteen years he would attempt to prevent others from committing similar crimes. This would be his gesture of compensation. But the compensation would never be adequate."[12]

## The Justice Commandos

On October 22, 1975, the Turkish ambassador to Austria, Daniş Tunaligil, was assassinated by three gunmen. Two days later, his colleague Ismail Erez, the ambassador to France, was killed, along with his driver outside the Turkish embassy in Paris.

A second Armenian terrorist organization, the Justice Commandos of the Armenian Genocide, claimed responsibility for the killings. The Justice Commandos were pursuing the same tactic as ASALA—but as rivals, not partners. Their name was less well-known at the time, primarily because the Turkish state and its Cold War allies preferred to focus on the left-wing and allegedly Soviet-funded ASALA as an enemy. But the Justice Commandos actually killed more Turkish diplomats than did ASALA.

It was never openly advertised, but was soon an open secret that the Justice Commandos were closely associated with the Dashnaks of the Armenian Revolutionary Foundation. A Justice Commandos statement of December 1975 made exactly the same claims as ASALA, the only difference being that they offered to lay down their weapons when Turkey "agrees to negotiate with Armenian Representatives in order to reinstate Justice"—a hint at Dashnaktsutiun. It is possible that the militant group had been planned at the ARF congress of December 1972 and was stung into action by the first ASALA attacks. A quick glance at the biographies of its members and the way the Dashnak press gave extensive coverage to their attacks (but not those of ASALA) leaves little doubt as to the connection.[13]

The Turkish diplomat Galip Balkar was a favorite of his contemporaries (Figure 7.1). Ilter Turkmen, who served as Turkey's foreign minister from 1980 to 1983, says, "He was Number Two in our NATO mission and we were looking to him as the next Secretary General

Figure 7.1  Galip Balkar, Turkey's ambassador to Belgrade, assassinated in 1983.
Source: Ministry of Foreign Affairs of Turkey

or Ambassador to Washington. He was so brilliant, but he had to do another embassy before that."[14] So in 1981, when Balkar was 45, the minister sent him to Belgrade to serve a term as Turkey's ambassador to Yugoslavia.

Balkar had a good friend in Brussels, Volkan Vural. They used to play tennis together. Vural describes Balkar as "a very liberal, extremely bright gentleman." Balkar had wanted to stay in his job in NATO. "He was reluctant, but he finally had to bow to pressure and go to Belgrade as ambassador. Of course, I mean to become an ambassador is the dream of every Foreign Service diplomat. But he was happy with his life, content with his life."[15]

On March 9, 1983, Balkar's ambassadorial car stopped at a red light in central Belgrade near the Turkish embassy. Two Armenian gunmen were waiting for him and opened fire. The embassy driver was wounded. Balkar was struck by two bullets and died two days later in the hospital. The two attackers fled from the scene, chased by Yugoslav policemen stationed near the parliament building. In an exchange of gunfire, a student, Zeljko Milivojevic, was killed. One of the gunmen escaped—he was arrested shortly afterward in the town of Novi Sad.

The other was shot in the legs by a policeman and fell to the ground, bleeding profusely.

"The guy who shot me came and he took my gun from the ground, of course I was feeling that my situation is hard, because of my wound, and also the blood was coming from my mouth, because my tooth was broken," the wounded assassin, Anto (Antranik) Boghossian, recalled 30 years later. "The first thing I did, I was trying to answer that this is a political action. . . . And after that I lost consciousness."

Boghossian, was then aged 26. He was paralyzed from the waist down by the shots and was confined to a wheelchair. He now lives in Yerevan. Boghossian was trained as a photographer and now works as a sculptor. It is probably not too fanciful to imagine that he, a well-educated man, and the "refined" Ambassador Balkar would have found subjects in common to talk about, if somehow they had met in a different peaceful setting, not at either end of a gun on a Belgrade street.

Boghossian learned to use a gun in a Dashnak-led self-defense unit protecting an Armenian neighborhood in Beirut during the Lebanese Civil War: "We were very active in those neighborhoods, not just in defending but also in passing on that thinking and that ideology. And that's when we first started feeling the potential in us that we could, in fact, get engaged in that other struggle."[16]

In July 1983, four months after the Belgrade attack, five young Beirut Armenians, aged between 19 and 21, staged an even more radical mission in Lisbon. They left behind a videotaped message saying they did not intend to come out alive. It said, "This is not suicide . . . but rather our sacrifice to the altar of freedom."[17] The five attacked the Turkish embassy in Lisbon. In the violent struggle for the building, the wife of a diplomat, Cahide Mihçioğlu, and a Portuguese policeman, Manuel Pacheco, as well as the five young Armenians, all died. The "Lisbon Five" subsequently became the subjects of Armenian militant martyrology, with portraits and commemorations, including church services, commemorating them as martyrs and comparing them to the men who seized the Ottoman Bank in 1896. Following the example of Irish, Palestinian, and Tamil militants, radical Armenians had acquired their own suicide martyrs.

Two years after Belgrade and Lisbon, Boghossian says, the violence "exhausted itself, it had done its job." Asked in 2013 whether it was time for Armenian-Turkish dialogue, he answered, "Not yet. They need to be ready. We've been ready for a long time. We've understood that we need to live side by side. We also know they can't rely on retreating from positions, from reality. They must become aware of what they've done and the consequences of that, and remove the consequences of that."

## End of a Campaign

The wave of Armenian terrorism in the 1970s polarized the Diaspora community. In Lebanon, the home of many of the assassins and a place immersed in political violence, it had a large base of support. An American journalist reported from Beirut in 1980, "Even the most pacific Armenian intellectuals do not hide certain satisfaction whenever a Turkish target is hit, although they criticize attacks on non-Turkish objectives."[18]

In Western countries, most Armenian Diaspora figures deplored the killings. New York politician Edward Costikyan wrote a letter to the *New York Times*, published on October 20, 1980, calling the killings "an insult to all living Armenians and an insult to the Armenian martyrs." He wrote, "What is most distressing is that these terrorists 'claim responsibility' in the name of a people that has survived in large part because it has adhered to the Christian faith Armenians embraced centuries ago. Shame! Shame! Shame!"[19] In 1986, the US anthropologist Anny Bakalian asked a survey sample of 586 American-Armenians to respond to the statement, "Armenian 'terrorism' in the last few years has soiled the good name of Armenians in the USA as a law-abiding and peace loving people." A total of 65 percent of respondents agreed, 28 percent disagreed, while 7 percent had no opinion.[20]

In 1982, both the terrorism and counter-reaction to it had reached a peak. The campaign began to peter out. ASALA disintegrated. The leader of its core group, Hagop Hagopian, exhibited signs of madness and became obsessed with the pursuit and sadistic killing of Armenian "traitors." He even murdered his Yugoslav wife, before he himself was killed on an Athens street in April 1988.[21] The murderous feud between

former ASALA members dragged a bloody trail in the 1990s into independent Armenia, when two of its veterans were assassinated by rivals.)

The groups' claims to nobility were discredited by alleged criminal connections with drug-traffickers, weapons smugglers, and radical Palestinian hijackers. A US journalist, Nathan M. Adams, testified
before Congress in 1984 that "Armenian terrorist groups of both the
left and the right were estimated a year ago to be 90 percent financed
through the sale or barter of narcotics." He cited the case of "Noubar
Soufoyon," an Armenian-born "terrorist broker" arrested in numerous countries for acts of terrorism and drug smuggling, who operated in Lebanon. Nathan told congressmen that Soufoyon owned a
house in Los Angeles not far from that of Patti Reagan, daughter of
the president.[22]

Before ASALA ended, however, Hagopian unleashed three extremely
bloody acts of terrorism, in the covered bazaar in Istanbul, in Ankara's
Esenboğa Airport, and in Orly Airport in Paris. Nineteen people died
and more than 150 were wounded, almost all of them random victims.
Many more people would have died at Orly on July 15, 1983, had the
hold-all bag containing the bomb, which was about to be loaded onto
an Istanbul-bound airplane, not exploded prematurely. Four French
citizens, two Turks, one American, and one Swede died.[23]

In response to the Orly bomb, the French authorities launched a
big security sweep, arresting more than 50 Armenian suspects. The
Turkish government was angry, believing that the French government had eliminated Armenian cells whose existence it had been
aware of for a long time, only after a particularly heinous incident.
"The French reacted because French citizens also died," said Foreign
Minister Ilter Turkmen with bitterness. Previously, the socialist government of François Mitterrand had the reputation of being
pro-Armenian, and Interior Minister Gaston Defferre had called the
militants' cause "just."[24]

Both in France and in Lebanon, the groups lost their capacity to
organize. The Israeli invasion of Lebanon in 1982 had dealt another
blow to both organizations. Apo Ashjian, rumored to be the master-
mind of the Justice Commandos and a prominent member of the ARF,
was assassinated. In August 1983, the *Wall Street Journal*, naming no
sources, reported that the Justice Commandos "have yielded to CIA

pressure exerted through Dashnag intermediaries and 'frozen' their own terror campaign."[25]

## A Meeting in Zurich

On November 27, 1977, at the height of the assassinations, the Turkish foreign minister, Ihsan Sabri Çağlayangil, secretly met the leaders of the three Armenian political parties in a hotel in Zurich. They had a frank and often acrimonious discussion of the major issues that divided them, came to no agreement, and parted. Only a few weeks later, the Turkish government fell, the minister lost his job, and the fragile initiative vanished.

The confidential meeting yielded no results, but offers a tantalizing glimpse into a "might-have-been world" in Armenian-Turkish relations. The story is little known, even to senior Armenian and Turkish politicians. On the Turkish side, it appears that only Çağlayangil and his prime minister, Süleyman Demirel, and one or two others knew about the planned meeting.[26]

Çağlayangil, born in 1908, was a close political ally of Demirel. In 1976 the prime minister was increasingly worried by the campaign of Armenian terrorism and its implications. He made Çağlayangil his foreign minister for a second time. Çağlayangil himself had both a professional and a personal stake in wanting to stop the killings: two of his friends, the Turkish ambassadors to Paris and Vienna, had recently been assassinated, and he feared for the lives of his colleagues.

In the spring of 1976, Çağlayangil sought the advice of an Armenian philanthropist and art collector with the first name Agop, who told him to approach the Armenian Cilician bishop in New York. On a visiting card, he wrote merely, "Dear Bishop, I want to introduce you [to] my good friend, H. E. Mr. I. S. Çağlayangil, Minister of Foreign Affairs of Turkey. Please do the necessary. Thank you. Best regards, Agop" (Figure 7.2). The minister only took up the opportunity that October when he traveled to New York to attend the United Nations General Assembly.

The minister's closest aide was Oktay Aksoy. Aksoy is now retired, living in Ankara, after a long career that saw him become Turkey's ambassador to Sweden. A courteous gentleman with a trim white

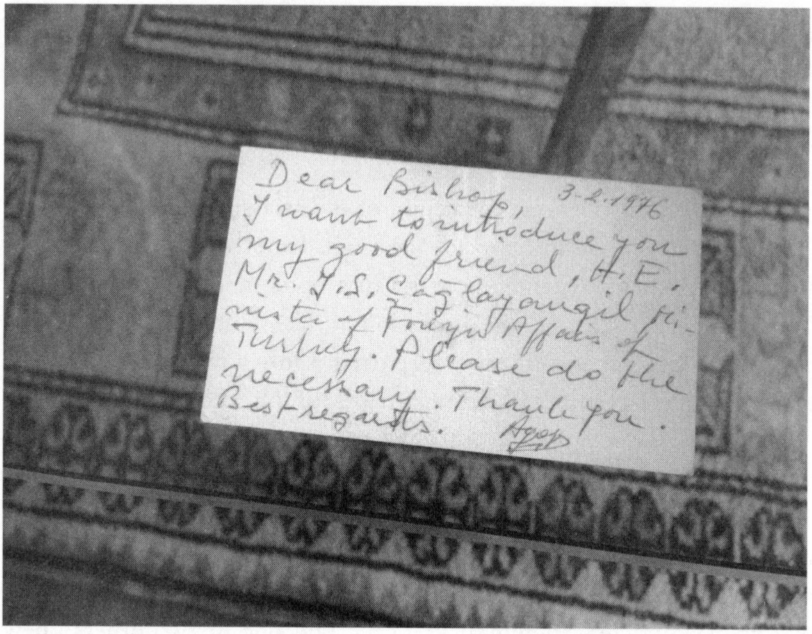

Figure 7.2 An Armenian introduction. Note to the Armenian Cilician bishop of New York, introducing Turkish Foreign Minister Çağlayangil, 1976.
Source: Thomas de Waal, courtesy of Ambassador Oktay Aksoy.

mustache, he is now the last surviving witness to the secret meeting in Switzerland.

Aksoy's family and personal history intersected with Armenians at several points. His grandfather, a controller on the Baghdad railway, was killed by Armenians after the French army and the Armenian Legion intervened in Cilicia in 1919. Aksoy still has a picture of him, an Ottoman gentleman with a fez and walking stick. He himself was born in 1938 in Adana on the Mediterranean coast, a city with a rich Armenian history. He went to school in Tarsus in the 1950s and had many Armenian school-friends there. In October 1992, it fell to Aksoy, as head of the Economic Section in the Turkish foreign ministry, to sign the first bilateral agreement with an Armenian minister, on shipment of wheat from the European Union to Armenia via Turkey.

In 1976, says Aksoy, "the wish of our minister was . . . 'How we can find a way to end these assassinations and discuss it with the Armenian leaders?'" In New York, Aksoy was commissioned to seek out the Armenian archbishop. But as the archbishop was not in town, he ended up meeting his assistant priest, Oshagan Choloyan (who in 1998 himself became archbishop).[27]

The priest contacted the well-known Washington-based ARF bureau member, the dentist Hratch Abrahamian, who summoned several of his colleagues for a clandestine meeting in New York with the Turkish minister. One day in early October 1976, the minister and his aide slipped away from their tight security detail—instructed to guard them against possible Armenian assassinations—and went to the Hilton Hotel in downtown Manhattan. There they met 10 Diaspora Armenians from different political groups. Çağlayangil told them he was prepared to hold a high-level secret meeting to discuss the assassinations. Abrahamian then traveled to Beirut and participated in a meeting of the three Armenian parties. It was agreed that the three leaders would take up the invitation, but they would do no "bargaining" on the territorial issue.

There had been sporadic contacts between the Turkish government and Armenian Diaspora politicians, especially the Dashnaks, since the early 1920s. Messages were exchanged. "I don't think there was ever a time when there was no communication at all," says veteran ARF politician Tatul Sonentz. He recalls that his father-in-law, Dr. Yervant Khatanasian, a one-time bureau member, was talking secretly with Turkish officials in Cairo in the 1950s.[28] But foreign minister Çağlayangil's approach was of a different order from anything that had previously passed between the two sides.

"Everyone was in high spirits," wrote Avedis Demirjian, the leader of the Hnchak Party, one of the three men delegated to meet the Turkish foreign minister. "For the first time, the Turkish state was beginning to talk to the representatives of the nation against which it carried out a genocide."[29]

Under conditions of absolute secrecy, a time and place were agreed upon in Zurich. On the morning of November 27, 1977, the three leaders met Çağlayangil and Aksoy in the Green Room of the illustrious Dolder Grand Hotel. The Armenians were represented by Demirjian on behalf of the Hnchak Party, the ARF leader Shavarsh Toriguian, and the Ramgavar leader Parounag Tovmassian.[30] They sat on either side of a long table, drinking tea. The conversation was conducted in English, with Aksoy interpreting, even though the Armenian leaders almost certainly knew Turkish. (Çağlayangil and Tovmassian were both born within two years of each other in 1908 and 1910, both near the town of Bursa, before their biographies diverged, with Tovmassian ending up as an orphan in Lebanon.)

"The atmosphere was tense," recalled Aksoy. The elderly Ramgavar leader was the friendliest of the three, Toriguian the most aggressive. Çağlayangil tried to lighten the atmosphere by telling his interlocutors jokingly that there was a rumor that his name had Armenian origins. He told them he had grown up on a farm with an Armenian boy, who took care of the horse-drawn carts and was part of his family. According to an Armenian memoir, the minister "added that, owing to his advanced age, it was possible that he would not be serving in subsequent Turkish governments, so he advised that the Armenians should take advantage of his presence."[31]

There was a predictably difficult exchange about 1915 and the Genocide. The minister made some comments about it being a "shared tragedy" from Ottoman times, brought on both peoples by the Great Powers. ARF leader Toriguian responded, "It is not possible to close the issue by not talking about it or by saying that both sides are guilty. The main thing is the resolution of the Armenian issue, the rights of the Armenian nation to live and thrive on its ancestral lands."[32]

When the conversation touched on the fundamental issues for both sides, all were disappointed. Çağlayangil's main objective was to halt the campaign of assassinations, but the three leaders told him they had no sway over a group of young militants who were out of control. (In the case of Dashnaktsutiun and the Justice Commandos of the Armenian Genocide, this was almost certainly not the case). According to one of the Armenians, the minister hinted that there might be Turkish retaliation if the terror campaign continued.

When the Armenians raised the issue of the eastern territories, the minister was intransigent. According to one of the Armenian reports of the meeting, Çağlayangil told the party leaders, "Material compensation, resettlement, and offering certain privileges for Armenians are acceptable issues, but your territorial demands are absolutely not acceptable. That demand is not acceptable to any Turk whatsoever, not even a traitor."[33]

The secret meeting in the Dolder Grand Hotel broke up at lunchtime with no result, except an exchange of telephone numbers. According to his aide, Turkey's veteran foreign minister was disappointed. In his view, he had reached out to the kind of people a foreign minister would never normally negotiate with and had achieved nothing. Çağlayangil, he says, "was not very happy with the way they were trying to pull Turkey, to negotiate. At that time we didn't have any independent Armenia. To negotiate with political parties was something out of the question at the time."

The minister's forecast that he was an elderly man who might be out of office soon proved correct all too quickly. Aksoy says the Zurich meeting was "exploratory, [to see] how the Armenians saw the issue. If we had had other meetings we could have probably come up with answers to some of the questions and demands of the Armenian parties." But only five weeks later, the Demirel government fell and Çağlayangil lost his job. The half-opened door closed shut, and the encounter in Zurich was buried in such secrecy that no one was able to open it again.

## A Turkish Counter-narrative

The assassinations kindled strong anti-Armenian feelings in the most Western-oriented section of the Turkish government, the foreign ministry. Everyone knew at least one of the victims. Ilter Turkmen, foreign minister from 1980, says, "When I was minister I attended many funerals. It was a very painful experience."[34]

Some Armenians say that the terror campaign raised consciousness and reminded Turkey of the Armenian problem. That is probably true, and it is also true that the foreign minister's decision to meet the Armenians in Zurich was a direct response to the assassinations. At the same time, the killings rekindled Turkey's "Sèvres syndrome," the perception that the country was under a concerted siege by foreign powers. In 1984, Dr. Tarik Somer, president of Ankara University, told a symposium on the Armenian terrorist issue, "[T]he motive is to wear down the Turkish Republic; it is to help the external enemies of Turkey to achieve their purposes."[35]

In 1946 Turkey became an electoral democracy, although the basic tenets of Kemal Atatürk's social order and nationalist consensus remained in place. Three military coup d'états, in 1960, 1971, and 1980, saw the army intervene to brutally reimpose its own vision of a secular Kemalist Turkey. On each occasion the army allowed elections to take place again after a suitable interval, but even when civilian governments were in charge, a so-called "deep state" of entrenched conservative security officials was detected in the background.

Political violence was still endemic in the system, and minorities often took the brunt of it. In September 1955, thousands of Istanbul's surviving Greeks were subjected to violence in two days of organized rioting and looting. Later, most would be deported from the city. In 1974, the Turkish military intervention in Cyprus prompted another backlash against Greeks and Armenians. In the 1970s, the Alevi religious minority suffered in a series of violent riots and massacres.

In Turkey, in the second half of the 1970s, left-right violence fed on economic turmoil, and public order all but broke down. In September 1980, the army again took power. Tens of thousands were arrested, and hundreds of political prisoners died of torture in jail. The general who led the coup, Kenan Evren, was elected president. The new military rulers of the country proclaimed a fight against the triple threat of Communism, Greek extremism, and Armenian terrorism. President Evren employed anti-Armenian rhetoric that had not been heard in 60 years. "Do you want to give your lands and homes to Armenians?" he asked an audience in a speech in Van in 1983. The president told a gathering in Niğde, "As in 1915, we did not declare war against the Armenians. The Armenians of those years, after their declaration of war, just as they were disappointed then by the results, they will be disappointed now." Behind the scenes, the president ordered a covert campaign of retaliation against the Armenian groups.[36]

The Turkish government also began an ideological counteroffensive. It was led by a class of men from the political elite who believed that the Turkish state was under attack and that the Soviet Union and the Kurdish separatist movement were probably supporting the Armenian militants.[37] The officials discovered that they had almost no Turkish narrative to set against the historical works of authors such as Yves Ternon and Vahakn Dadrian. The single exception was a long book by Esat Uras, published in 1950, which did not have a full narrative of the years 1915–1916.[38]

Nor were there any school or college textbooks. "[I]t was a narrative that was communicated through its *absence*," writes Professor Jennifer Dixon, who has written authoritatively on this issue. "Throughout the 1950s, 1960s and 1970s, Armenians were notably absent from history textbooks, and the 1915 deportation was not mentioned in *any* textbook in the period. Overall, the impression of Armenians that emerged from these textbooks was of their irrelevance and near non-existence within the Ottoman Empire."[39]

In 1981, the country's new army-led government created a new department in the foreign ministry entitled the Directorate of Intelligence and Research, tasked with dealing with all aspects of "the Armenian Question" except the security issue. Omer Lütem was the department's first director general. Now over 80 years old, Lütem still works full-time on the Armenian question as the head of a state-sponsored research institute in Ankara, describing it as an obsession he cannot abandon. At the start, however, he was a career diplomat who had very little acquaintance with the issue. Lütem says, "I was obliged to learn it. I remember I was working at least 16 hours a day because first I was doing the business of the department and in my spare time I was reading and reading and reading."[40]

Lütem sent Turkish diplomats and historians into the Ottoman archives to hunt for material. On the basis of what they found, he sponsored the publication of two books to form the foundation of the new Turkish narrative. One set out to prove that the alleged Talat Pasha telegrams, including the famous "Ten Commandments" document, obtained by the British in 1919, were in fact forgeries. (This is a view that most international scholars now share.)

The second book, *The Armenian File*, became a new guiding text. It was written by the second-ranking official in the foreign ministry, Undersecretary Kamuran Gürün, and was published in 1983. Its English version, published in 1985, with the subtitle *The Myth of Innocence Exposed*, made its intent clear. Gürün offered a new low figure for "Armenian casualties" of 300,000 and went further than his predecessors in pressing the case for Armenian treachery. Polemic is mixed with history, as in this passage:

The Armenians were forced to emigrate because they had joined the ranks of the enemy. The fact that they were civilians does not change the situation. Those who were killed in Hiroshima and Nagasaki during the Second World War were also civilians. . . . Turkey did not kill them, but relocated them. As it was impossible to adopt a better solution under the circumstances, it can not be accepted that those who died because they were unable to resist the hardships of the journey were killed by the Turks.[41]

Gürün's book was one among many. Twenty other books on the Armenian issue were published in Turkey between 1981 and 1985.[42] Armenian "traitors" invaded Turkish school textbooks. One 1989 textbook cited by Jennifer Dixon told schoolchildren, "They murdered tens of thousands of Turks with a brutality that has never been seen before. With these tragedies some Armenians added dark and shameful pages to the history of humanity." A 1995 textbook said, "Greeks and Armenians, who for hundreds of years as Turkish citizens had lived in tranquility and had benefited from all kinds of opportunities from the state, took advantage of the bad situation into which the Ottoman State had fallen, cooperated with the occupying states and worked to break up our lands."[43]

A permanent exhibition on the "Armenian Question" in Istanbul's Military Museum, set up in this era and still in place in 2013, informs the general public in great detail about Armenian treachery. On display is the striped shirt Talat Pasha was wearing on the day of his assassination, covered in bloodstains, along with his Webley Scott pistol, whip, sword, and scabbard. There are photographs of weapons and bombs said to be captured from Armenian fighters and of dead bodies of civilians said to have been massacred by Armenians. A brief summary of the "Armenian Question" gives an orthodox Turkish nationalist version of events, complete with capital letters in bold font: "These hostile activities of Armenians who made cooperation with the enemy, assaulted to Turkish army and relentlessly killed the innocent people and 'BETRAYED THEIR STATE' were hindered with the 'TEHCIR KANUNU (COMPULSORY IMMIGRATION LAW)' taken on May 27, 1915."

The inscription concludes: "The aim of these 'UNFOUNDED GENOCIDE CLAIMS' is to decrease the power of TÜRKIYE in the region by leaving TÜRKIYE alone in the international arena, to separate the country by taking some part of east and southeast of Anatolia, to establish so-called **GREAT ARMENIA** and to sentence **TÜRKIYE** to pay indemnities."[44]

## An American Battle

In the 1980s, the new Armenian-Turkish ideological dispute was fought out in Western countries and especially in the United States. History, terrorism, and Cold War politics all bled into one another as the Turkish government and the politically active Armenian Diaspora went into battle.

Each "side" in this battle now had a powerful lobby behind it. Armenian-Americans had become wealthier, more confident, and better connected to the world of high politics. There were Armenian politicians such as George Deukmejian, who became governor of California, and big businessmen such as Stephen Mugar, Kirk Kerkorian, and Alex Manoogian. In 1972, the Armenian Assembly of America was founded, which eventually turned into a major Armenian lobbying organization. Initially, the ARF was part of it, but in 1982 its members split away—with less acrimony than in previous times—to form its own Armenian National Committee of America.

Armenians focused most of their lobbying efforts on elected representatives in Congress, especially those with large Armenian communities in their districts, in regions such as California or Massachusetts. One such legislator was Thomas ("Tip") O'Neill, later speaker of the House of Representatives. O'Neill represented the 8th Congressional District of Massachusetts, which included Watertown, one of the densely populated Armenian electoral districts, and he was a friend of Armenian philanthropist Stephen Mugar. In 1975, he steered a resolution through the House, which "authorizes the President to designate April 24, 1975, as 'National Day of Remembrance of Man's Inhumanity to Man' for remembrance of all the victims of genocide, especially those of Armenian ancestry who succumbed to the genocide perpetrated in 1915." The House adopted a similar resolution in September 1984.

The Republic of Turkey based its case on a completely different set of arguments: its credentials as a core member of NATO, host to the US airbase at Incirlik near Adana, and political ally of the United

States. For a decade from 1979, Turkey's chief spokesman and ideological commander in the fight with Armenians was the ambassador to Washington, Şükrü Elekdağ. Because of the threat of terrorism, he permanently had four secret service agents with him. On vacation, he would check into hotels under a false name. After retiring as a diplomat, Elekdağ became a member of parliament for the main Kemalist party, the CHP. Lean and energetic in his eighties, he continued to campaign aggressively against the Armenian lobby.

Elekdağ made sure that the American voter was besieged by two lobbies, not just one. In April 1982, the newly-founded Assembly of Turkish American Associations sponsored a full-page advertisement, capped by a picture of a blond American little boy and the caption "Terrorism: Will it turn his American Dream into a nightmare?"

The ad begins by reporting the cancellation of a performance of a Turkish folk dance troupe at Disneyland, because of concerns about Armenian terrorism, and speculated that an American child visiting Disneyland with his Mom and Dad might become the victim of "an old, old story of a mindless blind Armenian vendetta against Turks." It gives a brief potted history of Turkish suffering at the hands of Armenians and concludes, "Our ancestral land is an important bastion of the NATO defense of Western democracy. We recognize that Armenian terrorists have confirmed ties with international communist and terrorist organizations."[45]

In this period, Armenian academic scholarship took a step forward with the foundation of several college departments and the work of scholars such as Richard Hovannisian, Ronald Suny, and Louise Nalbandian. In their work on Ottoman Armenians, Armenian historians used the archives of the Western Great Powers, missionaries' reports, and Armenian-language sources. The scholars of Turkey and the Ottoman Empire were part of Middle Eastern studies, and many of them were invested personally and professionally in Turkey. Some were Ottomanists, such as Bernard Lewis and Stanford Shaw. Others, like the influential political scientist Dankwart Rustow, described Turkey as a successful example of modernization in the Middle East. The two academic worlds rarely intersected.

In 1982, Ambassador Elekdağ founded the Institute of Turkish Studies, with a $3 million grant from Ankara. Its director was Heath

Lowry of Princeton University.[46] In 1985, it published a letter to Congress by 69 US academics, urging it not to pass a Genocide resolution. They wrote, "The weight of evidence so far uncovered points in the direction of serious inter-communal warfare (perpetrated by Muslim and Christian irregular forces), complicated by disease, famine, suffering and massacres in Anatolia and adjoining areas during the First World War." This added further fuel to the flames. Elekdağ says, "Let me tell you this, each of the 69 signatories of the declaration were threatened. They were instigating fear, the telephone used to call. . . . After what happened to Professor Shaw [whose house was the object of an arson attack] everyone started to be afraid. And they told them if they ever signed such a document you would know what would happen to you. So there was this academic terrorizing in the United States, which is a very bad thing."[47]

## Ronald Reagan's Switch

In 1981, Ronald Reagan took office in Washington. Within a few months, Reagan the Californian politician had changed into Reagan the Cold Warrior president. On three issues that Reagan cared about passionately—Israel, the Soviet Union, and the fight against "international terrorism"—Turkey fell on the right side of the debate and the Armenians on the wrong side. Secretary of State Alexander Haig and Secretary of Defense Caspar Weinberger shared the same worldview.

Ambassador Elekdağ says:

Naturally these were the Cold War years, and the Reagan administration, when looking at allies, when evaluating allies, was looking from a strategic perspective all the time and naturally Turkey at the time was seen as a dam stopping the communist expansion and Turkey, with its disciplined army, was stopping the Red Army in this area. That was the Cold War years, that was the outlook.

When I was in Ankara as undersecretary, General Haig was Supreme Allied Commander in Europe and used to come very often to Ankara naturally to meet, and normally he had to deal with the Turkish foreign minister but for one reason or another the Turkish foreign minister at the time had given this task to me so I was, when he used to come to Ankara, his interlocutor. . . .

So we knew each other very well. And when I went to Washington he became [Ronald Reagan's] secretary of state, as you remember, and he told me "Şükrü, the doors are open to you all the time." That created enormous support and facility to me to carry out my work. Because, just imagine, there are 190 ambassadors in DC and they all wanted to see either the secretary of state or one of the undersecretaries or the assistant secretaries.[48]

The two governments speculated that the Soviet Union was funding ASALA. A Turkish professor, Aydin Yalçin, told the US Senate in 1981 that his country faced a threat by "Soviet-supported terrorists" that was replicating Stalin's territorial claims of 1945. "This time, the threat is not direct but indirect. The demand is not direct but by proxy."[49] The following year, Fred Ikle, US undersecretary of defense, testified to the Senate, "It does not matter very much whether the Armenian Secret Army is directly commanded by Moscow. . . . It has intimidated governments allied with Turkey and law-abiding Armenian communities as well. It if it were to be successful in its aims, it would lead directly to the expansion of the Soviet Union."[50]

Until the 1970s, the issue of calling the deportations and massacres of Armenians in 1915–1916 a "genocide" had not been a big issue of controversy. Many parliaments and institutions around the world had done so, beginning with Uruguay in 1965, and only incurred pro forma resistance from the Turkish government in doing so. The US government had also several times listed the Armenian case as an instance of genocide, without elaborating as to whether this had any policy relevance for the present day.

In the late 1970s, the government in Ankara elevated resistance to the concept of an "Armenian Genocide" to being a top-level foreign policy priority. In 1982, the US government altered its policy—although not without getting confused as to what its policy actually was.

Ronald Reagan exemplified both the switch and the confusion. As governor of California, the state with the biggest Armenian community in the United States, Reagan had many Armenian friends and colleagues. In 1969, he had made an April 24 speech at the Genocide

Memorial at Montebello in which he bowed in memory of the Armenian dead. On April 22, 1981, in a proclamation on the Holocaust, Reagan's speechwriter Kenneth Khachigian encouraged him to include a mention of "the genocide of the Armenians before it, and the genocide of the Cambodians which followed it." Khatchigian cleared the phrase with the White House national security adviser and the president duly delivered it.[51]

Within a year, US policy had changed. The pivotal moment was a killing in Reagan's home state of California. On January 28, 1982, the consul of Turkey in Los Angeles, Kemal Arikan (Figure 7.3) was driving to work and stopped at an intersection. Two Armenians carrying handguns approached the car from each side and fired at Arikan. He died almost instantly. The men dropped their guns and fled. One of them was never caught. The other, a 19-year-old recent immigrant from Lebanon, Hampig "Harry" Sassounian, was arrested.[52]

Arikan was 54. He was on the point of leaving the foreign ministry. Poignantly, it emerged after his death that he had quietly been reaching out to Los Angeles Armenians. One of them, a lawyer named William

Figure 7.3  Kemal Arikan, Turkey's consul in Los Angeles, assassinated in 1982.
Source: Ministry of Foreign Affairs of Turkey

Mihrtad Paparian, wrote that the consul had arranged for him to meet a Turkish journalist, and they had talked on the telephone three times:

> I learned that [Kemal Arikan] was about to retire from the diplomatic service and return to Turkey to resume the practice of law. Our last conversation took place on Jan. 27. Our final words were that the doors of communication would remain open between the two of us. The following day Kemal Arikan was dead. What impressed me the most about Mr. Arikan was that, unlike his government, he had an apparent willingness to really listen and what seemed to be a sincere desire to understand.[53]

The assassination of Kemal Arikan on American soil stung the Reagan administration. The president himself called it a "vicious act." From this moment, every official in the administration associated the Armenian question and the genocide issue with terrorism. Visiting Ankara in May 1982, Secretary of State Alexander Haig was unstinting in his praise of Turkey, "the vital anchor of the southeastern flank of the alliance," and of its military leader, "General Evren, an old friend." Overlooking the mass human rights abuses being perpetrated at the time, Hague praised the general for "the return to law and order, the suppression of terrorist activities that Turkey was plagued by in the late 1970s and early 1980s." And he mentioned the Arikan assassination: "I, of course, used the opportunity to convey the deep sense of regret and sorrow that every American feels for the recent tragedies in our own country as a result of terrorist—vile terrorist—acts against Turkish officials."[54]

## Legislating Genocide

In August 1982, the official *Department of State Bulletin* published a special issue on terrorism, which included a piece by Andrew Corsun entitled "Armenian Terrorism: A Profile." A "Note" at the end said, "Because the historical record of the events in Asia Minor is ambiguous, the Department of State does not endorse allegations that the Turkish government committed a genocide against the Armenian people. Armenian terrorists use this allegation to justify in part their continuing attacks on Turkish diplomats and installations."[55]

Armenian organizations expressed outrage. The State Department later printed not one but two clarifications. The second one said, "The article . . . and its accompanying note and footnotes were not intended as statements of policy of the United States. Nor did they represent any change in policy." However, it did not explain what US policy was.[56]

Van Krikorian, a young lawyer from Massachusetts working for the Armenian Assembly of America, says of the original article, "That put the Armenian community into shock. Nobody ever thought that the US government would say that. Our congressional friends started complaining immediately but they also said 'OK, to correct that, why don't we just pass another resolution?' which they thought would be kind of easy. And that is where it restarted."[57] Krikorian later launched a Freedom of Information request to discover the history of the article. It took him 10 years to get a full disclosure of documents, which suggested that Corsun's original text had been heavily edited.

So began an epic battle between the Armenian activist community and the Turkish government, fought in the US Congress, over the validity of the word "genocide" to describe the Armenian massacres of 1915, which was still continuing 30 years later.

In February 1990, the Senate debated the issue for two days before failing to pass a resolution. Senior Republican Bob Dole spoke for the Armenians. He was strongly influenced by an Armenian friend, the surgeon and Genocide survivor Hampar Kelikian, who had restored him to health when he had suffered severe injury in World War II. He was opposed by Senator Robert Byrd, backed by the executive branch, which warned that a successful resolution "will unwittingly slap the face of a very important NATO ally."[58]

For Armenians there could be no turning back from the term. "Everybody here has family members that were killed," says Van Krikorian, who argues that the word "genocide" encapsulated the collective Armenian experience and could not be negotiable. "That particular word, I think, represents what it is. To compromise off of it would be starting down a slippery slope."

Krikorian says that they did discuss inserting different language into congressional resolutions instead of "genocide" but decided against it. "I suppose the fact that Turks are so allergic to it, is part of what makes it valuable," Krikorian adds with a laugh.

The Turkish government determined for its part that if the word "genocide" was used, it would eventually threaten the very existence of the Turkish state. Omer Lutem, one of the chief ideologists in the battle of the 1980s, says:

> Even at that time we had some indications that this is a kind of vehicle. Behind, there will be Armenian demands. Demands for what? Demands for land, demands for indemnities, demands for the return of properties. So just to realize these demands, they use this "genocide." In fact if Turkey accepts that an Armenian genocide took place, the other Armenian demands could be easily realized. When you accept to be guilty, naturally you should pay compensations, naturally you should give Armenian properties back. . . . But as Turks knew what is the Armenian way of thinking, they resisted it.[59]

This perception of danger was so intense that it drove the Turkish government into dire warnings—not just to recall its ambassador, but against the most sensitive area of US-Turkey relations: military cooperation. There were threats to close the Incirlik airbase and cancel defense contracts. In February 1985, Secretary of Defense Caspar Weinberger led the charge against a resolution, warning Congressmen, "Whatever the merits of such remembrance, we believe such resolutions are counter-productive in that they serve to encourage Armenian terrorists who have killed more than 50 Turkish citizens, mostly diplomats over the past years. Some murders have occurred in the United States."[60]

Another argument deployed by Turkey was its status as the only major Muslim-majority power that was an ally of Israel. Members of the pro-Israel group AIPAC helped lobby against Armenian genocide resolutions.

History and geopolitics intersected here. In the 1940s and 1950s, both Armenians and Jews had mentioned the tragedy of the other without controversy. Some Israeli scholars, such as Israel Charny and Elie Wiesel, continued to write sympathetically about the Armenians. However, 30 years later, Israel was invested in an alliance with Turkey. Many Jews insisted that the Holocaust should have a unique place in history and should not be compared with other mass atrocities. For example, Shimon Peres, then foreign minister of Israel, was quoted as saying, "We reject attempts to create a similarity between the Holocaust and the Armenian allegations. Nothing similar to the Holocaust occurred. It is a tragedy what the Armenians went through but not a genocide."[61]

This controversy dogged the planning of the US Holocaust Memorial Museum. After much deliberation on whether or not to include the Armenians (or others) in the public space of the museum, all that remained of them in the end was the famous quotation by Adolf Hitler, "Who, after all, speaks today of the annihilation of the Armenians?"

Professor Bernard Lewis of Princeton University was a favorite historian of the Reagan administration, a veteran scholar of the Middle East, and a key figure in the Turkish-Israeli scholarly compact. His 1961 book, *The Emergence of Modern Turkey*, was for years the standard English-language history of Turkey. The degree to which Lewis had, perhaps unwittingly, internalized some Turkish thinking is evident in the fact that he gave only a few lines to the Armenian deportations, which he summarized as "a struggle between two nations for the possession of a single homeland, that ended with the terrible holocaust of 1916, when a million and a half Armenians perished."[62]

Lewis would later become embroiled in a controversial court case in France in 1995 on the Armenian issue, being prosecuted for having denied the Armenian genocide. Whatever the merits of prosecuting a historian for expressing an opinion, his later comments suggested that this prominent Ottoman scholar had missed much of the historical scholarship on the Armenians. Writing about their fate in 1916, he made this strange utterance, "When the survivors of the Armenian deportation arrived at their destinations in Ottoman-ruled Iraq and Palestine they were welcomed and helped by the local Armenian communities. The German Jews deported to Poland by the Nazis received no such help, but joined their Polish coreligionists in a common fate." Evidently, Lewis was not aware of the massacres in and around Der Zor.[63]

The epic battle in the Senate in 1990 provoked a serious debate about the Armenians, their history, and the role of the United States in 1915. Thereafter, following that resolution's failure, the Genocide resolutions carried on, but became part of everyday legislative business. Heavyweight legislators, such as Senators George Mitchell, Edward Kennedy, and Joe Biden, supported the Armenian cause, but as soon as any of them was appointed to the executive, he immediately softened his stance.

By the 1990s, an air of cynicism had begun to descend on the entire exercise, even as it still took up enormous amounts of time in the legislature. For the US executive, the words "Armenian Genocide" came to be equated chiefly with an inside-Washington battle with Congress. One former State Department official recalls a lunch in 1992 in the office of Brent Scowcroft, the National Security Adviser, where those present calculated that the foreign policy issue that had consumed the most hours and energy within Congress that year was Armenian Genocide recognition.

The intense politics also drove the Turkish state into an even more extreme form of denialism. From 1993 until his dismissal in 2008, the director of the official Turkish Historical Society was Yusuf Halaçoğlu, an extreme nationalist who later became a member of parliament for the ultra-right Turkish party, the MHP. Under the influence of Halaçoğlu and others, versions of the Armenian Question were written that were far more starkly revisionist than even the memoirs of the Unionist leaders themselves. Halaçoğlu himself, in a 2001 essay, calls the deportations of 1915 "one of the most orderly population movement of the past century" and puts the death toll in massacres at just 9,000–10,000.[64]

"It acquired a life of its own," concedes Van Krikorian of the Genocide resolution drive. He argues, however, that the Genocide issue was "an outlet to the frustration" Armenians had, and that it mobilized the Armenian community around a peaceful cause that meant something to every member of it."

> We would probably have lost a lot more Armenians if we didn't do that. Because there are Armenians all over the United States. And if you call them up and say "Maybe you should do some Armenian cultural event" maybe they would say OK. If you say "Look we are pushing this Armenian Genocide resolution, we need you to go talk to a Congressman or Senator," they feel the burden of their family history and they all feel strongly about it.

In a generation that was already the great-grandchildren of Genocide survivors, Genocide recognition was a mark of collective identity. The anthropologist Anny Bakalian calls it an "equalizer":

The Genocide and its subsequent denial by Turkish governments is therefore a symbol of collective Armenian identity. It affected not only one segment of the population, but almost everyone. It serves as a common denominator, an equalizer of all differences between Armenians: national, religious, ideological, political, socioeconomic, generational, and so on. Armenian community brokers and intellectuals have used the Genocide as a tool to mobilize men and women of Armenian descent, to foster a sense of we-ness, and to maintain their ethnic allegiance. The Genocide has become an ideology. By selecting such a symbolic framework, Armenian-Americans have been provided with a sense of peoplehood, cultural rebirth, and historical continuity. So far, it has been fairly successful.[65]

# 8

## A Turkish Thaw

ON SEPTEMBER 24, 2005, an academic conference opened, one day late, at Bilgi University in Istanbul. The topic was "Ottoman Armenians during the Decline of the Empire." Despite its neutral title, it was a highly charged event. The conference participants were bussed in with a police escort, past a crowd of nationalist demonstrators throwing eggs and rotten tomatoes.

The conference was originally planned for May 2005, but was postponed after a concerted campaign to stop it. Justice Minister Cemil Çiçek told parliament that attempts to hold the meeting were "treason" and a "stab in the back of the Turkish nation."[1] However, Prime Minister Recep Tayip Erdoğan was more supportive, in part because the row threatened to overshadow negotiations on Turkey's EU membership. "If we have confidence in our beliefs, we should not fear freedom of thought," Erdoğan said.[2]

The controversial parts of Turkish history were one bone of contention in the protracted war between Erdoğan's more permissive AKP government and parts of the old Kemalist establishment. In February 2005, the country's most famous novelist, Orhan Pamuk, told a Swiss newspaper, "Thirty thousand Kurds and a million Armenians were murdered. Hardly anyone dares mention it, so I do. And that's why

I'm hated." Pamuk's comments caused an uproar, and he left the country, fearing for his life. Later in the year, he was prosecuted under the new controversial Article 301 of the Turkish Penal Code, "insulting Turkishness." The charges were eventually dropped, and Pamuk won the Nobel Prize for Literature in 2006.

In September, on the eve of the rescheduled opening of the Ottoman Armenian conference, its opponents struck again. Two more legal challenges in the Istanbul court threatened to entangle it in legal proceedings and prevent it from taking place. However, the petitions only named Bosphorus University, the planned venue of the conference, and Sabanci University, one of its cosponsors. Bilgi, a third Istanbul university supporting the event, was not mentioned and therefore was not tied up by the new legal delaying tactics. Taking advantage of this omission, the rectors of the three universities agreed to move the conference to Bilgi and to cram three days of discussions into two.

The impact of "the Armenian conference," as it was popularly called, was even bigger than its organizers had anticipated. "A dam broke," says the historian Halil Berktay, one member of the organizing committee. More than 200 academics took part. They realized that they constituted a group in Turkey able to have a new kind of conversation on historical issues.

Papers were given on the deportations of Armenians, the Adana massacres of 1909, and different versions of the famous Ottoman Bank raid—topics that had never had such a prominent public airing in Turkey before. Several Turkish scholars, such as Fikret Adanir of Ruhr University, declared that they now used the words "Armenian Genocide" in their academic writing.[3]

Some unexpected guests crossed the threshold of Bilgi University. A former minister of health, Cevdet Aykan, said he felt honor-bound to speak about the vanished Armenians of his home region of Tokat. Erdal Inönü, son of Turkey's second president, Ismet Inönü, and a former deputy prime minister, made his way through a crowd of angry demonstrators into the conference hall.[4] When the conference was over, a columnist in the newspaper *Milliyet* said, "Another taboo has been broken. The Armenian conference was held, and the world didn't come to an end."[5]

In another mainstream Turkish newspaper, *Hürriyet*, a well-known secularist journalist from the town of Urfa named Bekir Coşkun, then aged 70, wrote that the conference had prompted him for the first time to tell in public the story of his grandmother, his grandfather's second wife, who was an Armenian orphan:

> Never mind what may have been done to the Armenians, or why people are fighting about it now but I would like to know what power separated my grandmother when she was just a young girl from her nest, her home and hearth. I would like to know who was responsible for the pain she tried to hide from us, and for the life-long exile she had to lead. I don't know about the one million Armenians, just this one, the sad woman I loved so much.[6]

## The AKP Government

If a dam broke at the 2005 Bilgi conference, it was because waters had been building up for some time. At the turn of the millennium, Turkish society was changing. There was serious discussion of joining the European Union. The economy improved after what many described as the country's "lost decade" in the 1990s. Most important, a new generation was less invested in some of the rigid doctrines of the Turkish Republic that their parents and grandparents had grown up with.

In the general election of November 3, 2002, for the first time in years, a single party won a majority in parliament and formed a viable government without coalition partners. The party was the Justice and Development Party, known by its Turkish initials, AKP, an acronym which also played on the Turkish word *ak*, meaning "white" or "clean." Its leader, soon to be the new prime minister, was Recep Tayyip Erdoğan. Erdoğan was a very different type of Turkish leader: a combative fighter from a poor Istanbul neighborhood, an instinctive politician with a moderately Islamist and post-Kemalist ideology. He had a radical agenda to break the grip of the military and the "deep state" on Turkey and to empower millions of Turkish Muslims. His core constituents were the members of the rural and small-town population of

Anatolia and their kin in the poorer suburbs of Istanbul, who had been more or less taken for granted for most of the republican era.

In waging this fight, AKP resumed some of the pro-European reforms that former Prime Minister Turgut Ozal had initiated in the 1980s and opened up a space where entrenched interests could be challenged. The AKP did not actively endorse a new policy on the blank spots of Turkey's past, but it employed much more equivocal language. For example, in 2006, Prime Minister Erdoğan announced that the phrase "so-called Armenian genocide" (*sözde Ermeni soykırımı*) should not be used by government officials, who were instead instructed to use the more neutral phrase "the events of 1915" (*1915 olayları*).[7]

The change of tone was not dramatic, but what the AKP government chose *not* to do was very important. In 2013, Halil Berktay said, "What has happened is over the past few years the official production and reproduction of Turkish denialism has stopped. The factory is no longer operating. They are not dishing up this stuff on a daily basis. Few people have noticed it but the Turkish government has fallen silent on this question. It is an unnoticed silence, a reverberating silence—a loud silence."[8]

Intellectuals took advantage of the freedom that the official silence afforded them. For two decades there had been discreet centers of alternative thought in Turkey to the orthodox nationalist doctrine on its pre-1923 history. Two small Istanbul publishing houses, Belge and Aras, printed works of Armenian literature and history. The courageous owners of Belge, Ragip Zarakolu and his wife, Aysenur, had had their house firebombed by ultra-nationalists.

Now this space expanded. Several Turkish intellectuals who had lived abroad during the worst years of military rule returned in the 1990s and began to propagate alternative views. Despite political and personal differences, these thinkers had important elements in common. They generally came from a leftist background. They believed that Turkey's best hopes lay in the path of democratization and eventual European Union membership. And they all believed that Turkey could only democratize by confronting the dark issues in its past.

Cengiz Aktar spent much of the 1970s and 1980s in Western Europe, first as a student, then as an academic working on European politics and a United Nations official. Studying in France, he encountered the entirely different Western historical literature about the end of the Ottoman Empire and the fate of the Armenians. "As soon as we started to read two or three books we very quickly learned what it was all about really," he said.[9] When he returned to Turkey in the 1990s, Aktar says, "I realized very quickly that a redefinition of the social contract in this country for the twenty-first century can't happen without democracy for all, a democracy for all means also for non-Muslims, both with the past memories and today's citizenship rights."

Taner Akçam, who was born in Ardahan province in Turkey's far east, was the first Turkish historian to write a different narrative about the Ottoman Armenians. As a left-wing student, Akçam campaigned for Kurdish rights and opposed the Turkish military intervention in Cyprus in 1974. He was arrested and given a nine-year jail sentence in 1977, but he escaped to Germany, where he spent 16 years in exile and worked on a PhD thesis. In 1990, Akçam began to work on the Ottoman Armenians; he published his first book, *Turkish National Identity and the Armenian Question*, in 1992. He himself marks his own "turning point" as his attendance of an international conference in Yerevan in 1995, when he used the term "Armenian genocide."

A lonely and combative figure, Akçam became a lightning rod for Turkish nationalist anger in the 1990s. In 2000, he moved to the United States and in 2008 took a position at the Center for Holocaust and Genocide Studies at Clark University. In this period, Akçam was both a beneficiary and victim of the schizophrenia of the post-2002 Turkish thaw. He was able to return to Turkey, work in the archives, publish articles, and see his books published in Turkish. At the same time, he was vilified by Turkish ultra-rightists and received death threats.

Akçam's two main books, *A Shameful Act* of 2006 and *The Young Turks' Crime Against Humanity* of 2012, are important milestones in the historiography of the Armenian Genocide, not just for the new sources he cites but for the very fact that they were written by a Turkish scholar. Some critics have charged him with using his evidence selectively; no one has questioned the authenticity of the documents from the Ottoman archives he has unearthed, which give a more damning picture of how the Young Turk leadership planned the elimination of the Armenians.

Why was Akçam perceived by this segment of Turkish society as so dangerous? He argues that to raise the Armenian issue is to question fundamentals about Turkish identity:

As currently constructed, our existence as the Turkish nation, as well as the Turkish national identity, necessitate the non-existence of the Armenians, their conceptual annihilation, so to speak. The other's non-existence cannot be removed without bringing the parameters of our own existence into question. To put it another way, for the Armenian to again be able to "exist," for us to actually face our history and accept the reality of Armenian Genocide—means to wrestle with our very identity as Turks.[10]

Halil Berktay was a distinguished historian studying what he called "the historical memory of Turkish nationalism"—in other words, the ways in which modern Turkish political discourse mythologized the country's historical past. This research led him first to analyze how Greeks and Bulgarians were cast as "traitors" to their Ottoman masters. Later Berktay came, as he puts it, "into the inner sanctum, the inner temple, the holy of holies," to the Armenian question. Like several of his colleagues, he concluded that the 1915 Young Turk deportations of the Armenians constituted a genocide, although as a historian he says he is wary of the usefulness of the term "genocide" in academic history, saying that "a word, a cliché, a buzzword is substituted for real understanding, a descriptive analytical understanding of what actually happened."

Berktay says that he was offended by the persistent mainstream narrative about the Armenians in contemporary Turkey: "There was this deep viscous hypocrisy that seemed to be sticking on you like napalm." In October 2000, he decided to confront this taboo and gave a long interview to the left-wing daily newspaper *Radikal* in which he spelled out the current state of international scholarship on the Armenian deportations of 1915 and challenged several long-standing Turkish nationalist credos. *Radikal* had a large readership, and the interview touched a nerve. "All hell broke loose," says Berktay. There were calls to fire him from Sabanci University. He received a daily torrent of hate mail and threats, mostly from Turks living outside Turkey. But he also received support and congratulations from other readers.

Until the 1990s, the worlds of Armenian and Turkish scholarship were almost entirely separate. However, in 2000, two Armenian-American historians, Ronald Suny and Gerard Libaridian, decided to reach out. Together with a Turkish colleague based in the United States, Fatma Müge Göçek, they organized a small Armenian-Turkish history workshop at the University of Chicago. Most of their Armenian colleagues in the United States declined to attend, saying they saw no point in the exercise. Akçam and Berktay were among the Turkish scholars who accepted the invitation.

Halil Berktay recalls that in the introductory session in Chicago he uttered the phrase "Armenian Genocide" and realized that almost by accident this had broken the ice. The workshop was a meeting of professionals, more interested in sharing knowledge than scoring points. More scholars, including several of the initial Armenian skeptics, attended the next seminar. The project came to be called the Workshop for Armenian/Turkish Scholarship, or WATS. Six meetings were held over six years, and the initiative helped create the foundation for the Bilgi conference of 2005.

The organizers of the Workshop for Armenian/Turkish Scholarship decided to exclude several veteran Turkish historians who wanted an invitation. This was controversial, but Gerard Libaridian argued that they needed time to build something new and did not want to allow the traditionalists to set the terms of the debate:

> At first sight this [call for inclusion] may sound like a legitimate expectation. Yet there are a number of issues to be considered. First, it is worth repeating that this is not a workshop consumed by the use or non-use of the term "genocide." The whole idea is to move away from such argumentativeness to make possible research and discussion of the history of the period. Second, including one extreme position would also mean to include the other; on the Armenian side this would mean including those who cannot fathom any discussion of the genocide without a demand for territorial reparations. Under the circumstances, the Workshop meetings would turn into shouting matches, simply put.[11]

One of the achievements of WATS was that the former labels of "Armenian historian" or "Turkish historian" could no longer stick. There was now a mixed group of like-minded scholars from many different backgrounds working on the subject (although, despite efforts to find them, no historian from the Republic of Armenia could be found to attend the workshop).

Another American historian with a different background weighed into the debate in 2006. Donald Quataert was a distinguished Ottomanist. He had been one of the 69 signatories of the joint letter sponsored by the Institute of Turkish Studies in 1985. In a review essay of Donald Bloxham's history of the Armenian Genocide, he was critical of both himself and his peers for failing to confront this huge issue. Now, he observed, "After the long lapse of serious Ottomanist scholarship on the Armenian question, it now appears that the Ottomanist wall of silence is crumbling." Quataert found fault with Bloxham (and the British writer Robert Fisk) for misunderstanding aspects of Ottoman history, but he implied that Ottomanist scholars had only themselves to blame: "Those who have the linguistic and paleographic tools to unlock the truth must not leave the matter for others to debate and resolve. How can we expect Bloxham and Fisk to write accurately about the role of Ottomans (not Turks) in the deaths of so many Armenians when Ottomanists provide no guidance, no leadership, and no scholarship?"[12]

WATS completed its work and bridged some of these gaps in 2012 when its contributors published a book of essays in 2012, entitled *A Question of Genocide*, that established a new scholarly consensus on the Armenian Genocide.

## Hrant Dink

One community understood the complexities of Armenian-Turkish relations more deeply than anyone else: the surviving Armenians of Turkey. However, after the founding of the Turkish Republic in 1923, they lost a public voice. By the turn of the twenty-first century, they numbered around 80,000, almost all of them in Istanbul, centered on the Armenian Patriarchate. Their rights were nominally guaranteed by the Treaty of Lausanne, but they practiced self-censorship and endured routine discrimination. All Istanbul's minorities—Armenians, Greeks, and Jews—were especially bitter about the wartime Wealth and Revenue Tax, which bankrupted many of them for the second time in their lifetimes.

Despite this discrimination, Istanbul Armenians still endeavored to prove that they were loyal Turkish citizens. A group of Armenians chose to mark the fiftieth anniversary of the Genocide on April 24, 1965, by laying flowers at Atatürk's statue in Taksim Square. The Patriarch routinely disparaged radical Diaspora politics in Western countries and was among the first voices condemning Armenian terrorist acts. In 1982, an Armenian named Artin Penik immolated himself in front of the same statue in a tragic and strange protest at the ASALA terrorist attack on Istanbul airport.

Hrant Dink was different (Figure 8.1). Until his tragic assassination in 2007—and even after it—he did more than any single individual to advance understanding between Armenians and Turks. "He changed everything,"

Figure 8.1  Turkish Armenian editor Hrant Dink in Istanbul in 2007.
Source: Hrant Dink Foundation.

says his friend and biographer Tuba Çandar. Somehow, Dink managed to articulate, in his life and in his writings, a different approach: that of being both an Armenian proud of his ancestry and culture and a Turkish citizen, committed to the reform and democratization of the Turkish state. These went hand in hand. He did this without being an intellectual or knowing any other languages, other than Armenian and Turkish.

Almost everyone recalls Dink with affection and still refers to him by his first name, Hrant. He was a survivor, with an extraordinary biography. He was born in a poor Armenian family in the eastern city of Malatya in 1954. His parents were so poor that he and his two brothers ended up in an Istanbul Protestant orphanage. Later he worked for the Armenian Patriarch, studied zoology at Istanbul University, and with his wife Rakel ran a popular children's camp, which he described as a "lost Atlantis." He got involved in radical left-wing politics. He owned a bookshop with his brothers and made money. Then, in 1996, he found his mission when he founded and edited a new Turkish-Armenian newspaper named *Agos*.

Hrant Dink lacked the fear and circumspection of most of his Turkish-Armenian compatriots. Two days before his death, he said in an interview, "You have hardly any problems if you hold your tongue. As for me, I found it hard even in my teens to join the chorus singing how proud we were of being Turks. Certainly, this country has a great deal to be proud of, but I am not a Turk, after all."[13]

Despite a modest demeanor, he had a natural manner and gift for words. "Hrant was a born communicator," Cengiz Aktar says. "He was an Anatolian man, he was talking like Anatolians, he was not talking like an Istanbul intellectual. He was capable of convincing the worst denialist in 20 minutes—and this is probably why he was assassinated."[14]

Tuba Çandar first met him when she and her husband, the well-known journalist Cengiz Çandar, gave him a lift back from a funeral. Her first impression was of a rather old-fashioned Anatolian man. All she could see was Hrant Dink's broad neck as he sat in the front of the car talking to her husband. Then:

He said, "Are you hungry?" And I said, "Yes." And he said "Stop, stop the car" to Cengiz. . . . He just jumped from the car and he took me by my hand and he began to run, and I couldn't understand what was going on. There were fishermen, and he just ran behind this fisherman's place, and there we found a lonely fisherman making fish on a very primitive fire, and Hrant asked me if I wanted this or this, as if we were in a restaurant, and the fisherman made a fish sandwich. . . . And Hrant was there feeding me with fish. And I say, what kind of a man is this? The first day I met him he was feeding me. Can you imagine?[15]

Under Hrant Dink's editorship, *Agos* became an influential newspaper, despite a circulation of only 6,000. It ran articles in both Armenian and Turkish on a variety of themes that had hitherto been passed over in silence. Dink's stand and the platform provided by *Agos* were an example to Turkey's remaining Armenians. They now had a place where, for the first time, they could share family stories, memoirs, and problems. "We had built a ghetto," says Istanbul Armenian businessman Dikran Altun, "and the walls of that ghetto were very thick walls. For us, silence was a system to defend ourselves, without saying anything. Because of Hrant we started to pull down the walls and we came out of the ghetto. And we realized that silence is not good to defend ourselves. We had to speak. And because of Hrant we started to explain ourselves to the majority."[16]

Dink was preoccupied with the issue of how to talk about the Armenian question to the Turkish public. Tuba Çandar recalls:

My husband [Cengiz Çandar] asked once, "Hrant, What do you think? Do you think it was really genocide what happened in 1915?" And Hrant said, "Cengiz, I'm an Armenian, for every Armenian, we don't talk about this, we don't tell these things to our kids at home, but for every Armenian it's the knowledge that, you know, it was genocide." So we didn't use the word that much when Hrant was alive, but we knew what happened, we found out about those events, and I sometimes say, for every Armenian's knowledge inside, for every Turk the knowledge is also inside. Because when you learn about it, it's not a big astonishment, or big shock, and that's very very important. It's an inside information.[17]

Understanding both worlds, Dink took on Turkish denialism about the Armenian Genocide and framed it within a larger debate about Turkey's future. He argued that the overall goal should be democracy in Turkey. With that, everything else would follow:

> The problem Turkey faces today is neither a problem of "denial" or "acknowledgement." Turkey's main problem is "comprehension." And for the process of comprehension, Turkey seriously needs an alternative study of history and for this, a democratic environment. It is unfair, either through political pressure or laws, to impose denial or acknowledgement upon the individuals of a society who are in the middle of a process of comprehension. Such a method would be the greatest blow inflicted on the process of comprehension. After all, denial or acknowledgement without comprehension benefits no one. . . . In the process we are going through, it is impossible to say that, those who expect Turkey to accept historical reality or impose denial on it are reading the current reality of Turkish society well. After all, it is not that the society knows, or denies the truth; the society is defending the truth it knows.[18]

In this spirit, Dink spoke out for Kurdish rights and found common cause with the new AKP government in opposing the secularist ban on headscarves. "He was against all the taboos of Turkey, not only the Armenian issue," says Çandar.

But Dink's treading on taboos, especially in Armenian-Turkish relations, was too much for some elements of Turkish society to accept. In February 2004, an article Dink wrote in *Agos* caused an explosion. In it he aired a report that Sabiha Gökçen, the adopted daughter of Kemal Atatürk and Turkey's famous aviator, had in fact been born an Armenian. He wrote that an Armenian in Antep believed Gökçen to be her aunt, that her real name was Hatun Sebilciyan and she had been left an orphan when her father was killed in the deportations of 1915.[19]

Sabiha Gökçen is a legendary person in Turkey. Her story is that of a poor orphan, taken in by the childless Atatürk, who then trained to be the world's first woman combat pilot. The *New York Times* called her the "Flying Amazon of Turkey." Every Turkish schoolchild knows

Gökçen's story of emancipation, modernization, and Turkish patriotism under the tutelage of the father of the new Republic.

Dink's article caused uproar, thereby exposing some deep truths
about mainstream narratives in Turkish society. Why should it matter
that a famous person was not an ethnic Turk? The fact that it did matter revealed that ugly ethnic prejudices were still widely held. Atatürk's
other adopted daughter, Ulkü Adatepe, organized a press conference to
denounce the story and more or less accuse Dink of blasphemy: "The
defamation of such a respectable person who carries Atatürk's name
with honor makes me upset . . . the real purpose behind the news like
this is to defame Atatürk."[20]

Overnight, Hrant Dink became an enemy of the old establishment.
He faced a prosecution charge—the first of three—under the notorious Article 301 of the Turkish Penal Code for "insulting Turkishness."
Conspiracy theorists leapt into action. A columnist in *Cumhuriyet*
newspaper wrote that Dink was trying to "grease the wheels for imperialism" in what was a "scenario written about destroying Turkey."[21]

Finally came a verdict from the guardian of the Turkish state, the
military. The office of the chief of the general staff issued a statement
saying, "Sabiha Gökçen is at the same time a precious and reasoned
[*akilci*] symbol that shows the position Atatürk wanted the Turkish
woman to occupy in the Turkish society. Whatever the purpose is,
throwing such a symbol into a debate is an approach that does not
contribute to our national unity and social peace."[22]

However, this was not the Turkey of old. Many rallied to Hrant
Dink's defense, such as columnist Şahin Alpay, who urged Turks
to take the opportunity to grasp that Turkishness was a civic, not
an ethnic category. The AKP government did not support Dink
but did not endorse his accusers either, as their predecessors might
have done.[23]

Not one for shirking hard questions, Hrant Dink also challenged
long-standing Armenian shibboleths, both in Turkey and abroad. In
Istanbul, he argued with the Armenian Patriarchate about their role
in the community and said that the Armenians also needed secular
schools. During his life—but not after his death—Dink made himself unpopular in Armenian Diaspora political circles with his views,
and he received a chilly reception on a visit to Lebanon in 2005.

In a passage that offended both Armenians and Turks, Dink charged that too many Armenians had formed an identity not as themselves but in opposition to Turks, with predictably unhealthy results. "This 'Turk' lying at the core of the Armenian identity today became a source of pain, a trauma that—poisons the Armenian blood." This tendency prevented the development of a positive Armenian identity. He also criticized Diaspora Armenians for spending too much time worrying about their historical identity, rather than getting behind the project of supporting the new independent Republic of Armenia: "There exists a much more vital phenomenon that will fill the void left behind from the 'Turk' and this is the existence of the independent State of Armenia."[24]

Dink wrote of the Armenian Genocide that "the crime happened here [in Turkey], the recognition and the solution of it will happen here." This led him to oppose the practice of genocide resolutions in foreign parliaments because, he said, he saw no need for foreign "referees" to validate the experience of his Armenian ancestors:

It offends me to see my past history or present problems being made into a capital of some sorts in Europe and America. I sense some form of abuse and desecration beneath all this kissing. I no longer accept the vile refereeing of imperialism which tries to strangle my future in my past.

Those referees are the exact same dictators who in times past had gladiators fight each other in arenas, watched on as they clashed and gave the thumbs down to the winner to finish off the loser. Therefore I don't accept in this age the refereeing neither of a parliament, nor a state.

The true referee is the people and their conscience. And in my conscience the conscience of the power of no state can compete with the conscience of the people. All I want is to talk about our common past with my beloved friends in Turkey in the most comprehensive manner and without raising the slightest animosity.[25]

In 2006, this stance led Dink to oppose—on grounds of free speech— a resolution in the French parliament to make Armenian Genocide denial a criminal offense, even saying that he was ready to go to Paris to oppose the decision. A prominent Armenian-American commentator decried his position, saying "Mr. Dink's misguided words are providing support for genocide denialists in Turkey."[26]

## Death of an Oracle

Hrant Dink had received death threats ever since his article on Sabiha Gökçen was published. On January 19, 2007, at around 3 P.M., he received a phone call and hurried out of the offices of *Agos* onto the street. There, a Turkish teenager wearing a white beret shot him in the head and he died instantly. The boy was heard saying, "I shot the Armenian." Hrant Dink's body lay on the pavement for several hours, covered in a sheet, as Turkish television ran live coverage of the murder and its aftermath. Prime Minister Recep Tayip Erdoğan declared, "A bullet was fired at freedom of thought and democratic life in Turkey."[27]

The assassin was quickly identified as a 17-year-old man named Ogün Samast. He came from the Black City sea of Trabzon, a place with a strong Turkish nationalist tradition. Samast was detained and, after a long trial, given a 22-year prison sentence. Another young ultra-nationalist named Yasin Hayal, also from Trabzon, was given a life sentence for having organized the killing.

Despite the convictions, Hrant Dink's friends and human rights groups were frustrated that the court had ruled there was no wider conspiracy to murder the editor. Many leads that might have led to association with rogue security officials from Turkey's "deep state" were ignored. A video released on the Internet deepened the anger: it showed Samast posing with Turkish policemen in a police station in the town of Samsun, shortly after his detention, in front of a Turkish flag and an inscription by Atatürk. For some Turks, Hrant Dink's murderer was a hero, not a villain.

On January 23, 2007, Hrant Dink was buried. The funeral turned into a momentous event in the city of Istanbul, as his supporters and friends rallied to honor him (Figure 8.2). Tens of thousands of people joined a five-mile procession between the offices of *Agos* and the Armenian patriarchal church in Kumkapi on the other side of the Golden Horn. Armenian music played from loudspeakers. Many

Figure 8.2 The funeral of Hrant Dink. Mourners carrying placards saying "We are all Hrant Dink" at Dink's funeral, January 23, 2007.

Source: Murad Sezer/AP Photo.

carried placards saying "We are all Armenians" and "We are all Hrant Dink," in Turkish on one side and Armenian on the other.

Despite the tragic occasion, Hrant Dink's funeral was a catalyst for more change. The writer's influence grew with his death. Diasporan Armenians who had criticized Dink were now eager to embrace him. Two writers noted the irony that "many Armenians who, while disagreeing with his overtures during his lifetime, didn't hesitate to 'use' him as a new symbol, layered on old ones, of genocide by putting his death in the same category as the victims of the Genocide of 1915."[28]

Others spoke out more boldly on the issues for which Dink had broken ground: the Armenian taboo and democratization in Turkey. When Dink was still alive, Cengiz Aktar had discussed with him the idea of "a grassroots initiative," a public apology to which ordinary Turks could put their name. When Dink was killed, the idea became a "must." He worked on the idea with three colleagues, the academic Ahmet Insel, the politician and scholar Baskin Oran, and the journalist Ali Bayramoğlu.

The four men drafted a text and opened a secure website with the name "I Apologize," at http://www.ozurdiliyoruz.com/in 14 languages. They chose the Armenian term "Great Catastrophe," or *Medz Yeghern*, to define what had happened to the Armenians in 1915. The text read, "My conscience does not accept the insensitivity showed to and the denial of the Great Catastrophe that the Ottoman Armenians were subjected to in 1915. I reject this injustice and for my share, I empathize with the feelings and pain of my Armenian brothers and sisters. I apologize to them."

When the website opened in December 2008, 275 intellectuals signed the online petition. In early 2014, the number of signatures stood at more than 32,000.

The Turkish prime minister publicly disagreed, saying the petition was "irrational" and that there was no need to apologize. Sixty retired diplomats launched a counter-petition, calling the apology campaign a "betrayal" and warning that an official apology might lead to Armenian demands for reparations against Turkey. They called their website, http://www.ozurdilemiyorum.net/, "I do not apologize."[29]

Aktar says that he believes that what happened to the Armenians constituted a genocide but that they chose the Armenian formulation "Great Catastrophe" so as to be more inclusive and to make it easier for Turkish citizens to understand, empathize, and sign. He also argues that the term "Great Catastrophe" covers all the people of eastern Anatolia in this period and those who suffered indirectly because of the departure of the Armenians:

> When the genocide happened, the social, human, political, economic and cultural bonds of the entire Anatolia collapsed. And therefore this was a general and a "Great" catastrophe and this is understood when you talk this way to the Anatolian peasants because they know from their parents that it was really bad and everything collapsed when the Armenians were not there anymore. . . . The "Great Catastrophe" is very very powerful because it means a general catastrophe. Of course, those who suffered the most were the Armenians but those who stayed behind suffered by all means—even those who stayed behind.

Among those who signed the apology petition were the co-chair of the German Green Party, Cem Ozdemir and journalist Hasan Cemal, the grandson of the Unionist leader Cemal Pasha. The apology campaign proved that a large element of Turkish society was able to confront the taboo of the Armenian issue. However, they risked being characterized as an urban left-wing intellectual class, without broader representation in Turkish society. Armenian-Turkish reconciliation on a larger scale would be much harder to achieve without an open border and a rapprochement between the governments of Turkey and Armenia.

# 9

## Independent Armenia

IN FEBRUARY 1988, SOVIET Armenia erupted into protest. Hundreds of thousands of people poured onto the streets of Yerevan. A mass manifestation of people power in a republic that had the reputation of being quiet and loyal to Moscow came as a shock to everyone—including Armenians themselves.

The cause was the autonomous highland territory of Nagorny Karabakh, which had been part of Soviet Azerbaijan since 1921, but which had always had a majority Armenian population. After a carefully planned secret campaign, the Armenians of the Soviet of the Nagorny Karabakh Autonomous Republic pushed through a resolution in February 1988, demanding that their region leave Azerbaijan and be united with Soviet Armenia.

The resolution caused a chain reaction of events unprecedented in the USSR. In Karabakh itself, there were strikes and rallies. In Yerevan, up to one million people took part in the protest rallies. In Azerbaijan, there were counter-demonstrations and an angry backlash. In the Azerbaijani city of Sumgait, a rampaging crowd of young men killed 26 Armenians and wounded many others, and the Soviet armed forces were called in to restore order. The Soviet leadership, headed by

Mikhail Gorbachev, struggled to contain the situation and was gradually overwhelmed by it.

The Sumgait killings set in train a mass exchange of populations between Soviet Armenia and Azerbaijan, which ended with the displacement of more than half a million people. Around 350,000 Armenians, including the large old Armenian community of Baku, left Azerbaijan. About 200,000 Azerbaijanis fled from Armenia, where they had had a centuries-old presence. The Azerbaijani exodus turned Armenia into one of the most homogeneous states of Europe, with a population that was more than 98 percent Armenian.

As the power of the Communist Party disintegrated, a group of 11 opposition activists and intellectuals, known as the Karabakh Committee, claimed moral authority. Levon Ter-Petrosian, a Syrian-born scholar of Middle Eastern languages, emerged as its leader.

Armenia's tumultuous year ended with a huge tragedy. On December 7, 1988, a powerful earthquake struck northern Armenia. The small town of Spitak was almost completely leveled and there was extensive destruction to Armenia's second city of Leninakan. An estimated 25,000 people died—almost one percent of the population of Armenia. The tragedy of the earthquake had one good side-effect in that it reconnected Armenia with its Diaspora. Diaspora organizations raised up to $1 billion in emergency relief. American medical personnel returned to Leninakan, a town that the US Near East Relief organization had worked in as Alexandropol and that would soon be renamed Gyumri.

After visiting the Armenian earthquake zone, Gorbachev ordered the arrest of the Karabakh Committee, but this only accelerated the demise of his own authority in Armenia. The 11 men were released five months later. In August 1990, Ter-Petrosian became the speaker of Armenia's Supreme Soviet and de facto leader of the republic. A declaration of sovereignty that month proclaimed "the process of establishing independent statehood." Armenia shed the word "Soviet" from its name and took on the attributes of a state, calmly re-adopting the red-blue-and-orange tricolor flag of the First Republic, which had caused so much anguish in the 1930s.

## Misunderstandings

From 1988, eastern and western Armenians came together again. But the reunion was accompanied by multiple misunderstandings. Cultural and linguistic differences combined with different political agendas.

The politics and identity of the new Republic of Armenia were shaped irrevocably—and still are—by the conflict with Azerbaijan over Nagorny Karabakh. A political dispute gradually escalated into a full-scale war. By the time a ceasefire halted fighting and confirmed a de facto Armenian victory on the ground in May 1994, 20,000 people were dead and more than a million had been displaced, three-quarters of them Azerbaijanis. The Armenians won possession of not just Karabakh itself but, wholly or partly, seven regions around it. As of this writing, the Karabakh conflict is still unresolved and is the main issue holding back the future development of the South Caucasus.

Turkey, which had been hidden behind a Cold War frontier for two generations, excited fewer passions. In 1988 or 1989, eastern Armenians used the word "genocide" more in reference to the behavior of "Turks"—Azerbaijanis—than to the Ottomans of 1915. That made the killings of Armenians in 1915 more of a symbolic touchstone than an issue for the present day. Sociologist Nora Dudwick observed of Armenia in 1988:

> For Armenians living in Yerevan . . . the "root paradigm" with the most explanatory power is one of suffering, oppression and persecution, the most potent and inclusive symbol of which is the 1915 Genocide. Hence the "de-Armenization" of Nakhijevan (an autonomous republic under the jurisdiction of the Republic of Azerbaijan) is referred to as "white genocide," the severe air pollution of Yerevan is "ecological genocide," and the assimilationist policies of Azerbaijan are considered "cultural genocide." The massacre at Sumgait became simply "genocide." It seemed that every social and political problem took on additional significance as containing a threat to the Armenians' continued existence as a people.[1]

In this environment, the "Sumgait Genocide" became the new rallying point for Armenians. Symbolically, three young Armenians killed in fighting with Azerbaijanis in the village of Eraskh in 1990 were buried as martyrs next to the Genocide Memorial in Yerevan. (They were later reburied in a war cemetery.)

Yerevan-based scholar and diplomat David Hovhannisian sums up the difference in outlook between the Diaspora and the people of the republic of Armenia as follows:

> The mythical idea of "paradise lost" is built in to the self-consciousness, the self-identification of the Armenians of the diaspora. From that the ideological idea of *Hai Dat* [the Armenian cause] begins.
>
> Here it is a bit different. Here we have an accumulated identity. We were first citizens of Armenia in Soviet times. . . . We did not have a problem of preserving national identity. In Western Armenian there is the word *ergir* or country. For many Armenians who escaped Western Armenia the mythological homeland is *ergir*. But this Armenia is a surrogate homeland. The real homeland is there.
>
> For most Armenians who live in Armenia the problem of recognition of the Genocide is a problem of the guarantee of security against genocide, because if Turkey recognizes that genocide was committed against the Armenian people it means "Never Again," it won't happen again. For citizens of Armenia it is a security guarantee. For Armenians who are citizens of other states, who lost their homeland, recognition of genocide is the restoration of divine justice.[2]

In October 1988, the three main Armenian diaspora parties, the ARF, Hunchakian, and the Ramgavar Party, issued a rare joint statement, which urged the Soviet Armenian opposition not to harm "the good standing of our nation in its relations with the higher Soviet bodies, and other Soviet republics."[3] After positioning itself for more than 50 years as a staunchly anti-Soviet party, the ARF had changed tack a decade before and had supported Moscow's rule over Armenia. In January 1989, ARF leader Hrair Marukhian urged caution on moves toward independence, on the grounds of a Turkish threat. "The ARF considers Armenia's independence its main purpose. But we think that it is not the time to present demands for immediate independence, when our nation needs the help of the Russian nation. In order to understand this it is necessary to go to the bank of the Akhurian to see the Turkish soldiers standing on the opposite bank and the ruins of Ani."[4]

The Armenian National Movement reacted to these declarations with disdain. In March 1991, Ter-Petrosian would refer to "Armenian orange-eaters in Paris and New York" who valued an absolutist position vis-à-vis Turkey more than feeding ordinary Armenian children. It was a kind of replay of the controversy of 1918 when one of the leaders of the First Republic accepted wheat from Ottoman Unionist commander Halil Pasha—only with the Dashnaktsutiun now positioned on the other side of the debate.[5]

The acrimony between the new Armenian leadership and the Diaspora's main political party intensified until Armenia held its first presidential election in October 1991. The locals won a resounding victory, when Ter-Petrosian was elected president with 83 percent of the vote, while Dashnaktsutiun's candidate, the actor Sos Sarkisian, received just 4 percent of the vote. The quarrel would reach a peak in December 1994, when Ter-Petrosian banned the ARF completely, alleging that they were plotting to overthrow him.

## Turkey Seeks a Policy

Turkey was one of many neighbors of the Soviet Union not fully prepared for its demise in 1991. By the end of that year, five new independent Turkic states had formed, frontiers were open, and vast business opportunities opened up. But Turkey's political class was far from ready for the challenge. The country spent much of the 1990s in domestic political turmoil; between October 1989, when Turgut Ozal left the post, and March 2003, when another heavyweight, Recep Tayip Erdoğan, took charge, Turkey had nine prime ministers, many of them heading weak coalition governments. The foreign ministry had a traditional Western-looking bias and few specialists on the former Soviet Union.

For Ankara, the emerging eastern Armenian state was an especially strange creature. For 70 years, almost all contacts between Ankara and Yerevan had been handled via Moscow. The border was partially open for trains to pass between Kars and Gyumri, but only once or twice a week for foreign travelers.

Those Turkish officials dealing with the Soviet Union were granted latitude to act—and Turkey at this moment had an open-minded ambassador in Moscow, Volkan Vural. Vural saw the fact that he was ambassador to all 15 Soviet republics, including Armenia, as an opportunity. In March 1990, the Armenian Patriarch of Constantinople, Shnork Kalustian, died while on a visit to Armenia. Ambassador Vural arranged for the return of his body to Turkey via Moscow. In Moscow a service was held for the departed religious leader and the ambassador decided to pay his respects.

> They were surprised. They didn't expect that the Turkish ambassador would be present. They were filming me throughout the process, the religious ceremony. . . . And, after the funeral, according to their tradition, they hosted a lunch, and they asked me whether I will attend. And I said, "Yes, of course." We went together with some clergy, some people from Armenia and so forth, we had a discussion there, a very friendly conversation. And I said, "Of course the time has come to develop our relations." They said they all agreed that something has to be done. They were very enthusiastic about that. And I said I will visit Armenia on my own initiative, as I can because I was accredited to all the republics. So, that's why I decided to visit Armenia.[6]

Formulating its Turkey policy, the new Armenian leadership decided not to press for genocide recognition.

Ter-Petrosian himself had impeccable credentials on this matter. One of his grandfathers had fought in the famous defense of Musa Dagh in 1915. His father was politically active in Syria in the 1940s. He himself was arrested in 1966 as a student in a protest on the anniversary of the events of April 24, 1965.[7] However, Ter-Petrosian argued that it was in Armenia's interests to strive to normalize relations with Turkey without any pre-conditions. There were long debates in the new Armenian parliament over the text of a Declaration of Independence. Eventually, after many drafts were debated and discarded, a text was adopted on August 23, 1990. References to the 1921 Treaty of Kars—still hated for its confirmation of territorial losses—were not included. But, contrary to Ter-Petrosian's advice, Article 11 stated, "Armenia stands in support of the task of achieving international recognition of the 1915 Genocide in Ottoman Turkey and Western Armenia."[8]

In April 1991, Ambassador Vural made his long-planned visit to Armenia at the end of a long cold winter. He visited Echmiadzin and the Turkish border and waved at the Turkish border guards on the other side. Invited to an official dinner, the ambassador was intrigued to discover that several of his hosts spoke his language: "There were five or six ministers at the official guest house. It was cold. There was no heating. And I asked them whether we should talk in English or in Turkish or in the Armenian language, which I don't know and can't speak. They told me, 'You can speak in Turkish. We all understand Turkish.' I said, 'How come?' And one of them said, 'I am from Bursa.' The other said, 'I am from Van.'"

Vural and Ter-Petrosian discussed a resumption of bilateral trade. The Armenian leader said that, despite the article in the Declaration of Independence, he did not intend to seek genocide recognition. Soon afterward, the historian Gerard Libaridian moved from Cambridge, Massachusetts, to join Ter-Petrosian as a foreign policy adviser and negotiator with Turkey. Libaridian sums up the new Armenian state's thinking as follows:

Do we want Turkey to recognize the Genocide? Of course. But is that a pre-condition? Of course not. Why not? Because that doesn't resolve any particular issue that the country is facing, that our people are facing. We have no energy, we have no economy, we have a war with Azerbaijan and we are going to go to Turkey and say, "You guys are killers and you are killers if you don't recognize [the Genocide] and we want what from you? Territory." What kind of policy is that? That's not a policy, that's reflex.[9]

According to Ambassador Vural:

[Ter-Petrosian] told me clearly that, although he would not forget history, nevertheless it was his responsibility to look further beyond, think about his grandchildren, and pave the way for normalization of Armenian relations with Turkey. In principle, we had no objection to that. In fact, I welcomed that. But there were several obstacles to that. One was the domestic reaction to normalization of relations within Armenia. . . . Secondly, in Turkey, people said that in order to normalize our relations they have to amend the Declaration of Independence and they have to at least say something which would recognize Turkey's borders, that Armenia doesn't have territorial claims on Turkey, etc. I tried very hard in Ankara.[10]

On September 21, 1991, Armenians formally voted for independence in a referendum. On December 16, Turkey recognized the independence of most of the post-Soviet states, including Armenia, but in the Armenian case it declined to open diplomatic relations. The Turkish government set two conditions before it would do so: that the government in Yerevan would not demand genocide recognition and that Armenia would recognize the borders as established by the 1921 Treaty of Kars.

Vural believes that not opening diplomatic relations with Yerevan in 1991 was a mistake and that, had they done so, they could have worked on these disagreements inside Yerevan from a position of greater leverage:

My position at that time, personal position, was that we should establish diplomatic relations with Armenia anyhow. And that those controversial issues could be discussed later. And, of course, in Turkey there were other, more conservative or nationalist circles. They said, "No, they have to amend their position before we enter into a dialogue with Armenia." So, I wasn't successful in my efforts. . . . We are still the hostage of Nagorny Karabakh. So this is the situation in which we are now. Perhaps, if we had established diplomatic relations and opened our borders, perhaps it would have been more difficult for the Armenians to launch an attack in Nagorny Karabakh. It could pacify the situation.[11]

## War in Karabakh

In 1992, the Karabakh conflict escalated into a full interstate war between Armenia and Azerbaijan. Both countries again found themselves independent in a period of conflict and economic breakdown.

The Karabakh Armenians received almost all their support from or through Armenia. But they were semi-autonomous, and throughout the war there was constant tension between the agenda of the leadership in Yerevan, seeking to establish Armenia as a respected international state, and that of the Armenians of Karabakh, whose goal was to defeat Azerbaijan by any means on the battlefield.

With time, Karabakh—or sometimes a mythical version of it—would become more of a cause for Diaspora Armenians than Armenia itself, especially as corruption eroded the image of the new Armenia. Several Diaspora Armenians went to Karabakh to fight, among them the semi-legendary ASALA veteran Monte Melkonian, who was killed there in 1993. After the war, Diaspora telethons and benefactors financed the construction of a high-quality 40-mile highway linking Armenia and Karabakh, costing $10 million.

At the end of 1991, Azerbaijani forces rained missiles on Karabakhi Armenians in the town of Stepanakert. Several hundred people died in the siege. In the New Year, the Armenians broke out of their encirclement and attacked the Azerbaijani town of Khojali. On February 26, Azerbaijanis fled Khojali on foot and were shot at close range by Armenian paramilitaries. According to a later Azerbaijani parliamentary report, 485 Azerbaijanis were killed, the majority of them civilians.

The killings of Azerbaijani civilians at Khojali were the bloodiest episode of the Karabakh conflict and demonstrably a war crime. They stung ordinary Azerbaijanis into action, and for the first time in the conflict, international sympathies swung against the Armenians. A decade later, the Azerbaijani government would retrospectively elevate them to the "Khojali Genocide" to counterpose their own genocide against that of the Armenians. Paradoxically, although the Karabakh conflict was small in scale compared to the mass bloodshed of World War I, Azerbaijan developed an aggressive anti-Armenian rhetoric that was in excess even of that of Turkish ultra-nationalists.

Despite the Karabakh conflict, negotiations continued between Armenia and Turkey in 1992. As winter approached, Armenia was facing drastic food shortages. The European Economic Community, as it was then called, committed itself to send wheat as humanitarian aid, but the route through Georgia was too dangerous and from August

1992, the railway connection via Abkhazia was shut down by the outbreak of war there.

In September 1992, the Armenian government secured Turkey's approval to transport the wheat. As it did so, there was an awkward split in the government, as Foreign Minister Raffi Hovannisian—the 32-year-old son of famous historian Richard Hovannisian—made a fiery speech in Istanbul that he had not cleared with Ter-Petrosian. Hovanissian brought up the issue of the Genocide and mentioned Cyprus and the Kurds. Ter-Petrosian was incensed and forced his foreign minister to step down.

On October 7, 1992, Armenian agriculture minister Gagik Shakhbazian flew to Ankara and signed an agreement with the Turkish foreign ministry. His co-signatory was the head of the foreign ministry's economic department, Oktay Aksoy—the man who, as the aide of the then foreign minister, had taken the notes in the secret Armenian-Turkish talks in Zurich in 1977. The Turkish government agreed to open the border and deliver the European cargoes—they even agreed to loan their own wheat on the understanding that the Europeans would make up the difference later. The wheat deliveries began in November 1992 and helped Armenia through a harsh winter.[12]

At the same time, negotiations continued on signing diplomatic protocols. In early 1993, the two sides were said to be "95 percent" in agreement on a text. The main outstanding problem was the Armenians' aversion to a formal reference to the Treaty of Kars. After the last round of talks in February 1993, Armenian chief negotiator Gerard Libaridian was hopeful that this too could be solved with some ambiguous language. Events on the Karabakh front changed everything, however. In the last few days of March, Karabakh Armenian forces moved into the large mountainous Azerbaijani province of Kelbajar, situated between Armenia and Karabakh itself, acting in coordination with troops from the Republic of Armenia. Within a few days, the Armenian pincer operation had overrun the entire region. Fifty thousand Azerbaijani refugees were forced to flee in terrible conditions over the mountainous Omar Pass.

The Kelbajar operation marked a new escalation in the conflict. For the Karabakh Armenians, the capture of a province that lay directly between Karabakh and Armenia was a major victory. But it was a big diplomatic blow for the government in Yerevan. Ter-Petrosian had been very wary about the operation. According to the then Armenian defense minister, he was not properly informed about it. Once it had begun, Ter-Petrosian sent a letter to Karabakh Armenian leader Robert Kocharian asking him to halt it.[13] On April 30, 1993, a United Nations resolution explicitly criticized Armenia and called on it to withdraw its forces from Kelbajar.

More crucially, the operation killed the rapprochement with Turkey. On April 4, the Turkish government closed the land border with Armenia and shut down its airspace to Armenian flights. Turkish president Turgut Ozal made threatening statements and traveled to Baku in a show of solidarity.

Three days after his return from Baku, Ozal unexpectedly died of a heart attack. Four days after that, an Armenian delegation went to Ankara to attend his funeral. Turkish political veteran Süleyman Demirel, who was about to replace Ozal as president, invited Gerard Libaridian for a private meeting.

> I went to his official residence from the airport. We had coffee. Then he took me to his back office. There was a small armoire and he opened the drawer, took out a map, very rudimentary, and he said "*Bak*, look. *Bu Ermenistan*—this is Armenia, *ermeni topraklar*, Armenian lands. We have no problem with that. *Bu Karabagh*, this is Karabakh, it's not Armenian territory, it's part of Azerbaijan, but your people live on it and you took it, you said they're not secure, we swallowed that. Now, this is Lachin. It's not Armenian territory, it's Azerbaijan and there are no Armenians living on it, you took it and you said it's the security of your people in Karabakh. We got that. What business do you have in Kelbajar?" In Turkish it comes out as *Kelbacarda ne işle var*? He was a very foxy guy. And that was it.[14]

Armenian-Turkish relations nosedived. The full closure of the Turkish border blocked Armenia's main transport route to Europe and left it with only two of its four borders open: those with Georgia and Iran. The Armenian economy was crippled by these conditions, but the euphoric Armenian military barely noticed. In the summer of 1993, the nationalist government in Azerbaijan collapsed and Armenian forces took advantage, capturing, in whole or part, a further five Azerbaijani regions around Nagorny Karabakh itself. By May 1994, the Armenians had imposed a de facto territorial victory over Azerbaijan on the ground.

## President Kocharian

In February 1998, a group of Armenia's leaders mounted a palace coup and forced President Ter-Petrosian to step down. They strongly opposed his endorsement of a peace deal with Azerbaijan. A month later, Robert Kocharian was elected Armenia's second president (Figure 9.1).

A very definite personality took charge. Kocharian was a Karabakh Armenian whose political career had been formed as an outsider and in the war with Azerbaijan. As a *Karabakhtsi*, he represented a third strain of Armenian identity: less inclined to compromise with Azerbaijan, closer to Russia, and also further removed from the Ottoman Armenians.

Kocharian initiated a change in Armenia's foreign policy. He wanted to get closer to the Diaspora and decided that his administration

Figure 9.1 Levon Ter-Petrosian (right), first president of independent Armenia, and his successor Robert Kocharian, Yerevan, 1998.

Source: Ruben Mangasarian. <[crop]>

would push for acknowledgment of the genocide by foreign countries. He was encouraged by the French National Assembly, which passed a one-sentence resolution on May 29, 1998, saying, "France publicly recognizes the 1915 Armenian Genocide."

Vartan Oskanian was Kocharian's new foreign minister. Born in Aleppo from a family from Maraş, he had been educated in both Armenia and the United States. Oskanian says:

> Because nothing was happening in Armenian-Turkish ties, Kocharian was thinking that it was our moral obligation to talk more about this and to raise it in international organizations. He had seen that being reserved about it had not produced any positive results anyway—so by putting it on the foreign policy agenda, it was not deemed as something that will change the situation drastically.
>
> I think he was right. Raising that issue more openly, speaking about it at the UN, also helping our different communities in different countries to pursue recognition was not detrimental in any way to our obligations. On the contrary what transpired in my period and after, leading to the [2009] Protocols, was maybe the result of more openness about the genocide issue, this led to more debate within Turkey, as more countries recognized. And I think that helped the debate.[15]

In his speech to the United Nations General Assembly on September 25 1999, Kocharian duly hailed the recognition of genocide by parliaments around the world. Over the next 15 years, some 20 foreign parliaments would pass genocide resolutions, including such heavyweight powers as Canada, France, Germany, Italy, and Russia. But Kocharian's change of policy was less momentous than some in the Armenian Diaspora supposed. Asked in a television interview in 2001 by the Turkish television journalist Mehmed Ali Birand whether Armenia would claim reparations or territories from Turkey if Ankara recognized the genocide, Kocharian answered, "The Republic of Armenia will not have the legal basis for making such demands."[16] Yerevan and the Diaspora still had different priorities: in 2006, the Armenian foreign ministry clashed behind the scenes with the Armenian lobby in the US Congress. Senator Robert Menendez put a block on the nomination of Richard Hoagland as the US ambassador to Armenia for failing to affirm use of the word "genocide." The government in Yerevan tried to dissuade Menendez: it was more important for them to have a US envoy to their country than a vacant post, even if the envoy used equivocal language about 1915.

After the election of the AKP government in Turkey in 2003, high-level negotiations resumed again. A stable group of diplomats had been dealing with the issue behind the scenes. The Armenian side was represented by Karen Mirzoyan, a fluent Turkish speaker, who would become Armenia's de facto "ambassador in Istanbul" at the Black Sea Economic Cooperation organization, and later by the deputy foreign minister, Arman Kirakosian. Constant faces on the Turkish side were Unal Çeviköz, head of the Caucasus department, and Ertan Tezgör, who as ambassador in Georgia also had responsibility for Armenia.

This group now backed up the two foreign ministers, Vartan Oskanian and Abdullah Gül, who had five rounds of talks in 2003 and 2004. The same issues came round again. Trade had opened up via Georgia, meaning that Turkish goods found their way to Armenian shops and markets and there was a direct Yerevan-Istanbul flight. But for the Armenians the closed land border was the main issue.

Turkey still wanted to see an end to the genocide recognition resolutions, Armenian recognition of its borders, and progress in the Nagorny Karabakh conflict. Azerbaijan was a strengthening factor. In 2003, the Baku-Tbilisi-Ceyhan oil pipeline opened, giving Azerbaijan a new massive stream of revenue, a strategic link to European markets, and an umbilical connection with Turkey. Thanks to these revenues, Azerbaijan was the world's fastest-growing economy in the years 2005–2008.

Oskanian says that when the Armenian side pressed for "de-linkage" between the issues of Karabakh and bilateral Armenia-Turkey relations, Gül approved at first, but later backed away. He sensed, "they couldn't find the right trade-off between what they could do with us and the Azeris."[17]

The Turks had a different perspective. According to a Turkish diplomat, Gül asked Oskanian, "Give us a tool," meaning a step forward on Karabakh that they could present in Baku as progress—but the Armenians said this was not possible.

Prime Minister Recep Tayip Erdoğan had very different ideological convictions from his secularist predecessors, based on religious principles and a more positive conception of Turkey's Ottoman past. In 2011, Erdoğan apologized for the massacre of Kurds in 1938 and 1939 in Dersim/Tunceli. By doing so, he was taking a politically useful step by blaming his Kemalist predecessors, but also setting out a certain vision of reconciliation in Turkey. It was not so clear if this vision would also reach to the descendants of Christians who had suffered in Ottoman times. Erdoğan was not shy about using the word "genocide"—*soykirim* in Turkish—but he did so almost exclusively in reference to the persecution of Muslims around the world, whether Bosnians, Palestinians, or Uyghurs in China. Conversely, he rejected the charge that Sudan's government had committed genocide, on the grounds that a Muslim could not commit genocide, by definition.[18]

The prime minister did declare a vote of no confidence in the previous generations of state-backed history. On April 10, 2005, he sent a letter to the Armenian president proposing that "because of diverging interpretations of events that took place during a particular period of our common history," the two countries should establish a "joint commission of historians."[19]

To Armenian scholars, the letter was a trap, an attempt to re-legislate an issue that had already been decided. In his reply on April 26, Kocharian did not completely reject the proposal but suggested a group with a bigger mandate, saying, "an intergovernmental commission can meet to discuss any and all outstanding issues between our two nations, with the aim of resolving them and coming to an understanding."[20]

Two years later, Ankara re-launched the initiative, this time targeting it at the United States. On April 23, 2007, the Turkish government published a full-page advertisement in several US newspapers with the title, "Let's Unearth the Truth about What Happened in 1915 Together." This relayed an invitation to Armenia for "the establishment of a joint commission of historians which will also be open to third parties" and made the promise that "Turkey ensures full access to all its archives." It ended with the call, "Support Efforts to Examine History, not Legislate It." The offer won approval from, among others, US secretary of state Condoleezza Rice.[21]

## A Reconciliation Commission

In the year 2000, after the fallout from another genocide recognition debate in Congress, the US government promoted a plan for informal and confidential Armenian-Turkish negotiations. They would be conducted by nongovernmental figures with connections to the two governments. American scholar, expert in Track II diplomacy, and robust New Yorker David L. Phillips took up the challenge. The Turkish Armenian Reconciliation Commission, or TARC, was formed and met between 2001 and 2004. The title was something of a misnomer. TARC was more of an ad hoc discussion group with a serious agenda than a formal commission. The word "reconciliation" was also too ambitious: it was an exercise in dialogue that narrowed differences but could not begin to claim to reconcile two entire societies.

Two of the four Armenians who took part came from Armenia: former foreign minister Alexander Arzumanian and former ambassador to Syria David Hovhannisian. Andranik Migranian, a pugnacious adviser to Presidents Boris Yeltsin and Vladimir Putin, came from Russia. The heaviest responsibility lay on Van Krikorian, former head of the Armenian Assembly of America, the powerful Diaspora organization. Krikorian had excellent credentials in the US Armenian community, having crafted the genocide resolution of 1990, led by Senator Bob Dole. But he was aware that he would alienate many by entering into a dialogue with Turks. Why the change in approach? Krikorian says that in his early recognition campaigns, "I had not considered the receptivity of the host society," Turkey. He now wanted to engage in a debate directly with Turkey itself.[22]

Former Turkish Foreign Minister Ilter Turkmen later headed the Turkish side. Calm and diplomatic, he helped smooth things over at difficult moments. Like many Turks of his generation, Turkmen says that he knew Armenians in Istanbul but had never learned that they had a different version of historical events. As a diplomat he had also lost many friends in the Armenian terrorist attacks of the 1970s and 1980s. He describes Armenian-Turkish relations as "an insolvable problem," but believes that TARC paved the way for the Protocols process of 2007–2009.

Phillips later noted that there was "[a] gap in expectations between Turkish and Armenian members. Armenians pushed to achieve results; Turks preferred a slower process. There were more problems in between meetings than at meetings themselves."[23]

In the first meetings they discussed many issues, but "[t]he genocide issue was the 800 lb gorilla in the room," says Krikorian. David Hovhannissian says, "We said 'Genocide,' our Turkish colleagues said 'Events' at the first meeting. At the second meeting, they said 'massacres' or 'tragic events.' At the third meeting an interesting word was invented: 'G-word.' "

Phillips had briefed the *New York Times*, and the initiative went public in July 2001. While "the reaction to TARC in Turkey was mature and level-headed," much of the Armenian Diaspora press was very aggressive. Writers aired conspiracy theories on the credentials of the participants to represent the Armenian nation and questioned why there was no one from the ARF in the Armenian delegation. One ARF supporter wrote of "the putrid smell of a misguided and ill-conceived scheme."[24] Both Krikorian and Hovhannisian say that even as they were being assailed in the media as traitors, they got plenty of support in private. "For every stupid thing that was written, I got so many pats on the back," said Krikorian.

Confronting the genocide issue head on, TARC members commissioned a report on the legal status of the 1915 killings from the International Center for Transitional Justice (ICTJ), a nonprofit organization that helps societies address legacies of large-scale human rights violations. ICTJ's report, delegated to an independent expert, came out in February 2003. It reviewed the coining of the word "genocide" and the adoption of the 1948 UN convention. It concluded that the killing of the Ottoman Armenians in 1915 did constitute genocide under the Convention, as "the overwhelming majority of the accounts conclude that the Events occurred with some level of intent to effect the destruction of the Armenian communities in the eastern provinces of the Ottoman Empire, with many claiming that this was the specific intent of the most senior government officials."[25] However, the analysis also argued that the Genocide Convention did not have any retroactive force, as its "negotiators understood that they were accepting prospective, not retrospective, obligations on behalf of the States they represented, including the 'prevention of future crimes.' "[26]

In sporting terminology, the expert verdict on the gravest of issues was a draw. The Armenians were vindicated by a legal opinion that the crime against their ancestors was genocide. The Turkish side could be reassured that the verdict had no retroactive legal validity.

The legal analysis commissioned by the ICTJ deserves to be better known, but has made surprisingly little impact on the Armenian-Turkish debate. Perhaps this is because it was an advisory opinion with no formal status; it also did not help that the author of the report was anonymous and could therefore not defend it publicly.

"They tried to appease both sides . . . I think they did a good job," says Ilter Turkmen of the legal analysis. "At the end, we couldn't continue." In April 2004, the two delegations concluded their work by composing a joint list of seven proposals to strengthen Armenian-Turkish relations. Prominent among them was the recommendation to open the Turkish-Armenian border in 2004.

Its proposals were not acted on, but the commission had a catalyzing effect. In its wake, there was a proliferation of exchanges between Armenian and Turkish journalists, artists, and businessmen. David Hovhannisian says, "It was designed to destroy many taboos and stereotypes. . . . Afterwards, other meetings became possible." Ilter Turkmen says that the TARC paved the way for the attempted normalization process, which resulted in the 2009 Protocols signed in Zurich five years later. "We wrote letters to our respective foreign ministers exactly suggesting what the protocols have done."

# 10

## The Protocols

### A Swiss Breakthrough

ON OCTOBER 10, 2009, in the main auditorium of the University of Zurich, known as the Aula, the foreign ministers of Armenia and Turkey signed two historic documents on establishing and developing their relations. This moment of unprecedented hope for Armenian-Turkish relations was fraught with anxiety. The signing was only the first step, to be followed by a parliamentary ratification process. And the ceremony did not go as planned. The speeches by the two ministers were canceled at the last moment and they said nothing. The only person to speak was Micheline Calmy-Rey, the foreign minister of Switzerland, who told her two guests, "Your political courage, your relentless efforts and your generous vision has [sic] made this agreement possible."[1]

The mediation of Switzerland was key in bringing the two sides close to a success. Calmy-Rey had first floated the idea of a Swiss role to bridge the differences between Armenia and Turkey five years earlier. The first talks got underway in 2007. As one Swiss official explains it, "We could do it as a neutral country, with no colonial past, no interest in the region, no hidden agenda, not in the EU or NATO. There are not so many candidates like this. We had quite a good label."

The country's most senior diplomat, State Secretary Michael Ambühl, took charge of the process. He had previously won respect for his mediation work in United Nations talks with Iran.[2] Deputy Foreign Minister Arman Kirakosian headed the Armenian delegation. He was not only an experienced diplomat but also a historian with a fine pedigree in Yerevan; his father, John Kirakosian, had been a well-known scholar and diplomat in Soviet Armenia. Kirakosian was assisted by the Armenian foreign ministry's leading Turkey expert, Karen Mirzoyan.[3]

The Turkish side was led by Ertuğrul Apakan, another experienced diplomat who, as undersecretary, held the second most powerful position in Turkey's foreign ministry. Apakan also had a highly experienced "number two" in Unal Çevikoz, who had worked on the Armenia-Turkey brief and the Caucasus for the previous eight years and had also served as Turkey's ambassador to Azerbaijan.

In early 2008, the two sides started secret talks at a manor house named Gerzensee belonging to the Swiss Central Bank, situated by a lake outside Bern. Ambühl built up an atmosphere of trust by observing extremely careful procedural niceties on who should speak and what terms they should use. Fairly soon, there was a good personal relationship between the two chief negotiators and the mediator, who affectionately called the other two "Kira" and "Apa." He observed that they had a similar calm temperament and "[t]hey even look like they could be brothers."[4]

The United States was also looking for a rapprochement. In October 2007, another ferocious political battle in Washington over an Armenian Genocide resolution had just ended. After the House Foreign Affairs Committee had passed the resolution by 27 votes to 21 and sent it to a full floor vote, Turkey withdrew its ambassador in protest. The website of *Hürriyet* newspaper that evening carried an American and Turkish flag under the dramatic headline, "Is This the End of a Hundred-Year Partnership?" After no fewer than eight former US secretaries of state issued a joint appeal for the resolution to be scrapped, its backers caved in once again and canceled the vote.

"We told the Turks, 'We can't keep on doing this,'" says one State Department official of this episode. Two months later, Assistant Secretary of State for European and Eurasian Affairs Daniel Fried met Apakan by chance in the Lufthansa business lounge at Munich airport.

The Turkish diplomat informed him about the Swiss talks. After that, the Swiss kept Washington informed. In the words of a Swiss official, Bern and Washington made a "good tandem" with Switzerland negotiating the details of the agreement itself while the United States used its "bargaining power" with the two governments.

### "Football Diplomacy" in Yerevan

In 2008, Armenia acquired a new president in circumstances of extreme controversy. On February 19, Serzh Sarkisian competed as the official candidate to be Armenia's third present, after Robert Kocharian had finished two terms in office. A Karabakh Armenian who had been a close colleague of Kocharian for 30 years, Sarkisian had already served twice as Armenia's defense minister and as prime minister. In the election, Sarkisian faced an unexpected and serous opponent in the 63-year-old former president Levon Ter-Petrosian, who came out of a 10-year retirement to attempt a comeback.

Sarkisian was declared the outright winner in the first round of voting with 52 percent of the vote. The opposition challenged the result, claiming fraud, and protests began on the streets of Yerevan. These culminated on March 1, with a police crackdown. Ten opposition supporters died and hundreds were injured. The outgoing leader, President Kocharian, briefly declared a state of emergency.

Serzh Sarkisian thus assumed the presidency in a situation of domestic turmoil, with doubts cast on his legitimacy. Sarkisian was a hardened veteran of the Karabakh conflict, but also a more consensual politician than his predecessor. To assert his own legitimacy and win back international support, he began a rethink on the negotiations on Karabakh and made a new commitment to rapprochement with Turkey.

The economy was a crucial factor. Under Kocharian, Armenia had enjoyed several years of economic growth. That stalled in 2007, while the massive Diaspora investment program that Kocharian had hoped for never materialized. In 2009, as a result of the world financial crisis, the Armenia economy declined by a disastrous 14 percent. Even with a closed border, Turkey had become Armenia's fifth-largest trading partner, via the territory of Georgia. Economists predicted that an open border would give Armenia's economy a big boost. Ratna Sahay of the International Monetary Fund said, "Once the border opens up we think that the impact would be pretty quick because it would reduce [Armenia's] transportation costs tremendously. There would also be a lot of indirect impact through trade in goods and services with Turkey."[5]

Abdullah Gül, who had moved from being Turkey's foreign minister to the post of president the year before, was one of the first heads of state to congratulate Sarkisian, even as others were equivocating. A coincidence of sports scheduling gave the two men an opening. Armenia and Turkey were paired against each other in the qualifying rounds for the soccer World Cup of 2010. That meant that the Turkish team was due to play in Yerevan, and the Armenian team would play in Turkey. In June 2008, Sarkisian sent Gül an invitation to attend the first match in Yerevan in September. Gül agreed to come.

Turkey's anxiety that it was missing a role in the security of its neighboring region, the South Caucasus, was also a factor. To be a proper actor in the region and play a role in resolving the Karabakh conflict, Ankara needed to come out of its diplomatic freeze with Armenia. In August 2008, Georgia and Russia fought a disastrous five-day war. On August 13, 2008, the day after a ceasefire was signed, Prime Minister Erdoğan announced in Moscow a multilateral initiative called the Caucasus Stability and Cooperation Platform. The platform idea made no progress, but it provided an extra stimulus for rapprochement with Yerevan.

On September 6, 2008, President Gül traveled to Yerevan to attend the football match. He stayed only six hours—the engines on his airplane did not stop running—but the very fact of a visit by a Turkish head of state to Armenia was historic. Most Armenian dailies carried an advertisement in Armenian and English, which read, "Welcome Honorable President Abdullah Gül. Fair play beyond 90 minutes. That's our wish." Gül and Sarkisian watched the soccer game from behind bulletproof glass in a VIP box in the Hrazdan stadium. Dozens of unhappy but peaceful demonstrators held torches and flowers in silent vigil at the nearby Genocide Memorial. Then Gül went to the presidential palace for talks, and he and Sarkisian publicly shook hands outside, with the Armenian tricolor and the Turkish flag placed behind them (Figure 10.1).

Figure 10.1 A historic meeting in Yerevan. Presidents Abdullah Gül and Serzh
Sarkisian shake hands after their "football diplomacy" meeting in Yerevan,
September 6, 2008.
Source: AP Photo.

A group of Turks eager to pursue reconciliation accompanied their
president. Among them was Hasan Cemal, the grandson of one of the
Unionist leaders who had crushed the Armenians, Cemal Pasha. In
Yerevan, Cemal met the grandson of one of the Armenian assassins
who had killed his grandfather in 1921. As the Turkish president flew
back, he told journalists, "I believe that my visit broke the psychological barrier in the Caucasus. If this atmosphere continues, everything
will move forward and will stabilize. I concluded my meeting with
positive feelings and thoughts."[6]

Turkey's foreign minister Ali Babacan stayed behind for talks on the
diplomatic texts being negotiated in Switzerland with Armenian foreign minister Eduard Nalbandian. The discussions began at midnight
and lasted two hours. Nalbandian, an English and French speaker,
had been Armenia's ambassador in Paris and also had close ties to the
Russian foreign policy establishment. However, a Turkish diplomat
reported that he was dismayed by the outcome of the bilateral meeting,

as Nalbandian took charge of the process from his subordinates and took the negotiations in a different direction.

## Navigating Obstacles

By February 2009, the Armenian and Turkish diplomats had agreed on a draft text of two Protocols establishing and developing bilateral relations. For the Armenians, the biggest priority was to open the closed border as early as possible. The Turkish government was still wedded to its concept of a "joint commission of historians" as a solution to the genocide dispute. They argued that "leaving it to the historians" was a progressive step, a sign that the Turkish government was delegating judgment to scholars. The Armenian government was skeptical about the commission, but agreed to discuss it. An Armenian official says, "We said, 'Historians could sit and talk for 100 years. Let's open diplomatic relations.'"[7]

At the Swiss talks, the parties agreed to demote the historical commission to the status of one of seven branches of a single Armenian-Turkish intergovernmental commission. It was eventually named "the sub-commission on the historical dimension to implement a dialogue with the aim to restore mutual confidence between the two nations, including an impartial scientific examination of the historical records and archives to define existing problems and formulate recommendations." The formulation was ambiguous enough for the Armenians to present the commission as a body that would discuss historical issues in general and not adjudicate on 1915.

A Swiss official suggests that the Turkish diplomats at the talks saw the historical commission as a device that would open up debate within Turkish society and prepare the public for a shift in policy on the history of 1915. Gerard Libaridian also points out, "By agreeing that the truth has yet to be established, albeit by an ambiguous sub-commission, the Turkish Republic was also recognizing, as tacitly as the Republic of Armenia, that the official Turkish position of absolute denial, which was maintained for so long and at such cost, was being challenged and moderated—at least in principle."[8]

But the commission idea provoked strong opposition in the Diaspora from Armenian scholars, who saw it as a ploy. In October 2009, leading

Armenian-American historian Richard Hovannisian said, "It is a snare to be avoided and rejected. The proper order must be recognition of the crime and only then the formation of commissions to seek the means to gain relief from the suffocating historical burden."[9]

The final texts, drafted by the Swiss, navigated a way around other controversial issues. The first Protocol on establishing relations satisfied the Turks' demands that Armenia would recognize their shared border, while the phrase "as defined by the relevant treaties of international law" saved the Armenians from having to affirm directly the 1921 Treaty of Kars. With regard to the tricky issue of timing, the requirement to open the border "within two months" and to begin the work of the intergovernmental commission "within three months" of the Protocol coming into force allowed for ambiguity and ensured that these steps could proceed almost in parallel.

Such a sensitive deal needed some kind of public imprimatur to go forward and the draft text gave the two governments political cover by requiring the two Protocols to be ratified by the Armenian and Turkish parliaments "within a reasonable time-frame." The diplomats' work was all but done: it was up to the top leaders on both sides to endorse the drafts and a timetable for signing and ratifying them.

### The Azerbaijan Factor

As the draft texts awaited top-level political endorsement, the Turkish elite looked to be divided. President Gül had personally committed himself to the rapprochement and had even been nominated for the Nobel Peace Prize for doing so. But Prime Minister Erdoğan, the country's most powerful politician, was a consummate election-winner, who counted every vote, and saw negatives in the process, particular with regard to Turkey's alley, Azerbaijan.

Without at least Baku's tacit endorsement, there was every chance that it would seek to use its influence on its ally, Turkey, to torpedo an agreement opening the Armenian-Turkey border, which had been closed in an act of solidarity with Azerbaijan in 1993. In their talks in Switzerland, the Armenians and Turks had agreed to leave the issue of the Karabakh conflict and Azerbaijan's claims out of their discussions. The Armenians insisted that these were bilateral talks and that there was no reason to include the claims of a third party, Azerbaijan. However, they believed that "someone was talking to Baku." The Turkish diplomats agreed not to try to discuss Karabakh in Switzerland. But one of them also says, "We let it be known that the Turkish expectation was that if there is progress in one process, we expect progress in another."

If there was an Armenian-Turkish rapprochement and the border reopened, how would this impact the peace process over Nagorny Karabakh and Armenia's willingness to make a deal with Azerbaijan? The view in Switzerland was that the impact would be beneficial. One official says, "The general philosophy of the exercise was that if there was progress in Turkey-Armenia relations, it would make Armenians feel better and soften them up [on Karabakh]."[10] The International Crisis Group also made the case that a deal with Turkey would be the catalyst for new thinking in Armenia: "An open border could help break Armenian perceptions of encirclement by hostile Turkic peoples, making them less adamant about retaining the territories around Nagorno-Karabakh as security guarantees. It is important that Yerevan realize progress in bilateral relations will be sustainable only if it withdraws in due course from occupied Azerbaijani territory after a border opening with Turkey."

The Azerbaijani government feared the opposite: that it would lose leverage over Armenia in the Karabakh dispute as soon as the Armenia-Turkey border opened. Matthew Bryza was both the US negotiator mediating the Nagorny Karabakh conflict and the deputy assistant secretary of state responsible for Turkey and the South Caucasus region. As such, he worked on both processes in parallel. Bryza believes that the prospect of success with Turkey did indeed make the Armenians more stubborn with Azerbaijan. He says, "Of course, if you are Armenia you wanted to obtain one of your primary pay-offs early in the game [opening the border with Turkey] because you don't have to negotiate for that and so if you can obtain that then you can harden your position on other issues—that's just Negotiations 101."[11]

Quite probably, both arguments were right—within different time frames. Certainly, when the border opened and the Armenian government established diplomatic relations with Turkey, it would be able to proclaim an immediate public relations victory, while Azerbaijan would lose face. However, in the longer term, a deal would make Turkey an inside rather than an outside player in the Caucasus, with much more influence. Most important, the rapprochement would change Armenia's worldview. The Armenians would finally emerge from out of the shadow of a Turkish threat, whether real or imagined. In so doing, they would be compelled to confront the enormous security issue of the Karabakh conflict and their own role in perpetuating it.

As the talks progressed, US officials, from President Obama downward, had a simpler calculation: a window of opportunity in a dispute that had bedeviled US interests for years was open. One State Department official argued, "We should not tie the outcome of one extremely difficult process [Armenia-Turkey] to that of another extremely difficult process [Armenia-Azerbaijan]."

In 2008, Russia's new president, Dmitry Medvedev, injected new energy into the Karabakh peace process by taking personal charge of the talks. In 2008 and 2009, Medvedev convened seven rounds of direct talks between himself and the two presidents and personally worked on the language of draft texts. With Medvedev leading the Armenia-Azerbaijan talks and Switzerland handling the bilateral Armenia-Turkey negotiations, it fell to the United States to try to promote both tracks, without saying that there was an explicit link between them. Bryza worried, "Maybe it's impossible to do both processes, but if you can't do both you are not going to get either." Asked about the linkage, US officials emphasized that the two processes were "in parallel" and "mutually reinforcing."

However, this was easier said than done. The Karabakh negotiations were extremely opaque, and the Armenian and Azerbaijani presidents were very cautious about sharing their views with outsiders. In 2008, Serzh Sarkisian began his presidency by telling the mediators that he was ready to be more flexible in the Karabakh talks than his predecessor Robert Kocharian. Later in the year, mediators found the Armenian president much more equivocal. It was possible that Kocharian had reined him in.

The thinking of the Azerbaijan president, Ilham Aliev, was even harder to read. In 2008, he made no public comment, and in private he gave foreign visitors the impression that he was relaxed, and would not oppose an Armenian-Turkish rapprochement—even as his subordinates spoke out against it.

In March 2009, Turkey's foreign minister, Ali Babacan, finally put his initials to a draft text of the two Armenian-Turkey Protocols, which made no mention of Azerbaijan or the Karabakh conflict. He did so, having received only verbal assurances from US secretary of state Hillary Clinton that Washington would put more energy into the Armenian-Azerbaijani peace process. Either the Azerbaijani president had been dissembling, or no one in Turkey had been briefing him properly. Either way, he exploded in anger. On April 3, 2009, Aliev and his foreign minister received Bryza and the US ambassador in Baku. Bryza said that Secretary of State Hillary Clinton had commissioned him to hear Azerbaijan's concerns about Armenia-Turkey normalization and delivered an invitation from President Obama to join talks in Istanbul in three days' time. According to the US Embassy cable,

> Aliyev responded with a lengthy and bitter indictment of Turkey as a "liar, cheat and betrayer" of Azerbaijan. Noting that the consequences of the current volatile situation in the region are unpredictable, he complained that Azerbaijan had quietly supported the recent improvement in Turkish-Armenian relations, including President Sargsian's "football diplomacy," never dreaming that Turkey "would cheat us" by delinking progress on NK [Nagorny Karabakh] from that process. President Gül had promised that there would be no doors or borders opened for Armenia without progress on NK, Aliyev asserted. "He lied, I no longer trust him."

The Azerbaijani president then said that he had warned Turkish foreign minister Babacan of "all the possible consequences for Turkey and this region" if the Turkish government did not heed Azerbaijan's concerns.[12] Somewhere between Azerbaijan, Switzerland, Turkey, and the United States, there had been a serious breakdown in communication. Regardless of whether some of this was political theater, the Armenia-Turkey rapprochement looked to be in serious trouble, just as its backers were urging it over the finishing line.

## Obama and the Armenians

Just as draft texts of the Armenia-Turkey Protocols were being agreed in January 2009, President Barack Obama took office. In 1990, President George H. W. Bush had set a precedent of issuing a presidential declaration on April 24, which expressed sympathy with Armenians on their tragic anniversary, but avoided using the "G-word." Since then, in what became a well-trodden ritual, almost all US presidential candidates cultivated the Armenian vote by pledging to use the term "Armenian Genocide" if elected, only to back away from the promise once they took office. The foreign policy imperative of avoiding a dispute with an important ally, Turkey, always trumped the promises made to Armenian-Americans.

As a senator and candidate, Obama went further than his predecessors had done on the Armenian question. He also had as an advisor the journalist and historian Samantha Power, whose book *A Problem from Hell*, devoted to the story of genocide in the twentieth century, began with the Armenians. In 2005, US ambassador in Yerevan John Evans used the word "genocide" in public—a decision that he later said was deliberate. Evans was later recalled and was dismissed from the State Department for disobedience. The US government's nominee to replace Evans as ambassador to Armenia, Richard Hoagland, was blocked by Senator Robert Menendez—contrary to the advice of the government in Yerevan—on the grounds that Hoagland was not prepared to use the word "genocide." It was two years before the United States had an ambassador in Yerevan. In this dispute Senator Obama emphatically backed the Armenian lobby against the State Department, saying,

> I criticized the Secretary of State for the firing of US Ambassador to Armenia, John Evans, after he properly used the term "genocide" to describe Turkey's slaughter of thousands of Armenians starting in 1915. . . . The facts are undeniable. An official policy that calls on diplomats to distort the historical facts is an untenable policy. As a senator, I strongly support passage of the [2007] Armenian Genocide Resolution (H. Res. 106 and S. Res. 106), and as President I will recognize the Armenian Genocide.[13]

Elected president, Obama visited Turkey on his first major foreign tour. In a wide-ranging speech to the Turkish Grand National Assembly in Ankara on April 6, 2009, Obama came around to the Armenia issue tactfully, beginning, "Another issue that confronts all democracies as they move to the future is how we deal with the past. The United States is still working through some of our own darker periods in our history. . . . Our country still struggles with the legacies of slavery and segregation, the past treatment of Native Americans." He went on,

> Each country must work through its past. And reckoning with the past can help us seize a better future. I know there's [sic] strong views in this chamber about the terrible events of 1915. And while there's been a good deal of commentary about my views, it's really about how the Turkish and Armenian people deal with the past. And the best way forward for the Turkish and Armenian people is a process that works through the past in a way that is honest, open and constructive.
>
> We've already seen historic and courageous steps taken by Turkish and Armenian leaders. These contacts hold out the promise of a new day. An open border would return the Turkish and Armenian people to a peaceful and prosperous coexistence that would serve both of your nations. So I want you to know that the United States strongly supports the full normalization of relations between Turkey and Armenia. It is a cause worth working towards.
>
> It speaks to Turkey's leadership that you are poised to be the only country in the region to have normal and peaceful relations with all the South Caucasus nations. And to advance that peace, you can play a constructive role in helping to resolve the Nagorno-Karabakh conflict, which has continued for far too long.[14]

Just before the president arrived in Turkey, Ambühl had secured the initials of both foreign ministers to the latest draft documents. Nalbandian was invited to Istanbul to meet Obama after the speech and confirm the deal. Nalbandian demurred, saying that there was no available flight to Istanbul. Ambühl then arranged for him to be flown in on a Swiss air force plane. Obama, Swiss president and Foreign

Minister Micheline Calmy-Rey, Babacan, and Nalbandian duly met and reaffirmed the agreement (Figure 10.2).

Hillary Clinton and Abdullah Gül also telephoned Azerbaijan president Ilham Aliev to repeat the invitation to join the Istanbul meeting. Aliev declined to come, evidently not wishing to offend the new American president by opposing the rapprochement to his face. However, by simply not showing up in Istanbul, he had not raised a red flag that President Obama would notice.

It now remained for Armenia and Turkey to reveal their planned deal to the world. On April 18, Bryza traveled to Yerevan. He went through a 13-hour session in Minister Nalbandian's office over the wording of a public statement, sustained only by cans of processed meat and a 24-year-old bottle of Chivas Regal whiskey. Vice President Joe Biden called President Sarkisian to encourage him to cross the line. On April 22, a joint statement by the Armenian, Turkish, and

Figure 10.2 Trying to fix a deal in Istanbul. President Barack Obama with (left to right), Armenian Foreign Minister Eduard Nalbandian, Swiss Foreign Minister Micheline Calmy-Rey, Turkish Undersecretary Ertuğul Apakan, Turkish Foreign Minister Ali Babacan, April 6, 2009.
Source: White House.

Swiss foreign ministries was released, announcing a road map. It said that the two countries had "agreed on a comprehensive framework for the normalization of their bilateral relations in a mutually satisfactory manner."

Armenians were less nervous about the message itself than about its timing, coming two days before the April 24 commemorations. In his first White House statement as president, Obama described the Armenians' loss in the language employed in the Turkish apology campaign of a few months before: the Armenian phrase, "Great Catastrophe."

> Ninety four years ago, one of the great atrocities of the 20th century began. Each year, we pause to remember the 1.5 million Armenians who were subsequently massacred or marched to their death in the final days of the Ottoman Empire. The Meds Yeghern must live on in our memories, just as it lives on in the hearts of the Armenian people.
>
> History, unresolved, can be a heavy weight. Just as the terrible events of 1915 remind us of the dark prospect of man's inhumanity to man, reckoning with the past holds out the powerful promise of reconciliation. I have consistently stated my own view of what occurred in 1915, and my view of that history has not changed. My interest remains the achievement of a full, frank and just acknowledgment of the facts.

The president also strongly endorsed "the efforts by Turkey and Armenia to normalize their bilateral relations."[15]

The president said, "my own view . . . has not changed," but he did not use the "G-word." Turkish Prime Minister Erdoğan called the characterization of 1915 "unacceptable" and said "Turkey is not a country that can be deceived easily." The Armenian reaction was even angrier—the president was accused of using the normalization process to avoid promises he had made. The ARF-affiliated Armenian National Committee of America paid no attention to the words Obama had chosen, and homed in solely on the one he had not: "genocide." It said, "[T]he President chose, as a matter of policy, to allow our nation's stand against genocide to remain a hostage to Turkey's threats."[16]

## The Process under Attack

With the Armenian-Turkish road map now made public, its opponents went on the offensive. Azerbaijani president Ilham Aliev again said nothing in public but sent loyal officials to Turkey to lobby against the deal. A group of women Azerbaijani parliamentarians traveled to Ankara and took with them a box of earth, apparently from Nagorny Karabakh, to protest the Turkish betrayal. On April 24, Bryza, who was engaged in almost permanent shuttle diplomacy between his two mediation briefs, went to Azerbaijan:

> I saw [defense minister] Safar Abiev in Baku airport in the lounge and I say "Oh no, Safar, where are you going?" "Yup, I'm going to Ankara." "Oh no. You going to kill the thing?" "Yup. I am going to tell them that if they do this, we are going to wreak havoc in their domestic political system." I don't remember what his exact words were but [the message was] "We will cause problems in Turkish domestic politics." And so they did.

Things got more complicated on May 1, when Ali Babacan was replaced as Turkey's foreign minister by Ahmet Davutoğlu. Davutoğlu was both an adviser to the prime minister and Turkey's main foreign policy strategist. He had formulated a new slogan for Turkey of "zero problems with neighbors" and pushed for Turkey to play a bigger role in the Middle East and the Balkans. Some called his and Erdoğan's approach "neo-Ottomanist." There was a logic to making Davutoğlu the foreign minister, rather than the inexperienced Babacan. But the change dismayed the Armenians, who believed they had a done deal with Babacan, whereas "Davutoğlu wanted to start from zero."

On May 13, Erdoğan and Davutoğlu traveled to Baku and signaled an entirely different approach from that of their diplomats. In a joint press conference with President Aliev, the Turkish prime minister flatly squashed the premise of "de-linking" the Turkey-Armenia process from Nagorny Karabakh. Erdoğan said, "There is a cause-and-effect relation here. Occupation of Karabakh is the cause here and closing of the border is the effect. It is impossible for us to open the border unless that occupation ends." He went on, "Ankara will take no steps as long as we do not agree with our Azeri brothers." Aliyev said he was "grateful" for Erdoğan's words.[17]

Nonetheless, President Obama and Secretary of State Hillary Clinton still pressed both sides to complete the agreement. It took the Swiss two months to agree on the final texts, with the Armenian foreign ministry haggling over every last word. One frustrated official recalls that they debated for almost three weeks over whether to use the word "questions" or "issues."[18]

There was a final deadline. The return Turkey-Armenia soccer match was scheduled to take place on October 14 in the Turkish town of Bursa. President Sarkisian made it clear that he would not attend unless a normalization agreement had been signed before then. On August 31, the foreign ministries of Armenia, Turkey, and Switzerland released the texts of the two Protocols and issued a three-paragraph statement, announcing that the pacts would be signed after a six-week phase of "political consultations."

If there was to be a parallel breakthrough in the Armenia-Azerbaijan talks that allowed Erdoğan to honor the commitments he had made in Baku, there was only one small window for it, at scheduled talks on Karabakh in the Moldovan capital, Chisinau, on October 8. Erdoğan told the *Wall Street Journal*, the day before the talks, "The Armenian-Turkish agreement will be signed on the 10th. It doesn't have anything to do with what happens in Moldova. But of course a positive development in Moldova will definitely have a positive impact on the process altogether."

The Turkish prime minister was expecting too much of one meeting. President Medvedev was shepherding the presidents of Armenia and Azerbaijan toward acceptance of a brief two- or three-page framework agreement on the conflict called the Basic Principles. The best that could be hoped from each occasional meeting of the two leaders was an incremental step forward. In Chisinau the mediators found the two leaders seriously engaged, but there was no major breakthrough.

Serzh Sarkisian had arrived in Moldova exhausted from a four-country tour, selling the Protocols to the Diaspora. At each step of the way, he met resistance. The perennial contradictions between the Armenians of the Republic of Armenia (*Hayastansi*) and the Diaspora boiled up, as vocal Diaspora groups, especially the ARF, questioned his right to do a deal with Turkey, In Beirut thousands of Armenians turned out with signs that said, "The genocide is not subject to bargaining." In Paris, police had to drag away demonstrators who were trying to block the president's route to the memorial of the composer Komitas and prevent him from laying a wreath there. In New York, protestors held up placards objecting to the joint historical commission, saying, "Armenian History not for Sale" (Figure 10.3)[19]

These demonstrations set the tone of the tour. At the same time, influential but less visible organizations, including the Armenian General Benevolent Union, the Armenian Assembly of America, and the Apostolic church, all backed Sarkisian and the Protocols, only more quietly than the opponents. In an interview for the *Armenian Reporter* newspaper, the Armenian president said that the mandate of the historical sub-commission was different from what its critics alleged: "This is a long-term process, which encompass a broad range of issues: issues of the Armenian heritage in Turkey, issues of restoring and preserving that heritage, issues of the heirs of the victims of the Genocide."[20]

Figure 10.3 Demonstrating against the Protocols and Armenian president Serzh Sarkisian, New York, October 3, 2009.

Source: Scout Tufankjian.

## Meeting in Zurich

On October 10, 2009, the embattled foreign ministers of Armenia and Turkey came to Switzerland for the signing ceremony of the two documents establishing their relations.

A host of foreign luminaries gathered to bless the event in the University of Zurich. As well as the host, Swiss president and Foreign Minister Micheline Calmy-Rey, US Secretary of State Hillary Clinton, Russian Foreign Minister Sergei Lavrov, French Foreign Minister Bernard Kouchner, and EU foreign policy chief Javier Solana were also present. The plan was that the two foreign ministers would sign the two Protocols in the main auditorium at 5 P.M. and then make brief speeches hailing the breakthrough in relations.

Just before the ceremony was due to start, the process hit a new hitch. When the two sides exchanged the texts of their speeches, Nalbandian was aghast at a line in Davutoğlu's statement referring to the historical commission and demanded that it be taken out. The Turkish minister refused. A Western official says that the line was "innocuous," but a clearly nervous Nalbandian said that he would not go through with the ceremony.

The VIP guests had already assembled at the university for the ceremony. The French, Russian, and EU foreign ministers watched a Germany-Russian football match on television as they waited. At one point, the famous Armenian singer Charles Aznavour, who was acting as Armenia's ambassador to Switzerland, borrowed Nalbandian's ministerial car to drive to the university, briefly sparking a rumor that Nalbandian had been sacked and Aznavour had been appointed in his place.

Clinton was on her way to the university when she heard about Nalbandian's démarche. Her motorcade turned around and took her back to her hotel. For an hour she sat outside in the rain, talking on two mobile phones to Nalbandian and Davutoğlu in turn. A strange coincidence and bad omen—of which no one was aware—was that the hotel where Clinton and Nalbandian were both staying was the Dolder Grand Hotel, the same location where the secret and inconclusive Armenian-Turkish talks had been held in November 1977.

Later Ambühl arrived in a police vehicle with blue flashing lights, bearing compromise proposals. Clinton and Ambühl went to

Nalbandian's hotel room to find him "visibly agitated." He had talked on the telephone several times to his president. A face-saving compromise was negotiated whereby the two ministers would sign the two Protocols but would make no speeches. Lavrov wrote a note to Nalbandian, under which Kouchner and Solana also put their signatures, saying "Eduard! Agree to the ceremony without statements." Clinton gave Nalbandian a lift back to the university in her official car.[21]

At 8 P.M. Swiss president Calmy-Rey welcomed everyone with a brief opening speech. Then the ministers sat and took more than five minutes to sign multiple copies of the two Protocols, one on establishing diplomatic relations and one on "the development of relations." All the dignitaries crowded around the table. The two ministers then stood up and shook hands. Anxiety gave way for a moment to relief and smiles.

### Aftermath

The signing of two Protocols was the first step. They still required parliamentary ratification, after which the closed Armenia-Turkey border would be opened within two months and the intergovernmental commission established within three months.

President Sarkisian flew to the scheduled Turkey-Armenia return soccer match in Bursa on October 14. It was a tightly controlled occasion in which all seats had been allocated in advance and the sale of Azerbaijani flags had been banned, which sparked anger in the Turkish media. White doves were released above the pitch. Abdullah Gül again gave his personal backing to the process, saying, "We are not writing history. We are making history."[22]

But the process looked to have stretched both sides to their limits. Sarkisian had ridden out the Diaspora storm—even though he was still being assailed for "surrender" or "one of the biggest blunders in Armenian history." In Yerevan, there was still some criticism, but he could be sure that a compliant parliament would ratify the two Protocols as soon as he wanted them to. Some Armenian officials urged Sarkisian to submit them for immediate ratification, so as to keep up the momentum. But he decided on the more cautious approach of having the two parliaments ratify them in tandem. Nor were Armenian officials pro-active in publicly promoting or endorsing the Protocols.[23]

In January 2010, Armenia's Constitutional Court issued a legal judgment on the Protocols, a requirement for them to be submitted to parliament for ratification. The judgment noted that the documents were in accordance with Armenia's Declaration of Independence of August 1990. Turkey's foreign ministry objected that the Declaration of Independence explicitly aspired to recognition of the Armenian Genocide and that the court had therefore introduced a new pre-condition. The Armenians dismissed this argument as a pretext for inaction by Turkey. Both sides accused the other of bad faith.

However, the fatal issue was Nagorny Karabakh. Turkish Prime Minister Erdoğan again raised the question of Azerbaijan's claims within 24 hours of the Zurich ceremony. He told a meeting of party officials on October 11, "We want all the borders to be opened at the same time . . . , but as long as Armenia has not withdrawn from Azerbaijani territory that it is occupying, Turkey cannot have a positive attitude on this subject." At the same time, Azerbaijan put Erdoğan under more pressure, by signing a gas deal with Russia and threatening to renegotiate planned gas sales to Turkey.

Erdoğan and Davutoğlu made public appeals to Washington to put pressure on both parties to win progress on Karabakh—but their statements made the Armenians more intransigent. In December 2009, at a meeting in Athens, in the words of one US official, "the Armenians slammed on the brakes" on Karabakh and Foreign Minister Nalbandian refused even to accept a copy of a latest draft document. The following month, President Sarkisian arrived for the next trilateral summit with Medvedev and Aliev in Sochi with a much tougher position. The meeting was a failure. The problem for the Armenian president was that it was hard for him to be seen to be making concessions on his "number one" issue, Karabakh, under pressure from Turkey—domestic opinion in Armenia would accuse him of betrayal.

In April 2010, President Obama invited both Erdoğan and Sarkisian to his Nuclear Summit in Washington in a last attempt to save the normalization process. President Aliev of Azerbaijan was conspicuously not invited. In a meeting at the White House, Erdoğan called for a limited withdrawal of Armenian forces from the occupied territories around Nagorny Karabakh, but Sarkisian repeated that he would not negotiate with Turkey on this issue.

On April 22, a year after the road map had been announced and two days before the annual April 24 commemorations, Sarkisian publicly announced that he was suspending Armenia's participation in the Protocols process. He publicly thanked President Gül for his cooperation, but he accused Turkey of dragging out a process without result.

The failure of the normalization process promised by the Protocols illustrated how vested interests had made untying the knot of Armenia-Turkey normalization much harder, 20 years after Armenia won independence in 1991.

No one benefited from the failure. Turkey still faced all the same disadvantages of having rejected rapprochement with Armenia, both in the Caucasus and internationally. Without a Turkey border opening, Armenia's foreign policy options were again limited, and Moscow took advantage. In August 2010, Armenia signed a new military agreement with Russia, deepening their military cooperation and extending the lease on the base in Gyumri until 2044. That guaranteed that Azerbaijan also gained no new traction it is dispute with Armenia. All the main leaders involved won some short-term political advantage for the stance they had taken. But distrust predominated. The Armenian foreign ministry cut off all but the highest-level contacts on the grounds that the only agenda item to discuss was the ratification of the Protocols. The unfortunate result was that, for all the new contacts between Armenian and Turkish societies, the new deadlock put state-to-state relations in a deeper freeze than they had been for 20 years.

# II

## Hidden Histories in Diyarbakir

ARMEN DEMIRJIAN PULLED THE rope, and the bell of Saint Giragos Church clanked one hundred feet above us in its belfry in a still blue sky. It was five o'clock on a September afternoon, and I had returned to Diyarbakir to dig deeper into its hidden histories.

The flagstones of the courtyard were a haven in the noise of the town. A slow stream of visitors came to look at the reopened Armenian church, buy books, and drink tea. A balding Armenian wearing a gold necklace, who had returned here from Los Angeles, plucked notes from an instrument shaped like a half-pear, called the *ud*.

Everywhere, showing guests into the church, serving tea, sweeping the courtyard, selling books and watering the flowers, was Armen, one of two men looking after the church. Small, wiry, and gregarious, Armen (Figure 11.1) was the dynamo that kept the place whirring.

Armen was not his given name. When I persuaded the church deacon and caretaker to pause, he told me his story. "Till the age of 25, I did not know I was Armenian," he said. He was now 52. He had grown up in the town of Lice. His mother was Kurdish, his father an Islamized Armenian, who hid his identity all his life from his children. "My father and mother talked in Kurdish. I thought I was Kurdish." Armen learned that he was Armenian only after his father's death. He

Figure 11.1 Armen Demirjian at Saint Giragos Armenian Church in Diyarbakir, September 2013.
Source: Thomas de Waal.

recalled episodes from his childhood, when people had taunted him. "When I grew up, people called me *filleh* [a derogatory word for an Armenian in Kurdish]. Later everything made sense."[1]

Armen kept his discovery to himself until the publication of *Agos* newspaper and visits by Hrant Dink to Diyarbakir. "Hrant was the turning point," he said. He scrolled through his mobile phone and proudly showed me the former editor's number, beginning with the digits 0533. "After his death, I decided to take risks. There is a limit to fear."

There are no secrets in this part of the world, if you persevere. The newly emboldened Armenian found out from old people in the town what his father's surname had been and began to call himself Armen Demirjian. His Muslim name was still on his Turkish government ID card, but he said, "I don't want you to write it down! I am proud of my new identity." Armen also sought out and eventually found his Armenian relations: two cousins were in Amsterdam, another in Marseilles. One relative had become an antiques dealer in New York.

When the church in Diyarbakir was restored and reopened in 2011, the position there became vacant. Armen dropped his job as a driver and came here. The church was his life and he worked 13-hour days. He assiduously asked every visitor to donate a few coins to make up the remaining shortfall in the restoration budget. He was indignant that, with so many wealthy Armenians around the world, so few of them had wanted to contribute to the restoration fund of the largest Armenian church in the greater Middle East.

"Where is Kim Kardashian?" he asked.

For two days, one of the shiny walnut tables in the church courtyard became my office—the most pleasant one you can imagine. I was introduced to locals from Diyarbakir who had stories to tell and views to offer. Every now and again, Armen brought tea in a slender-waisted glass, inscribed with a picture of the church, keeping careful tally of the bill over the course of the day. It was quiet, except for when the bell sounded twice a day and the noise of the call to prayer from the next-door mosque weaved its way through the courtyard.

Gaffur Ohanian runs the church foundation. He told me that up until the Turkish invasion of Cyprus in 1974 there had been a small community of Armenians—around 50 or 60 families—in the area of narrow alleys around the church known as the "*Gavur* [Infidel] Neighborhood." Most of them left when the Cyprus conflict broke out. A crowd chanted the menacing slogan, "*Ya Kıbrıs'ın yarısı ya Agop'un karısı,*" meaning, "Either half of Cyprus or the wife of Agop [an Armenian name]."

A few Armenians clung on until the next disaster, the scorched-earth counterinsurgency campaign by the Turkish state against the Kurdish guerrillas of the PKK, which began in 1992. Hundreds of villages were destroyed and people uprooted. At that point, the last Armenian priest left and the church began falling down. Within a few years, it was a ruin.

"THIS PLACE HAS BECOME a center of attraction," said Gaffur. His family had moved to Diyarbakir 25 years before. Two generations back, the

Ohanians were wealthy landowners, but they were almost all wiped out in the Catastrophe. His family was dispersed across the world, "like little pieces of pomegranate scattered all over the place."

Since the church opened in Diyarbakir, Armenians have been tentatively coming out of the shadows. This is a part of a big phenomenon over the last decade in Turkey: almost a century after the Armenian Genocide, enormous numbers of people in Anatolia have begun to own up to Armenian roots.[2]

In 1915, tens of thousands of Armenian women and children were violently abducted or voluntarily surrendered to live with Kurdish and Turkish families. Missionaries reported on their losses; eyewitnesses recalled parting with them forever. From around 1920, these women and children disappeared entirely from view. They lost their Armenian names and identities and converted to Islam. Most subsequently hid the truth about their background from all but close family members.

The big implication of this is that there may be hundreds of thousands of people in what is now central eastern Turkey who know they have Armenian family roots. The anthropologist Leyla Neyzi says that when she did field research with a team of students, collecting interviews on people's memories around Diyarbakir, "[w]e couldn't find a family who didn't have some kind of Armenian relative."[3]

In Diyarbakir, bearing Kurdish names, speaking no Armenian, sometimes only dimly aware of their family history, these people came to the newly restored church, evidently feeling it was a place where they belonged and could feel pride in being Armenian. Six or seven hundred people came to the first Easter service at Saint Giragos in 2011, of whom only a tiny number were practicing Christians—most of the rest were Islamized Armenians, some open about their identity, some not. Afterward, they held a traditional Armenian dinner of the famous Diyarbakir lamb stew and consumed 100 kilograms of meat.

Gaffur introduced me to several of these Armenians, and they came and sat at my table in the courtyard and told their stories. All were still midway in a difficult process of "coming out" as Armenians and said that people they worked with or knew well did not know about their true identity. I therefore decided not to give their names.

A middle-aged teacher shared the tale of his family. In 1915, his father, who was 10 years old, had run away when the family was deported.

He took refuge in a Kurdish village where he learned to become a leather-worker and saddle-maker and was adopted by a local *sheikh*. The teacher's father became a Kurd on the outside. He told his children they were Armenian—but mainly as a warning. "During my childhood, when fighting with kids, whether right or wrong, my father beat us up for fighting with Kurds—'We have no one else, how dare you fight? We are all alone, how dare you?'"

There was an air of sadness about my interlocutor. He said that it was still easy not to tell others that he was Armenian. "I am not able to overcome the worry." But the church helped. "I'm neither Muslim nor Christian. Before it was renovated I came here every Sunday, I felt I am coming to the place that my grandparents visited. I feel at peace, I am sharing the place with my grandfathers."

He endorsed Hrant Dink's vision that the most important goal was civil rights and a democratic Turkey. "We don't want anything special for Armenians. It will be enough if Turkey becomes a democracy. Every ethnic group will be better, including Armenians and Turks."

Another teacher came and sat at my table. He carefully laid out his family story, piece by piece. He came from a village named Askar northeast of Diyarbakir. Both of his parents were Islamized Armenians. They married after being matched up by older women through "secret signals" that indicated they were suitable Armenian marriage material. "I first learnt about 1915 from my grandmother, I never knew my grandfather. She said the village used to be inhabited by Armenians, they used swords to decimate us."

He went to school only at the age of 10. "Of course we were discriminated against because we were not Muslim. People called us *filleh Askare*. But there was no physical violence, just abuse. In response to this bullying behavior, my grandmother used to say, 'Even if a Kurd is a lovely red apple in your pocket, you must still cut your pocket, so the apple falls out.'"

I asked him what was the hardest part about growing up as an Armenian. His answer was poignant. "An absence of stories. When I started high school, I realized the other children all had stories, fairy tales, legends, songs, but I felt the lack of all this culture. My mother and family never raised me with this unique culture. Others shared common stories, you didn't."

He did not know if his parents did not know the Armenian traditions or had simply failed to pass them on. "It was hard not having a single song or story that belongs to me. The only thing that I could associate myself with was the traumatic story. We didn't even learn a childhood game from our parents. Maybe their childhood was so tragic that they forgot how to play."

FOR THREE GENERATIONS, TURKEY's Armenians were like a secret society, unable to tell their stories. Even those in Istanbul lay low, despite keeping the Christian faith and the Armenian language.

From around the 1970s, a younger generation began to put the pieces together again. Dikran Altun, a businessman born in Erzurum, now resident in Istanbul, told me some of his family stories. I was moved by the story of his father-in-law. In 1915, at the age of four, he was being deported to Syria by train with his mother and sister. He got out in the desert, played with some rocks—and the train left without him, separating him from his mother and sister forever. He was taken in by a Bedouin, before being adopted by an Armenian family. "Our grandfathers or even our parents did not want to talk about this. They started to talk about this 20, 30 years ago. After Hrant, every family started talking about this."[4]

In his twenties, Altun traced two missing uncles and began to reassemble his own broken family. Altun's grandmother, who came from Kayseri in central Anatolia, had lost her two eldest sons in 1915. Her first husband was killed and then she was separated from the children during the deportations. She managed to stay in Turkey, while they were taken by an American orphanage to Aleppo. After World War I, she remarried and had four more children, including Altun's father.

As a student in Beirut, Altun began to look for his uncles from his mother's first marriage. Through Beirut Armenians who came from their home village, he learned that the younger uncle, Tatul Torosian, had emigrated to San Francisco. He contacted the Armenian church there, and they located his uncle. In 1973, Altun flew to San Francisco and brought his Uncle Tatul to Istanbul to be reunited with his mother. He was now 58 and she was 85, and an entire life had gone by—they had last seen each other when he was one. "He had two brothers, two sisters living in Istanbul, he didn't have any idea." Did mother and son manage to reforge a relationship? I asked. Altun tried to put what he had seen into words, but found it hard. "If you don't see each other. . . . It was very sad. I cannot explain."

As for Altun's elder uncle, Aram Torosian, he had emigrated as a repatriate from Beirut to Soviet Armenia in one of the convoys of 1948. In 1991, Altun followed his trail, too, to the Armenian town of Ijevan— only to find that his uncle had died the year before. Altun found the widow and children—his cousins—but his mother and her elder son were never reunited.

Almost all Armenians in Turkey have stories like these. Had they been able to tell them earlier, it would have helped to breach the wall of silence and mendacity the Turkish state had erected around the Armenian issue. Armenians would have been humanized for the Turkish public.

In 2004, one book broke the barrier of silence. It was *Anneannem*, or *My Grandmother*, by Fethiye Çetin, a lawyer. She had been close to her maternal grandmother, Seher, having lived with her in childhood. In 1975, her grandmother, then aged 65, surprised her by saying that her parents and brother were in America and she wanted to find them. This made no sense to Çetin, who knew only that her great-grandparents were a Turkish army corporal and his wife. The truth was that the couple who had brought her grandmother up were not her real parents; she was Armenian, and her real name was Heranush Gadarian, not Seher. "What she told me did not fit with anything I knew. It turned the known world on its head, smashing my values into a thousand pieces."[5] Çetin strived to reunite her grandmother with her parents or brother, but she did not succeed in seeing them before she died and never met a sister born in the United States.

When her grandmother died in 2000 at the age of 95, Çetin decided to tell her story. She told me she was frustrated by the contrast between the arid fashion in which people in Turkey discussed the Armenian deportations—"It was a debate reduced to how many people were killed"—and the real story she knew. A friend of Hrant Dink, and also his lawyer, Çetin declined his invitation to publish the book with *Agos*, wanting to see it come out with a mainstream Turkish publisher. She also decided not to use the word "genocide" in the book so as to reach out to the general Turkish reader. "I decided to write this book, I didn't make any use of this 'G-word,' I just wanted to tell a human story, which I hoped would open another horizon for people."[6]

In *My Grandmother*, Fethiye Çetin tells the tale of how her grandmother slowly confided in her, interleaved with her grandmother's story itself. It was a slow unburdening. "We formed a special and very secret alliance. I sensed her longing to rid herself of the burden she had been carrying all these years—to open the curtains that hid her secret, to tell this story she had never shared with a soul—but I think she also knew that, having gone through life knowing none of it, I would find it deeply upsetting. She was protecting me."[7]

Later Çetin realized that she had missed clues about the life of Heranush/Seher, which might have alerted her to her Armenian identity. In Maden, every year her grandmother and several other women in the town would make the same *çörek*, a sweet braided pastry, decorated with eggs and dried cherry powder and fennel seeds, at the same time. They were, she later understood, a club of Armenian ladies secretly baking together for Easter.[8]

The story of Heranush's young life is heart-rending. She grew up in a village called Habab (or Palu) near the River Tigris. Her father had emigrated to work in America. In 1915, when she was 10, all the Armenian men in the village were rounded up and she, her mother, and the other women and children in the village were shut inside a church courtyard. A girl climbed up on someone else's shoulders to look over the high wall of the courtyard. When she came down, the girl said, "They're cutting the men's throats and throwing them into the river."

The women and children were then sent on a deportation march. The elderly and infirm and those who lagged behind were killed on the road. When the convoy reached the town of Maden, two of her cousins could no longer keep up. Heranush's grandmother threw them in the River Tigris and then drowned herself. Two Muslim men wanted to take Heranush and her brother away, but her mother refused. She and her brother then were seized and taken to different households. Her abductor was an Ottoman corporal named Colonel Hüseyin, who adopted her, bringing her up with kindness, although his wife treated her as a servant. Her brother eventually escaped to join his father and mother in America. Aged 15, she was married to a man from Maden.

Heranush's family in the United States found her, but after a period of communication, the connection was lost again. Fethiye Çetin tracked down her cousins in America only after her grandmother's death. She learned that when Heranush's father died in the United States in 1965, his other daughter found an old letter folded in four in his wallet. It was a letter that Heranush had sent to him in New York as a child, more than 50 years before.

*My Grandmother* came out in 2004. The initial print run of 3,000 sold out in three days. Çetin said she received "hundreds" of telephone calls and letters, very many of them from people who had similar family stories to hers. It was a catalyst for others to open up. "There was this great silence. But once the book was published, people started telling all these stories." In the next four years, at least eight more books came out, telling the stories of Islamized Armenian women in Turkey.[9]

AS ORDINARY PEOPLE IN Turkey felt they had permission to speak about the past, and the political environment became more tolerant, researchers began collecting oral histories in Anatolia. British journalist Christopher de Bellaigue lived for a year in the small town of Varto, northeast of Diyarbakir. He excavated layers of oral history, each of them filled with episodes of violence between Sunnis, Armenians, Alevis, and Kurds, from the early twentieth century to the war with the PKK in the 1990s. The Armenians were at the bottom of the pile. In the town, there were 10 surviving families of Islamized Armenians, whom everybody knew to be such, a "self-perpetuating subset" to whom local Sunnis would not marry their children. De Bellaigue writes, "there was no pride in this survival. The qualities that enabled one to escape death and carry on living in Anatolia were not heroic ones: guile; mendacity; opportunism; selfishness. Gold and a pretty daughter helped. So the eyes of the survivor do not sparkle as he recounts the story of his ancestors' escape."[10]

In Varto, people remembered well, de Bellaigue found, but selectively. Near the village of Emeran, a farmer pointed out to him some old pear trees and meadows that were still called after their Armenian owners, a century later: "Those trees were in Hagop's meadows, and those ones in Khoren's."[11] In June 1915, a great number of Varto's Armenians were massacred in a valley named Newala Ask. One morning, de Bellaigue set out for a walk near the town and two locals stopped him and engaged him in conversation, stopping him from going any further. Later he discovered that they had prevented him from walking into the Valley of Newala Ask, "where, it is said, the soil remains ashen from the bones of the dead."[12] De Bellaigue concludes:

> I learned the meaning of the past in a society whose members, until twenty or thirty years ago, had nothing to do at night except discuss the exploits of ancestors, to regale and sing. The fractures running through this society mean that dramatically different versions of history are being recounted in neighbouring valleys, even next-door houses. Occasionally in Varto, or among the *Vartolus* of the diaspora, you will meet a man or a woman who confesses that a close relative—a grandfather, say—committed an appalling crime. But this is the exception. In general *Vartolus* use the past to acquit their ancestors and string up their enemies.[13]

Leyla Neyzi, the Sabanci University anthropologist who has conducted several studies in different parts of Turkey, also urges caution about the uses of oral history. In contrast to the approach of some Armenian researchers, she believes that it is no longer possible to use oral histories for historical corroboration of the Armenian Genocide—because all the eyewitnesses are dead. We know what happened [to the Armenians]," says Neyzi, but "[t]here is no truth out there."

Neyzi and her team conducted 100 interviews in four different parts of Turkey. She decided that they needed to approach the subject of Armenians sideways because to this day in parts of Turkey, "the word Armenian is a very problematic word." (The phrase *ermeni dölü*, or "Armenian sperm," is still an insult). The interviewers tried not to introduce the word "Armenian" themselves but rather to stimulate their subjects into using it. "We would ask about craftsmen. We would ask about houses. We would ask about land, about agricultural practices in the past, heritage, everyday life in the past, neighbors, weddings, what could evoke personal stories about real Armenians."

Neyzi was interested in what had been transmitted down to ordinary people in Turkey about Armenians and 1915, despite years of state directives on history.

There was a contradiction between the way [they] talked about the local situation and the way they generalized, because of how Turkish people are stuck between what was lived locally and the knowledge of it, and what they are taught at school and through the media. They had overall very positive stories and vivid stories about Armenian people and their relations with them, their forebears' relations with them. So generally it was fine, everything was good and so on at the local level. And they didn't want to talk about how is it was that things changed. So there was a silence about what happened and how it happened. So there was no agent. There was a silence there—and somehow the Armenians left.

One interviewee in the town of Divriği, a 70-year-old retired teacher named Necmi, was a good storyteller, with many tales about former Armenian neighbors. But his retelling of his father's story of the day of the Armenian deportations in 1915 seemed to conceal some painful silences. Necmi told his interviewer:

And my father used to say, "We woke up one morning and there weren't any Armenians left in Divriği. We went into the houses and they just stood empty. In one of the houses, the dinner table was set, with a soup pot with spoons around it." It seems that the order came so suddenly. In the marketplace it was announced: "Let the Armenians gather." They said, "It was announced, the town crier cried, the shops were closed. They took the Armenians behind the municipality. We don't know what happened. Everyone ran to their homes. We don't know what happened afterwards." We can't find the witnesses of that moment.[14]

IN CONTEMPORARY TURKEY OF 2015, the collective memory and perception of Armenians is evidently very different in different places. In parts of middle-class Istanbul, it has become normal, even fashionable, to know about Armenian culture and to claim Armenian roots.

In Turkey's provinces, Leyla Neyzi says that she and her team came on great variations of narrative in different places. In central Anatolia, they found the most confusion and contradictions, with narratives such as the story above. In Van, the scene of the Armenian-Ottoman warfare of 1915, there was "hatred, it was much more black and white, there was fear that the Armenians are going to come back."

In Diyarbakir and other Kurdish areas of southeastern Turkey, society has opened up the most and has dug the deepest into the past. There are divisions between old-fashioned and more Islamic Kurds, and politicized and more secular Kurds. Representing the latter and the left-wing Kurdish party, the BDP, the two elected mayors in Diyarbakir, Osman Baydemir and Abdullah Demirbaş have sponsored a comprehensive outreach campaign to Armenians. This has included an apology to Armenians by the party, the opening of a memorial called "Collective Conscience," the rebuilding of St. Giragos church, and the sponsoring of Armenian-language classes.

This campaign comes under a general ideology of multiculturalism, which the BDP uses to challenge the Turkish state in its bid for Kurdish autonomy. Demirbaş said, "When we started restoring the church, the mosque, the synagogue, we were aiming to restore not just buildings but a mentality. When we recruit staff to the municipality, we need them to know another language. Our aim is to make people protect their own language. We fire people who practice hate speech."[15]

The narrative of 1915 and the Kurds' role in the killings have been reframed to anticipate that the Kurds would be the next victim of the centralized state, after the Armenians. A direct thread is drawn between 1915 and the persecution of Kurds in 1925, 1937, and the 1990s. Demirbaş said:

> The state used the Kurds to achieve two things at once. The state used religion. They issued a Fatwa that whoever kills a *filleh* will go to heaven. We believe the Kurds were used as killers in this operation. These Kurds did not have an awareness of their own Kurdishness, they betrayed both Christians and themselves. Some of them also attacked Yezidi Kurds and Alevis. During the Dersim slaughter [of 1937], Kurds were also used. So we say the sovereign state used one group of people against another.

The stance is still controversial with some, said Sehmuş Diken, a well-known Kurdish historian in Diyarbakir. Others had objected when he had signed the "I Apologize" petition in 2008:

When I put my signature on it, some Kurdish intellectuals criticized me and said it was the Turkish state which conducted the Genocide and that the Kurds were only used as hired killers. I told them that we should put our signatures on it because it is a confrontation with the past. Then, if one day we have a state called Kurdistan it can't be established on the basis of denial. If Kurds played a role in the Genocide, the Great Catastrophe, we need to put it on the table.

Diken is one of those excavating the past. He knows the history of the *gavur* neighborhood, the labyrinth of narrow streets around the Armenian Apostolic Church in Diyarbakir, which is the city's old Christian quarter, better than anyone. On a bright fall morning, he walked me through the cobbled alleyways, some the width of a span of two arms, pointing out clues and details of its past. There were bell pulls and metal door knockers in the shape of birds that denoted old Christian houses. There is an old Chaldean (Assyrian) church in the neighborhood, beautifully kept but now a parish to only a dozen or so people. We saw the old Armenian Catholic church, now a weavers' workshop.

Our walk ended at the domed Armenian Protestant church, its cavernous space surrounded by first-story galleries. In 1925, when the Armenians had gone, Diken explained, spectators had looked down from these galleries at the show trial of Sheikh Said, the Kurdish tribal leader who led an uprising against the new Turkish state. Sheikh Said and 46 of his comrades were found guilty and publicly hanged. After its role as a courthouse, the old church then turned into a silent movie theater.

Now both the Armenian Protestant and Catholic churches in the old town are scheduled for reopening, despite the small number of Armenians who can actually use them. It is another hopeful sign in Diyarbakir. But the question remains of whether this "Armenian opening" can spread to other areas of Turkey or will be limited to the Kurdish regions. The outing of the hidden histories of the Armenians is still strongest in a place that calls itself "Kurdistan."

# 12

## Two Memorials in Istanbul

TWO MEMORIALS ARE SITUATED not far from each other in the district of Şişli in the center of Istanbul. The gate of the Armenian cemetery is easy to miss, but it opens to a broad space, orderly and well kept, thick with cypresses and cedars. The Marriott Hotel towers above. Paths paved with white and violet marble chips lead through a stone city of tombs and family mausoleums. The alleys are lined with sculpted figures of Istanbul notables—parliamentarians, actors, musicians, and footballers—with their names and stories recorded in both Armenian and Turkish.

In the middle of the cemetery stands a memorial to the poet Daniel Varoujan (1884–1915). He sports a trim mustache and neat necktie and seems to be stroking his chin in meditation. Varoujan's murder, at the age of 31, was one of the greatest losses for the Armenians. He was one of the Armenian leaders arrested in this city on April 24, 1915 and was killed four months later. He had been hailed as the great Armenian lyric poet of his generation.

Less than a mile away lies a semi-abandoned park next to an eight-lane highway, in the shadow of the Florence Nightingale Hospital and Istanbul's Hall of Justice. No one comes here, and the caretaker had to open a creaking gate to let two visitors in. Trash was strewn about. This was once a famous landmark, and the Monument to Liberty in the middle of the park, a broken obelisk, was erected in 1911 to honor Young Turk warriors. Around it are eight tombs. One of them is a 10-foot high marble arch, inscribed with the name of Talat Pasha (1874–1921). The Young Turk leader was reburied here in 1943, when his body was brought back from Berlin. Nearby is his comrade, the fiery minister of war Enver Pasha.

These two memorial sites, within walking distance of one another, say something about the schizophrenia of modern Turkey regarding its past. On the one hand, an Armenian poet killed in 1915 is memorialized, along with hundreds of his ethnic kin. On the other, the man who ordered the poet's arrest and murder—and directed one of the twentieth century's worst atrocities—is also still afforded a memorial, albeit one kept in far worse condition.

Since 2000, Turkey has begun seriously to address the blank spots in its past and the issue of its lost former citizens, the Armenians, Assyrians, and Greeks, as well as the rights of the Kurds. In Istanbul and Ankara, an urban class is conversant with these issues. They may buy a copy of Elif Shafak's novel *The Bastard of Istanbul*, which reflects on the Armenian deportations, or listen to a CD of the Armenian musician Armen Gasparian playing with his Turkish counterpart Erkun Ogur. Bookstores stock books that use the term "Armenian Genocide"— one written by the grandson of the Unionist leader Cemal Pasha. Anthropologist Leyla Neyzi compares the attitude of herself and her contemporaries on Turkish history to the generation who challenged state orthodoxy in Germany in the 1960s. "I converted my mother. She's converting her friends. Some of my friends think I'm betraying the country."

Sooner or later, as Turkey connects more to the world, it seems likely that Turkish society will come to terms with the vexing issue of how up to 2 million native Armenians "went missing" at the end of the Ottoman Empire. Turkey would be following the example of the United States, in its recognition of its legacy of slavery and the slaughter of Native Americans, or British and French officials who acknowledge crimes that their countries committed in colonial times. Cengiz Aktar likens nationalist Turkey's futile attempts to forget the issue to the denouement of the plot of a French crime thriller, quoting the phrase, "The dead body is too heavy to keep in the wardrobe." (In French, *"Le cadavre est trop grand pour tenir dans l'armoire."*)

Yet, for descendants of Ottoman Armenians, there is frustration that this is happening too slowly. Commenting on the changes in Turkey ahead of the 2015 centenary, one Armenian, from Diyarbakir but living in New Jersey, observed, "For the Turks 100 years is too soon, for us it is too late."

In 2004, Hrant Dink wrote, "Turks and Armenians and the way they see each other constitute two clinical cases: Armenians with their trauma, Turks with their paranoia." Armenians' trauma has been transmitted through the generations. While private grief for family members lost in 1915 has been constant, public expression of the loss has changed radically over time. The story might have closed in 1919, when Armenians regathered in Constantinople and spoke publicly about the slaughter, and the first trials of former Unionist perpetrators were held. That process ended before it could deliver a sense of justice. Then the Catastrophe began to recede from the world's memory as Armenians were dispersed and two regimes were established in Turkey and the Soviet Union, both based on organized forgetting. From the 1930s Diaspora, Armenians themselves suppressed the issue, fighting a bitter political feud over the legitimacy of Soviet Armenia. When Armenians mobilized in public in the 1940s, it was on the encouragement of Stalin around the issue of territorial claims against Turkey.

When private grief and public politics came together again, around the time of the fiftieth anniversary of the deportations in 1965, it transpired that the trauma was still strong. Occasionally, the Armenian press published a brave call to stop grieving. In an essay in 1977 entitled, "The Time for Crying Has Passed," Elise Antreassian urged, "The time for crying is past. It is time to grapple with this immobilizing grief and harness its power to do a job that would truly honor the memory of all our martyrs."[1] If that call failed, on a collective Armenian level at least, it was in large part because of a feeling of affront from Turkey. In 1980, at the height of the terror attacks against Turkish targets, the Armenian author Michael J. Arlen condemned the Armenian assassins unequivocally, but also sought to explain why this old historical wound was still so fresh. He compared his ethnic kin to traumatized survivors of a 60-year-old hit-and-run car accident:

They do themselves no favor by assassinating Turkish officials; the murder of innocent persons is just what it sounds like and victims become no less victimized for being linked to some abstract political or national generality by their murderers. On the other hand, if some Armenians are still walking around, decades after the original car crash, with a crazy look in their eyes, perhaps it has something to do with the fact that the other car, after knocking over nearly one million people, turned to be a hit-and-run job. Maybe, one of these days, the descendants from the Turkish car will come forward and at least admit that the dreadful business took place; and then the descendants from the Armenian car can begin to escape from the prison of their "revenge" and stop dreaming murderous dreams— and, better still, stop acting them out.[2]

Turkey's official refusal to acknowledge the crimes of 1915 tied Armenians and Turks together. To quote Hrant Dink again, "It is evident that the 'Turk' is both the poison and antidote of the Armenian identity."[3] Armenian public organizations felt the need to prove and shame Turkey into facing up to what its Ottoman predecessors had done. On April 24, the centerpiece of most commemorations is still not a ceremony of mourning for the Armenian dead but a demonstration in front of the Turkish embassy or consulate.

Turkey's slowness to change—until recent times—is a reflection of the second part of Hrant Dink's formulation: that its clinical condition is paranoia. Turkey has been said to possess the Sèvres Syndrome, named after the treaty that was never ratified in 1920, describing the fear that the state is vulnerable to dismemberment by the Great Powers. Militant Armenians twice contributed to reviving this siege mentality, once with Stalin's territorial claims on Turkey on behalf of Armenia and Georgia in 1945, and later with the ASALA and Justice Commandos terror attacks of the 1970s. The angry reaction of some Turkish politicians to Armenian Genocide resolutions in the parliaments of latter-day "Great Power" nations, such as France and the United States, speaks of the same siege syndrome. Typically, at the points of greatest insecurity in the twentieth century, in the 1940s, 1950s, and 1970s, Turkey's minorities, including Armenians, have suffered. Istanbul Armenian Dikran Altun comments, "To see such a small minority as a threat means they don't have self-confidence. If you have self-confidence why should you be afraid of a 0.1 percent minority?"[4]

TURKS SOMETIMES ASK THE rather naïve question, "What do Armenians want?" There are almost as many answers to this as there are Armenians. In the documentary film *Twenty Voices*, the Canadian-Armenian filmmaker Araz Artinian asks her elderly interviewees what they would like from Turkey. One of them, an old lady named Armine Dedekian, says, "Nothing," then adds, "My youth."[5]

Dikran Altun, both an ethnic Armenian and a Turkish citizen, answers the question by contrasting his own view with that of those American-Armenians who say they want reparations:

In Burun my grandfather had a vineyard. When a general asked me "What do you want as an Armenian?" I said "I don't want anything but when I am passing through Burun, I want to eat some grapes from there." So if as a Turkish citizen, I want to eat some grapes, US citizens of Armenian origin will ask for compensation. So the biggest problem is the compensation and . . . I do not want any compensation because to take compensation means to sell our grandfathers' blood for money. I don't want that compensation. The only thing that I want from Turks is to recognize what they have done. Even if they offer compensation I will not take that money.

Others have put together a list of measures that would mark symbolic gestures by the Turkish state toward reconciliation with Armenians, both past and present. These include offering Turkish citizenship to the descendants of Ottoman Armenians; the removal of Talat Pasha street signs and memorials to officials associated with the Armenian deportations; working to restore some of the hundreds of ruined Armenian churches on Turkish soil, as well as the city of Ani; and rewriting school textbooks to record a more equitable version of what happened in the late Ottoman period.

Bigger steps require greater political will. In 2014, full normalization of Armenian-Turkish relations appeared to be still dependent on the agreement of Azerbaijan, which has its own interests, insecurities, and

traumas. The analysis that the current deadlock hurts all three countries has still not persuaded Baku to lift its de facto veto over Ankara.

In April 2014, Prime Minister Recep Tayip Erdoğan issued a
statement of condolences to the Armenians. It said more than any
Turkish leader had said previously, declaring, "We wish that the
Armenians who lost their lives in the context of the early twentieth
century rest in peace, and we convey our condolences to their grandchildren." As the historian Ronald Suny has pointed out, this put
an end to the old nationalist narrative that Armenians were "traitors," as you do not offer condolences to traitors. But what was a big
step for a Turkish leader was only a small beginning as far as most
Armenians were concerned: they still held out for a formal apology
from the Turkish state.

Armenians in the Republic of Armenia and the Diaspora have
shown that they have different goals. These differences go back to the
time of the 1918 First Republic and the Paris Peace Conference, when
the ARF government and Ottoman Armenians could not agree on a
common agenda. Since Levon Ter-Petrosian became leader of Armenia
in 1990, he and other leaders have had the same goal: to normalize relations between Armenia and Turkey without pre-conditions. Building
a viable state in Armenia is the top priority, and that requires a rapprochement with Turkey. These tensions between the Diaspora and
Yerevan emerged again during the negotiation of the Protocols, when
the government of Armenia saw the formation of some kind of historical commission as a price worth paying for the opening of the border;
for critics in the Diaspora, however, it was a price too high to pay,
on the grounds that it would be a ruse intended to cast doubt on the
authenticity of the Genocide.

The proposal for a "sub-commission on the historical dimension,"
as agreed in the Zurich Protocols, may have been a clever diplomatic
device that allowed Turkey to sell the agreement to the Turkish public
and to open a new phase of debate on the "Armenian Question." But
it also looked like an outmoded answer to the problem. It promised
to form a group of "lawyer-historians" to make a political adjudica-
tion on an issue about which scholars from both countries, such as the
Workshop on Armenian/Turkish Scholarship, had already been writing sophisticated analysis for years.

As observed in Chapter 3, the history of Anatolia and the Caucasus of 1914–1921 is still awaiting its version of *Bloodlands*, the boundary-crossing book by Timothy Snyder that covers all parts of Eastern Europe between 1933 and 1945 and the interconnected traumas and horrors of the region. Armenians should not be afraid of such a project, as the Genocide of 1915–1916 would stand out as the biggest atrocity of this period; yet it would also establish a context that would allow others to come to terms with what happened and why, and also pay homage to the many Muslims who died tragically in this era. A young Turkish scholar might be up to the challenge of such a book, given the emergence of a new generation of Turkish academics who write without fear about the Armenian Genocide and the late Ottoman period. This is one of the most hopeful phenomena of the last few years. For all the imperfections of Turkish democracy, it is a good omen of things to come.

By contrast, there is a paucity of good historical writing from the Republic of Armenia—a result of Armenia's continued democratic deficit. Many Armenian publications simplify Armenia's history, employing Turcophobic language that is just as racist as Turkish nationalist writing on the Armenians and placing Armenian-Turkish relations only within the framework of genocide. In 1997, the head of Armenia's Academy of Sciences, Fadey Sarkisian, wrote a letter to the president of UNESCO, objecting to UNESCO's plans to mark the 700th anniversary of the Ottoman Empire. He wrote, "In its 700 years—the Ottoman Empire oppressed and planted seeds of fear in its neighbors—eliminating their cultures beginning with the Greek Byzantines. The climax of the Ottoman barbaric policies came with the 1915 Genocide of the Armenians in the Empire."[6] Yet by objecting to a commemoration of Ottoman culture, Sarkisian was also denigrating the achievements of famous Armenian Ottomans such as the architect Mimar Sinan or the inventor of the cymbals, Avedis Zildjian.

SINCE THE 1960S, ARMENIAN public consciousness has crystallized around "genocide," a word with totemic power. The disputes about the use of the word have become an issue within an issue and have taken on a life of their own.

As Chapter 6 shows, from the late 1940s Armenians and others embraced the word as something that encapsulated their experience—and the coiner of the word, Raphael Lemkin, endorsed the Armenians' cause. Since then, "genocide" has had a troubled history. The definition adopted in the United Nations convention of 1948 has ambiguities that international lawyers have argued over ever since. Devised in the aftermath of the murder of the European Jews with the noble message of "never again," the term "genocide" was debased by its use as propaganda in the Cold War. Anti-Soviet Diaspora Armenians were among those who fired the charge of genocide at the Soviet Union.

From the 1970s, Armenian Diaspora organizations promoted the cause of genocide recognition in parliaments around the world. Those who led the campaigns in the United States say that they were a peaceful tool which mobilized the Armenian community, reminded the US government of the history of 1915, and put pressure on the Turkish government. And it is true that the Turkish government's outreach to Armenians appears in part to be a response to a desire to remove the millstone of genocide resolutions from around its neck.

It is also clear that the term "genocide" was the cause of unforeseen consequences that Lemkin and others had not anticipated. From the 1960s, Armenians jostled for attention with other groups around the world that had experienced collective historical trauma, from Palestinians to Native Americans to Tibetans. With the word "genocide" enshrined as the "crime of crimes," these groups naturally aspired to have the term applied to them as well.

The Armenians have used the phrase "the Forgotten Genocide" to describe their tragedy and the phrase is in the title of several books about 1915. But at the same time, Assyrians could claim with some legitimacy that theirs is a "forgotten genocide"—and it is certainly less well known than the story of the Armenians. The Herero of Namibia have told the world that in 1904 they were the victims of the "first genocide of the 20th century," at the hands of German colonialists—a phrase sometimes used to refer to the Armenians.[7] These definitional disputes have pushed some analysts into the morally problematic exercise of creating hierarchies and categories of suffering. It is good to bear in mind the rebuke of the Israeli scholar of the Holocaust and the Armenian Genocide, Israel Charny:

> I object very strongly to the efforts to name the genocide of any people as the single, ultimate event, or as the most important event against which all other tragedies of genocidal mass death are to be tested and found wanting. . . . For me, the passion to exclude this or that mass killing from the universe of genocide, as well as the intense competition to establish the exclusive "superiority" or unique form of any one genocide ends up creating a fetishistic atmosphere in which the masses of bodies that are not to be qualified for the definition of genocide are dumped into a conceptual black hole, where they are forgotten.[8]

Genocide is real—and it is also used for political purposes. As Tzvetan Todorov has written, "If it can be convincingly shown that a group has been the victim of a past injustice, the group in question obtains a bottomless line of moral credit. The greater the crime in the past, the more compelling the rights in the present—which are gained merely through membership in the wronged group."[9]

This process is visible in the Caucasus, where the trauma of 1915 has impacted the more recent Armenian-Azerbaijani conflict over Nagorny Karabakh. Azerbaijanis have asserted that they were the victims of a "genocide" committed by Armenians near the town of Khojali in 1992, in an effort to oppose their own genocide to that of 1915. The killing of Azerbaijani civilians by Armenians at Khojali is better described as a "war crime" than "genocide." But some of the arguments and evasions that Armenians have used to deny it or minimize what happened in Khojali are uncomfortably reminiscent of the tactics of which they have rightly accused "denialist" Turks.

In the United States, the use or non-use of the word "genocide" has also come to define the Armenian issue. On April 24, 2010, President Barack Obama gave an annual statement honoring the Armenian dead of 1915:

> On this solemn day of remembrance, we pause to recall that ninety-five years ago one of the worst atrocities of the 20th century

began. In that dark moment of history, 1.5 million Armenians were massacred or marched to their death in the final days of the Ottoman Empire.

Today is a day to reflect upon and draw lessons from these terrible events. I have consistently stated my own view of what occurred in 1915, and my view of that history has not changed. It is in all of our interest to see the achievement of a full, frank and just acknowledgment of the facts. The Meds Yeghern is a devastating chapter in the history of the Armenian people, and we must keep its memory alive in honor of those who were murdered and so that we do not repeat the grave mistakes of the past.[10]

This dignified statement earned the president a withering response from the Armenian National Committee of America (ANCA): "In yet another disgraceful capitulation to Turkey's threats, President Obama today once again failed to properly recognize the Armenian Genocide, offering euphemisms and evasive terminology to characterize this crime against humanity."[11]

The ANCA's angry response would surely have baffled Armenian survivors of the 1915 deportations, which they called *Medz Yeghern*, had they been able to read it. Yet, despite a thoughtful statement that went further than US presidents before him, President Obama had set himself up for this protest. As a candidate, he had promised Armenians to use the word "genocide" if elected president—a promise that he did not keep.

The US government has hung itself on a nail on the genocide issue, with formulations that satisfy neither the Armenian Diaspora nor the Turkish government. As narrated in Chapter 7, the issue was handled clumsily, and the Reagan administration drew a thick red line in 1982, which has hemmed in official policy ever since. The Turkey-US military relationship is so strong that it is hard to imagine Washington using the word "genocide" if it elicits any threat to American military personnel in Turkey.

Both the Turkish government and its assailants have become invested in an all-or-nothing effort to prevent or adopt the use of the "G-word." This is the case even though most legal analyses, including that commissioned by the International Center for Transitional Justice (ICTJ), conclude that the UN genocide convention of 1948 had no retroactive force. It is an issue of pride and respect. Most Turks, given their own difficult history, instinctively reject a label that, in their eyes, equates the actions of their grandfathers with those of the Nazis. For their part, Armenians have come to believe that no other term can deliver "justice" for the sufferings of their own grandparents.

This battle has costs. One of them is that it risks making the real experiences of 1915 an abstraction. Halil Berktay is one of the first Turkish historians to use the term "Armenian Genocide," but he also states that the term does not have much application in academic history. Berktay suggests that making the discussion into a debate about "genocide" is useful for Turkish statists:

> When it boils down to a question of "Was it genocide or not?" if you don't use the word you are a denialist, as far as Armenians are concerned. If you use the word you are a traitor as far as the Turkish establishment is concerned. And in fact die-hards on both sides have acquired a vested interest in keeping the discussion to that word. And I think Turkish denialism likes this. It finds it easier to defend itself against so-called slanders about genocide than against a detailed analysis of how the deportations and massacres were organized and orchestrated et cetera et cetera.[12]

One effect of this is that Armenians have engaged in their own campaigns to "prove" the Armenian Genocide evidentially, with photographs and documents. It is as though, almost 100 years later, they are still registering a crime scene with bodies, surrounded by yellow tape—hardly an environment conducive to mourning.

The Armenian scholar and literary critic Marc Nichanian prefers to use the term "Catastrophe" instead of "Genocide" because he says that Armenians need to mourn, remember, and honor their grandparents, rather than use them as evidence in a courtroom. He writes, with David Kazanjian:

> By using the word "Genocide," we survivors are only repeating again and again the denial of the loss. We probably cannot help it. We are doing what the executioner wanted us to do, from the beginning

on. We claim all over the world that we have been "genocided": we relentlessly need to prove our own death. We are still in the claws of the executioner. We still belong to the logic of our executioner, through and through.[13]

What is to be done about this dilemma? The issue is bigger than Armenians and Turks. Some scholars argue that the concept of "genocide" should be phased out and that it is time to revive the more general and overarching concept of "Crimes against Humanity." In the Armenian case, it will be recalled that the phrase "Crimes against Humanity" was used in the famous démarche of March 1915 by Great Britain, France, and Russia, delivered in person to the Ottoman government by US ambassador Henry Morgenthau. The scholar of mass atrocities William Schabas says that the world needs a "Crimes against Humanity Convention," which would free prosecutors from the definitional and legal shackles imposed by the word "genocide" and thus allow more mass murderers to be brought to justice.[14]

For all the good sense this makes, this seems unlikely to happen. The word has acquired an aura. Even though the idea of "cultural genocide" was removed from the definition in the UN convention, contrary to Lemkin's advice, "genocide" is also taken to describe the destruction of a civilization, rather like the extinction of a species. For Armenians who in 1915 lost not only their homes but also their culture and ancient churches in their ancient homeland, that definition makes the word applicable to their experience.

Almost no one, it seems, admits to genocide. But the only other way forward requires that Turkey shed its paranoia about the implications of the word "genocide." This is a long-term aspiration that is more likely to come about through enhanced Armenian-Turkish dialogue than through confrontation. The word then could become normalized and acceptable throughout Turkish society, as it already has become for a small progressive group. Possibly, the day when Turkish society as a whole accepts the word "genocide" in relation to the Armenians is the day when the Genocide can become a Catastrophe again.

# GREAT CATASTROPHE CHRONOLOGY

| | |
|---|---|
| Around 301 | Traditional date of Armenia's conversion to Christianity. |
| Around 405 | Traditional date of invention of Armenian alphabet by Mesrop Mashtots. |
| 1375 | Fall of the Armenian kingdom of Cilicia. |
| 1514 | Division of Armenians between Ottoman and Persian empires. |
| 1828 | Eastern Armenian lands incorporated into Russian Empire by Treaty of Turkmenchai. |
| 1851 | First Ottoman novel, *Akabi Hikayesi*, published in Armeno-Turkish. |
| 1876 | Sultan Abdülhamid II accedes to the Ottoman throne. |
| 1878 | Under Treaty of Berlin, Ottoman authorities promise to protect Armenians. |
| 1890 | Armenian Revolutionary Federation (ARF), or Dashnaktsutiun, founded in Tiflis (Tbilisi). |
| 1894–1896 | "Hamidian" massacres of Armenians in eastern Anatolia. |
| 1896 August 26 | ARF militants raid Ottoman Bank in Constantinople. |

| 1908 | "Young Turk revolution" brings in constitutional rule in Ottoman Empire. |
| 1909 March–April | Failed counter-coup against the Young Turks, massacre of Armenians in Adana. |
| 1913 January 23 | Cemal, Enver, and Talat Pasha seize control of Ottoman government. |
| 1914 October 28 | Ottoman Empire enters World War I on side of Germany and Austro-Hungary. |
| 1914 December | Ottoman offensive against Russians ends in disaster at Sarakamiş. |
| 1915 | |
| April 24 | Arrest of Armenian leaders in Constantinople (most are later killed). |
| April 25 | Allied landings at Gallipoli. |
| May 23 | Russian forces enter city of Van. |
| May 24 | Great Britain, France, and Russia accuse Ottoman government of "crimes against humanity." |
| June 21 | Talat Pasha orders the deportation of all Armenians from eastern Ottoman provinces. |
| 1916 Summer | Mass killings of Armenians in Der Zor region of Syrian desert. |
| 1918 | |
| March 3 | Bolsheviks cede territory to Ottoman Empire at Treaty of Brest-Litovsk. |
| May 21 | Armenians halt Ottoman advance at Battle of Sardarapat near Yerevan. |
| May 28 | Armenia declares independence, following example of Georgia and Azerbaijan. |
| September | Ottoman military commander Halil Pasha visits Yerevan. |
| October 30 | Ottoman Empire concedes defeat to Allies at Armistice of Mudros. |
| 1919 | |
| January 18 | Paris Peace Conference opens. |
| March | First American food shipments from Near East Relief reach independent Armenia. |

| April 10 | Mehmed Kemal, former governor of Yozgat, hanged in Constantinople for crimes against Armenians after trial. |
| April 24 | First mourning ceremony for Armenians held in Constantinople. |
| May 19 | Mustafa Kemal lands at Samsun, begins Turkish War of Independence. |

**1920**

| February 10 | Turkish forces recapture town of Maraş. |
| August 10 | Treaty of Sèvres declares division of Ottoman Empire. |
| October 30 | Turkish forces capture Kars. |
| December 2 | First Armenian Republic falls to Bolsheviks. |

**1921**

| March 15 | Assassination of Talat Pasha in Berlin. |
| June 3 | Soghomon Tehlirian, assassin of Talat Pasha, acquitted by Berlin court. |
| October 13 | Treaty of Kars draws new Soviet-Turkish border. |
| 1922 November 1 | Office of Sultan abolished. |

**1923**

| July 24 | Treaty of Lausanne. |
| October 29 | Turkish Republic proclaimed, Mustafa Kemal (Atatürk) becomes first president. |

**1925**

| March | Sheikh Said Kurdish rebellion suppressed. |
| December 17 | Soviet-Turkish Friendship Treaty signed. |
| 1928 | Ottoman script abolished, replaced by Latin alphabet. |

**1933**

| July 1 | Armenian groups fight at World's Fair in Chicago. |
| November | Franz Werfel's *The Forty Days of Musa Dagh* published. |
| December 24 | Archbishop Leon Tourian assassinated in Holy Cross Cathedral, New York. |
| 1934 | Armenians and Greeks in Turkey forced to take Turkish surnames. |

1936

| | |
|---|---|
| July 9 | Armenian Communist Party leader Aghasi Khanjian murdered. |
| December 5 | Armenian Socialist Soviet Republic formed. |

1938 November 10    Mustafa Kemal Atatürk dies.

1945

| | |
|---|---|
| February 23 | Turkey declares war on Germany. |
| March 19 | Soviet Union annuls Soviet-Turkish Friendship Treaty, makes territorial claims on Turkey. |
| April | United Nations San Francisco Conference. |
| December | Repatriation plan announced, with plans for up to 300,000 Armenians to emigrate to Soviet Armenia. |

1946 April 6    The USS *Missouri* warship sails into Turkish Straits.

1947 December    Azerbaijanis deported from Soviet Armenia to Azerbaijan.

1948 December 9    United Nations General Assembly adopts convention on prevention of genocide.

1949

| | |
|---|---|
| February | Repatriation to Soviet Armenia stops. |
| June | Dashnaks and others deported to Siberia from Armenia. |

1952 February 18    Turkey joins NATO.

1956    Schism between Armenian churches of Antelias (Lebanon) and Echmiadzin.

1958 July–October    Armenians take different sides in small civil war in Lebanon.

1960 December 28    Yakov Zarobian becomes party leader in Soviet Armenia.

1962 April    Stalin's statue taken down in Yerevan.

1965 April 24    Mass commemorations and protests in Yerevan and other cities on fiftieth anniversary of Armenian Genocide.

1966    Controversy over Gurgen Mahari's novel, *Burning Orchards*.

| February 5 | Yakov Zarobian removed from office. |
| 1967 November 29 | Genocide memorial opens in Yerevan. |
| 1972 | Armenian Assembly of America formed. |
| 1973 January 27 | Turkey's consul and vice-consul in Los Angeles, Mehmet Baydar and Bahadir Demit, assassinated by Gurgen Yanikian. |
| 1975 | |
| January | Armenian terrorist group ASALA begins operations in Beirut. |
| April 9 | US Congress votes to designate April 24 day of "National Day of Remembrance of Man's Inhumanity to Man," honoring Armenians. |
| April 24 | Mass commemorations of Armenian Genocide anniversary in Beirut. |
| October 22 | Turkish ambassador to Austria, Daniş Tunaligil, assassinated in operation by rival terrorist group, Justice Commandos of the Armenian Genocide (JCAG). |
| 1977 November 27 | Turkish foreign minister Ihsan Sabri Çağlayangil holds talks with Armenian party leaders at secret meeting in Zurich. |
| 1980 September 12 | Military coup in Turkey. |
| 1981 | Turkish government forms Directorate of Intelligence and Research for "Armenian question." |
| 1982 January 28 | Turkish ambassador to United States Şükrü Elekdağ founds Institute of Turkish Studies. |
| 1983 | |
| March 9 | Turkey's consul in Los Angeles, Galip Balkar, assassinated. |
| July 15 | Bombing of Turkish Airlines desk at Orly Airport, Paris, kills 19, triggers crackdown on ASALA. |
| 1988 | |
| February | Beginning of Nagorny Karabakh dispute between Soviet Armenia and Azerbaijan. |
| December 7 | Earthquake in northern Armenia kills 25,000. |

| | |
|---|---|
| 1990 February | US Senate debates Armenian Genocide resolution for two days. |
| 1991 | |
| September 23 | Armenia declares independence following referendum. |
| October 16 | Levon Ter-Petrosian elected president of Armenia. |
| December 16 | Turkey recognizes Armenian Republic but does not open diplomatic relations. |
| 1992 October 7 | Turkish government agrees to wheat deliveries to Armenia. |
| 1993 April 4 | Turkey closes border with Armenia following Armenian capture of Azerbaijan's Kelbajar region. |
| 1994 May 12 | Ceasefire agreed, confirming Armenian military victory over Azerbaijan in Karabakh conflict. |
| 1996 | Turkish Armenian journalist Hrant Dink founds *Agos* newspaper in Istanbul. |
| 1998 | |
| February 3 | Levon Ter-Petrosian forced to resign as president of Armenia. |
| March 30 | Robert Kocharian elected Armenia's second president. |
| September 2 | Kocharian calls for genocide recognition in speech at United Nations General Assembly. |
| 2000 | Historians found Workshop on Armenian Turkish Studies (WATS). |
| 2001 | First meeting of Turkish Armenian Reconciliation Commission (TARC). |
| 2002 November 3 | Justice and Development Party (AKP) wins outright victory in Turkey's parliamentary elections. |
| 2004 | Publication in Turkey of memoir *My Grandmother* by Fethiye Çetin. |
| 2005 | |
| April 10 | Turkish prime minister Recep Tayip Erdoğan proposes historical commission to Armenians. |

| September 24 | Conference "Ottoman Armenians during the Decline of the Empire" opens at Bilgi University, Istanbul. |
| 2007 | Armenia and Turkey begin secret Swiss-mediated talks. |
| January 19 | Hrant Dink murdered. |
| January 23 | Tens of thousands attend Dink's funeral in Istanbul. |
| 2008 | |
| February 19 | Serzh Sarkisian elected third president of Armenia. |
| September 6 | Turkish president Abdullah Gül flies to Yerevan to attend Armenia-Turkey soccer match. |
| December | Turkish intellectuals begin "I Apologize" campaign to Armenians. |
| 2009 | |
| April 6 | US president Barack Obama gives speech to Turkish National Assembly. |
| April 22 | Road map presented for Armenia-Turkey normalization. |
| May 13 | Turkish Prime Minister Erdoğan and Foreign Minister Ahmet Davutoğlu visit Baku. |
| October | Sarkisian tours Armenian diaspora to sell Armenia-Turkey Protocols. |
| October 10 | Foreign ministers of Armenia and Turkey sign two Protocols in Zurich. |
| 2010 | |
| April 22 | Protocols suspended after lack of progress. |
| September 19 | Religious service in restored Armenian cathedral of Akhtamar on Lake Van. |
| 2011 | Armenian church re-opens in Diyarbakir. |
| 2014 April 23 | Erdoğan offers condolences to grandchildren of Armenians killed in deportations. |

# NOTES

## Introduction
1. Theodore Roosevelt, *Letters and Speeches* (New York: Library of America, 2004), 736.
2. Michael J. Arlen, *Passage to Ararat* (New York: Farrar, Straus and Giroux, 2006), 102.
3. Arlen, *Passage to Ararat*, 248.

## Chapter 1
1. Ara Sarafian, *United States Official Documents on the Armenian Genocide* (Watertown, MA: Armenian Review, 1995), 51–52.
2. Cansu Çamlıbel, "Turkish FM: 1915 Armenian Deportations Inhumane," *Hürriyet Daily News*, December 13, 2014. http://www.hurriyetdailynews.com/turkish-fm-1915-armenian-dep ortation-inhumane.aspx?pageID=238&nID=59487&NewsCatID=355.
3. Taner Akçam, "The Young Turks and the Plans for the Ethnic Homogenization of Anatolia," in *Shatterzone of Empires: Coexistence and Violence in the German, Habsburg, Russian, and Ottoman Borderlands,* edited by Omer Bartov and Eric D. Weitz (Bloomington: Indiana University Press, 2013), 250.
4. Sarafian, *United States Official Documents on the Armenian Genocide,* 372.
5. Phillip Mansel, *Constantinople: City of the World's Desire, 1453–1924* (London: St. Martin's Griffin, 1998), 127–128.
6. Frederick Davis Greene and Henry Davenport Northrop, *Armenian Massacres or the Sword of Mohammed* (Philadelphia: International Publishing, 1896), 450.

7. Robert Curzon, *Armenia: A Year at Erzeroom, and on the Frontiers of Russia, Turkey and Persia* (London: John Murray, 1854), 285.

8. Taner Akçam, *A Shameful Act: The Armenian Genocide and the Question of Turkish Responsibility* (New York: Metropolitan, 2006), 32.

9. Corinna Shattuck, "Armenian Massacres, An American Missionary Writes," in *Sword of Islam*, edited by J. Castell Hopkins (Brantford and Toronto: Bradley-Garretson, 1896), 341.

10. Caleb Frank Gates, *Not To Me Only* (Princeton, NJ: Princeton University Press, 1940), 103–104.

11. Gates, *Not To Me Only*, 109.

12. Richard G. Hovannisian, *Foreign Dominion to Statehood: The Fifteenth Century to the Twentieth Century*, vol. 2 of *The Armenian People from Ancient to Modern Times* (Basingstoke, UK: Palgrave Macmillan, 1997), 224.

13. Greene and Northrop, *Armenian Massacres or the Sword of Mohammed*, 357.

14. Verjine Svazlian, *The Armenian Genocide: Testimonies of the Eye-Witness Survivors* (Yerevan: Gitutiun, 2000), 557.

15. Michael A. Reynolds, *Shattering Empires: The Clash and Collapse of the Ottoman and Russian Empires, 1908–1918* (Cambridge: Cambridge University Press), 98.

16. Raymond Kévorkian, *The Armenian Genocide: A Complete History* (London: I. B. Tauris, 2011), 270.

17. Reynolds, *Shattering Empires*, 51–52.

18. Sean McMeekin, *The Russian Origins of the First World War* (Cambridge, MA: Belknap Press, 2011), 162–163.

19. William Schabas, *Unimaginable Atrocities: Justice, Politics, and Rights at the War Crimes Tribunals* (Oxford: Oxford University Press, 2012), 6.

20. Fuat Dündar, *Crime of Numbers: The Role of Statistics in the Armenian Question (1878–1918)* (New Brunswick, NJ: Transaction, 2010), 283.

21. Taner Akçam, *The Young Turks' Crime Against Humanity: The Armenian Genocide and Ethnic Cleansing in the Ottoman Empire* (Princeton, NJ: Princeton University Press, 2012), 373–379.

22. Kévorkian, *The Armenian Genocide*, 542.

23. Dündar, *Crime of Numbers*, 284.

24. Donald Bloxham, "The First World War and the Development of the Armenian Genocide," in *A Question of Genocide: Armenians and Turks at the End of the Ottoman Empire*, edited by Ronald Grigor Suny Fatma Müge Göçek, and Norman M. Naimark (Oxford: Oxford University Press, 2011), 263.

25. David Gaunt, *Massacres, Resistance, Protectors: Muslim-Christian Relations in Eastern Anatolia during World War I* (Piscataway, NJ: Gorgias, 2006), 259.

26. "Jackson from Aleppo, September 10, 1916", in Sarafian, *United States Official Documents on the Armenian Genocide*, 557.

27. Bloxham, "The First World War and the Development of the Armenian Genocide," 271.

28. Djemal Pasha, *Memories of a Turkish Statesman* (London: Hutchinson, 1922), 280.

29. Michael Mann, *The Dark Side of Democracy: Explaining Ethnic Cleansing* (Cambridge: Cambridge University Press, 2005), 140.

30. Hagop Arsenian, *Towards Golgotha: The Memoirs of Hagop Arsenian, a Genocide Survivor*, translated and annotated by Arda Arsenian Ekmerji (Beirut: Haigazian University Press, 2011), 55.

31. Rafael de Nogales, *Four Years Beneath the Crescent* (New York and London: Charles Scribner's Sons, 1926), 60.

32. Henry H. Riggs, *Days of Tragedy in Armenia: Personal Experiences in Harpoot, 1915–1917* (Ann Arbor, MI: Gomidas Institute, 1997), 138–139.

33. Leslie A. Davis, *The Slaughterhouse Province: An American Diplomat's Report on the Armenian Genocide, 1915–1917* (New York: Aristide D. Caratzas, 1989), 86. In 2000, a local woman told a *New York Times* reporter how her grandmother had told her that Armenians were massacred by the lake. Stephen Kinzer, "Turkish Region Recalls Massacre of Armenians," *New York Times*, May 10, 2000.

34. Grigoris Balakian, *Armenian Golgotha*, translated by Peter Balakian with Aris Sevag (New York: Alfred A. Knopf, 2009), 149.

35. Reprinted from *The Missionary Herald*, Boston, 1915. See Viscount Bryce, *The Treatment of Armenians in the Ottoman Empire: Documents Presented to Viscount Grey of Falloden* (Frankfurt: Textor Verlag, 2008), 307.

36. Riggs, *Days of Tragedy in Armenia*, 137.

37. Riggs, *Days of Tragedy in Armenia*, 98–99.

38. Donald E. Miller and Lorna Touryan Miller, *Survivors: An Oral History of the Armenian Genocide* (Berkeley and Los Angeles: University of California Press, 1999), 186.

39. Riggs, *Days of Tragedy in Armenia*, 98.

40. Miller and Miller, *Survivors*, 108.

41. Arsenian, *Towards Golgotha*, 100.

42. Hagop Assadourian, in Araz Artinian, *20 Voices* (Canada: Films Inc. and Araz Artinian Productions, 2005), documentary film.

43. J. Michael Hagopian, *The River Ran Red* (United States: J. Michael Hagopian, 2009), documentary film.

44. Svazlian, *The Armenian Genocide*, 571.

## Chapter 2

1. Arnold J. Toynbee, *The Western Question in Greece and Turkey: A Study in the Contact of Civilisations* (London: Constable, 1922), 50.

2. For a good list of press articles, see: http://en.wikipedia.org/wiki/ Press_coverage_during_the_Armenian_Genocide.

3. E. F. Benson, *Crescent and Iron Cross* (New York: Hodder and Stoughton, 1918), 197.

4. Herbert Adams Gibbons, *The Blackest Page of Modern History* (New York: G. P. Putnam's Sons, 1916).

5. Henry Morgenthau, *Ambassador Morgenthau's Story* (New York: Cosimo Classics, 2010), 213.

6. Morgenthau, *Ambassador Morgenthau's Story*, 231–232.

7. Caleb Frank Gates, *Not to Me Only* (Princeton, NJ: Princeton University Press, 1940), 222, 224.

8. V. N. Dadrian, "For a Free Armenia," *New York Times*, August 10, 1964.

9. Dadrian has been criticized for using quotations out of context to buttress his argument. Hilmar Kaiser, "Germany and the Armenian Genocide, Part II: Reply to Vahakn N. Dadrian's Response," *Journal of the Society for Armenian Studies*, vol. 9 (1996): 139–140.

10. Vahakn N. Dadrian, *The History of the Armenian Genocide: Ethnic Conflict from the Balkans to Anatolia to the Caucasus* (Providence, RI: Berghahn, 1995), xv. Vahakn N. Dadrian, *Warrant for Genocide: Key Elements of Turko-Armenian Conflict* (New Brunswick, NJ: Transaction, 1999), 20.

11. Margaret Lavinian Anderson, "Who Still Talked about the Extermination of the Armenians? German Talk and German Silences," in *A Question of Genocide: Armenians and Turks at the End of the Ottoman Empire*, edited by Ronald Grigor Suny, Fatma Müge Göçek, and Norman M. Naimark (Oxford: Oxford University Press, 2011), 199–217.

12. Dadrian, *The History of the Armenian Genocide*, 407.

13. Erik J. Zürcher, *Turkey: A Modern History* (London: I. B. Tauris, 2004), 117.

14. Mann, *The Dark Side of Democracy*, 18.

15. Mann, *The Dark Side of Democracy*, 178.

16. Leon Z. Surmelian, *I Ask You, Ladies and Gentlemen* (London: V. Gollancz, 1946), 63.

17. Kévorkian, *The Armenian Genocide*, 810.

18. Riggs, *Days of Tragedy in Armenia*, viii.

19. Riggs, *Days of Tragedy in Armenia*, 96.

20. Kévorkian, *The Armenian Genocide*, 809.

21. Akçam, "The Young Turks and the Plans for the Ethnic Homogenization of Anatolia," 266.

22. Ara Sarafian, *Talaat Pasha's Report on the Armenian Genocide* (London: Gomidas Institute, 2011), 10.

23. *Leslie Davis and Other American (and Western) Consuls.* Accessed at http://www.tallarmeniantale.com/Leslie-Davis.htm.

24. Kévorkian, *The Armenian Genocide*, 243.

25. Akçam, *The Young Turks' Crime Against Humanity*, 22–24.

26. Nogales, *Four Years Beneath the Crescent harles* harles and London, 57–58.

27. Nogales, *Four Years Beneath the Crescent*, 146–147.

28. Uğur Ümit Üngör, *The Making of Modern Turkey: Nation and State in Eastern Anatolia, 1913–1950* (Oxford: Oxford University Press, 2011), 106.

29. Akçam, *The Young Turks' Crime Against Humanity*, 434–436.

30. Hovhannes Katchaznouni, *The Armenian Revolutionary Federation (Dashnagtzoutiun) Has Nothing to Do Any More: The Manifesto of Hovhannes Katchaznouni, First Prime Minister of the Independent Armenian Republic*, translated by Matthew A. Callender, edited by John Roy Carlson (Arthur A. Derounian) (New York: Armenian Information Service, 1955), 6.

31. Gurgen Mahari, *Burning Orchards*, translated by Haig Tahta and Hasmik Ghazarian (Cambridge: Germinal/Black Apollo, 2007), 204.

32. Morgan Philips Price, *War and Revolution in Asiatic Russia* (London: George Allen & Uwin, 1918), 245–246.

33. Reynolds, *Shattering Empires*, 150.

34. Reynolds, *Shattering Empires*, 147.

35. Bloxham, "The First World War and the Development of the Armenian Genocide," 269.

36. Sean McMeekin, The *Russian Origins of the First World War* (Cambridge, MA: Belknap Press, 2011), 174. This *realpolitik* thesis may help explain why Ottoman Greeks were left relatively unscathed in 1915, while their Armenian neighbors were being slaughtered. Greeks were deported from the coast of the Aegean Sea in 1914 but their patron state, Greece, was then neutral in World War I and posed no direct threat to the Ottoman government. After Greece entered the conflict in 1917, calculations changed again.

37. Bloxham, "The First World War and the Development of the Armenian Genocide", 263. Balakian, *Armenian Golgotha*, 34.

38. Donald Bloxham, *The Great Game of Genocide: Imperialism, Nationalism, and the Destruction of the Ottoman Armenians* (Oxford: Oxford University Press, 2005), 133.

39. McMeekin, *The Russian Origins of the First World War*, 150.

40. Mann, *The Dark Side of Democracy*, 139.

41. Akçam, *The Young Turks' Crime Against Humanity*, 356, 431–439.

42. Ahmed Emin, *Turkey in the World War* (New Haven, CT: Yale University Press, 1930), 221.

43. Bloxham, *The Great Game of Genocide*, 139. Djemal Pasha, *Memories of a Turkish Statesman, 1913–1919* (New York: George H. Doran, 1922), 278.

44. Arsenian, *Towards Golgotha*, 87.

45. Kévorkian, *The Armenian Genocide*, 501–513.

46. Peter Balakian, *The Burning Tigris: The Armenian Genocide and America's Response* (New York: Harper Collins, 2003), 336 n. 30.

47. Raffi Bedrosyan, "The Real Turkish Heroes of 1915," *Armenian Weekly*, July 29, 2013, http://www.armenianweekly.com/2013/07/29/the-real-turkish-heroes-of-1915/.

48. Margaret Lavinia Anderson, Michael Reynolds, Hans-Lukas Kieser, Peter Balakian, A. Dirk Moses, and Taner Akçam, "Taner Akçam, The Young Turks' Crime Against Humanity: The Armenian Genocide and Ethnic Cleansing in the Ottoman Empire (Princeton, NJ: Princeton University Press, 2012)," *Journal of Genocide Research*, vol. 15, no. 4 (2013):, 491–492

49. Guenter Lewy, *The Armenian Massacres in Ottoman Turkey: A Disputed Genocide* (Salt Lake City: University of Utah Press, 2005), 95

50. Bloxham, *The Great Game of Genocide*, 92.

51. Ara Sarafian, "Study the Armenian Genocide with Confidence, Ara Sarafian suggests," *Armenian Reporter*, December 18, 2008, http://www.reporter.am/go/article/2008-12-18-study-the-armenian-genocide-with-confidence-ara-sarafian-suggests.

## Chapter 3

1. Morgan Philips Price, *War and Revolution in Asiatic Russia* (London: George Allen & Uwin, 1918), 234.
2. Price, *War and Revolution in Asiatic Russia*, 135.
3. Riggs, *Days of Tragedy in Armenia*, 177.
4. Price, *War and Revolution in Asiatic Russia*, 140–141.
5. Justin McCarthy, "The Report of Niles and Sutherland," *Kongreye Sunulan bildirler: XI Türk Tarih Kongresi* [*Papers Presented to the Conference: XIth Turkish History Congress*] (Ankara: 1990), 1850.
6. Sir Harry Luke, *More Moves on an Eastern Checkerboard* (London: L. Dickson & Thompson, 1935), 141.
7. Jenny Phillips, *Symbol, Myth, and Rhetoric: The Politics of Culture in an Armenian-American Community* (New York: AMS, 1989), 81–84.
8. Richard G. Hovannisian, *Armenia on the Road to Independence, 1918* (Berkeley: University of California Press, 1967), 193–194.
9. Tatul Hakobyan, *Armenians and Turks: From War to Cold War to Diplomacy* (Yerevan: 2013), 20.
10. Reynolds, *Shattering Empires*, 210.
11. Hakobyan, *Armenians and Turks*, 34–35.
12. Arshavir Shahkhatuni, quoted in Hakobyan, *Armenians and Turks*, 36, 37.
13. Halil Paşa, *Bitmeyen Savaş* [*Endless War*] (Istanbul: Yaylacik Matbaasi, 1972), 241.
14. Hakobyan, *Armenians and Turks*, 21.
15. "Antranik," *Blackwood's Magazine*, vol. 206, no. 1248 (October 1919): 441–477.
16. Anahide Ter Minassian, *Nationalism and Socialism in the Armenian Revolutionary Movement (1887–1912)*, translated by A. M. Bettet (Cambridge, MA: Zoryan Institute, 1984), 189.
17. Richard G. Hovannisian, *The First Year*, 1918–1919, vol. 1 of *The Republic of Armenia* (Berkeley and Los Angeles: University of California Press, 1971) 450.
18. Hovannisian, *The First Year*, 461.
19. Hovannisian, *The First Year*, 473.
20. Ter Minassian, *Nationalism and Socialism in the Armenian Revolutionary Movement*, 195.
21. Herbet Hoover, *Memoirs: Years of Adventure, 1874–1920* (New York: Macmillan, 1952), 385.
22. Mabel Evelyn Elliot, *Beginning Again at Ararat* (New York: Fleming H. Revell, 1924), 174. Nora Nercessian of Harvard University is writing a definitive study of the Armenian orphanages, where she will bring out the side of the story that has been suppressed: the experience of the orphans themselves in these institutions.
23. *The New Near East*, April 1922, 1.
24. Gates, *Not to Me Only*, 268.
25. The Brookings Institution, A Statesman's Forum with H. E. Recep Tayyip Erdoğan, Prime Minister of Turkey, Washington, D.C.,

Friday, May 17, 2013. Accessed at http://www.brookings.edu/~/media/events/2013/5/17%20erdogan/20130517_turkey_erdogan_transcript.pdf.

26. Lerna Ekmekcioğlu, "A Climate for Abduction, a Climate for Redemption: The Politics of Inclusion during and after the Armenian Genocide," *Comparative Studies in Society and History*, vol. 55, no. 3 (2013): 534.

27. Lerna Ekmekcioğlu, *Improvising Turkishness: Being Armenian in Post-Ottoman Istanbul (1918–1933)* (PhD diss., New York University, 2010), 122, 123.

28. Gary Jonathan Bass, *Stay the Hand of Vengeance: The Politics of War Crimes Tribunals* (Princeton, NJ: Princeton University Press, 2000), 123.

29. Bass, *Stay the Hand of Vengeance*, 125–126.

30. Bass, *Stay the Hand of Vengeance*, 257.

31. French prime minister Georges Clemenceau reportedly told Nubar in July 1918, "I am happy to confirm to you that the government of the Republic, like that of Great Britain, has not ceased to place the Armenian nation among the people whose fate the Allies intend to settle according to the supreme laws of Humanity and Justice." *The Armenian Herald*, vol. 1, no. 10 (September 1918): 525.

32. Katchaznouni, *The Armenian Revolutionary Federation (Dashnagtzoutiun) Has Nothing to Do Any More*, 12.

33. Firuz Kazemzadeh, *The Struggle for Transcaucasia, 1917–1921* (New York: Philosophical Library, 1951) 25, 258.

34. Paul C. Helmreich, *From Paris to Sèvres: The Partition of the Ottoman Empire at the Peace Conference of 1919–1920* (Columbus: University of Ohio Press, 1974), 50.

35. Alfred Rawlinson, *Adventures in the Near East* (London: A. Melrose, 1923), 151.

36. Rawlinson, *Adventures in the Near East*, 189.

37. Rawlinson, *Adventures in the Near East*, 218.

38. Maj. Gen. James G. Harbord, *Conditions in the Near East: Report of the American Military Mission to Armenia* (Washington, DC: Government Printing Office, 1920), 7.

39. Harbord, *Conditions in the Near East*, 8.

40. Harbord, *Conditions in the Near East*, 8–9.

41. Reynolds, *Shattering Empires*, 255.

42. Helmreich, *From Paris to Sèvres*, 321.

43. Hakobyan, *Armenians and Turks*, 91.

44. Andrew Mango, *Atatürk: The Biography of the Founder of Modern Turkey* (Woodstock, NY: Overlook, 2000), 294.

45. Hakobyan, *Armenians and Turks*, 94–95.

46. Hakobyan, *Armenians and Turks*, 94.

47. Hakobyan, *Armenians and Turks*, 95.

48. Hakobyan, *Armenians and Turks*, 96–97.

49. Charles Evans Hughes, "The Hour of Liberation Has Come," *Armenian Herald*, vol. 2 (1919), 164, 165.

50. James L. Barton, *Letter to Mark L. Bristol, January 14, 1921*. Letter. From Library of Congress, *Mark L. Bristol Papers, 1882–1939*. Container 33.

51. Vahan Cardashian, *Wilson: Wrecker of Armenia* (New York: Armenian Press Bureau, 1921), 11.

52. Cardashian, *Wilson: Wrecker of Armenia*, 9.

53. Barton, *Letter to Mark L. Bristol, May 6, 1921*. Letter. From Library of Congress, *Mark L. Bristol Papers, 1882–1939*. Container 34.

54. Charles Evans Hughes, "Recent Questions and Negotiations" (speech at Council on Foreign Relations, Washington, DC, January 23, 1924), *Foreign Affairs*. Accessed at http://www.foreignaffairs.com/articles/68473/honorable-charles-e-hughes/recent-questions-and-negotiations.

## Chapter 4

1. Marc Nichanian, "Testimony: From Document to Monument," in *The Armenian Genocide, Cultural and Ethical Legacies*, edited by Richard Hovannisian (New Brunswick, NJ: Transaction, 2007), 41–64.

2. Surmelian, *I Ask You, Ladies and Gentlemen*, 172.

3. Mann, *The Dark Side of Democracy*, 140.

4. Hratch Dasnabedian, *History of the Armenian Revolutionary Federation: Dashnaktsutiun, 1890–1924* (Milan: Oemme Edizioni, 1989), 155–156.

5. Quoted in Bloxham, *The Great Game of Genocide*, 212.

6. Interview with Tatul Sonentz, Boston, September 10, 2013.

7. Svazlian, *The Armenian Genocide*, 579.

8. Svazlian, *The Armenian Genocide*, 589.

9. Benjamin F. Alexander, *Armenian and American: The Changing Face of Ethnic Identity and Diasporic Nationalism, 1915–1955* (PhD diss., City University of New York, 2005), 91–92.

10. *Report of Near East Relief to the Congress of the United States of America For the Year Ending December 31, 1920*, US House of Representatives, December 31, 1920, no page number.

11. Herant Katchadourian, *The Way It Turned Out* (Stanford, CA: Pan Stanford, 2012), 13. The film *Grandma's Tattoos*, by Swedish-Armenian Suzanne Khardalian, unusually deals with the issue of rape. Khardalian investigates the story of her taciturn late grandmother, eventually discovering that she was raped as a 12-year-old girl and then brought up in a Bedouin family. Another memoir that is frank about this formerly taboo topic is Mae M. Derderian, *Vergeen: A Survivor of the Armenian Genocide* (Los Angeles: Atmus, 1996).

12. Erik Zürcher, *Turkey, A Modern History* (London and New York: I. B. Tauris, 2004), 163, 164.

13. Harold Armstrong, *Turkey and Syria Reborn* (London: John Lane, 1930), 142, 143.

14. Armstrong, *Turkey and Syria Reborn*, 145.

15. Gates, *Not to Me Only*, 309.

16. Fatma Ulgen, "*Sabiha Gökçen's 80-Year-Old Secret*": Kemalist Nation Formation and the Ottoman Armenians (PhD diss., University of California, San Diego, 2010), 321–323.

17. Ulgen, *Sabiha Gökçen's 80-Year-Old Secret*, 291.
18. Akçam, *Shameful Act*, 346–347.
19. Ulgen, *Sabiha Gökçen's 80-Year-Old Secret*, 281.
20. Nicole Pope and Hugh Pope, *Turkey Unveiled: A History of Modern Turkey* (Woodstock, NY: Overlook, 2004), 49. The authors note that "Koç always made a point of underlining in respectful terms how much he had learned from the non-Muslim merchants who were his first employers."
21. Şener Aktürk, *Regimes of Ethnicity and Nationhood in Germany, Russia, and Turkey* (Cambridge: Cambridge University Press, 2012), 124.
22. "Istanbul Ermenilerinin F. Werfele mukabelesi [Istanbul Armenians answer F. Werfel]," *Cumhuriyet*, December 16, 1935. My thanks to Ekin Ozbakkaloglu and Charles King for this reference.
23. Jacques Derogy, *Resistance and Revenge: The Armenian Assassination of Turkish Leaders Responsible for the 1915 Massacres and Deportations* (New Brunswick, NJ: Transaction, 1990), xix–xxiv.
24. Enver's remains were brought back from Tajikistan to be reburied on the same spot in 1996. Footage of Talat's funeral ceremony of 1943 can be seen at http://www.youtube.com/watch?v=wSq_fX8NFRw.
25. Katchaznouni, *The Armenian Revolutionary Federation (Dashnagtzoutiun) Has Nothing to Do Any More*, 16.
26. Sarkis Atamian, *The Armenian Community: The Historical Development of a Social and Ideological Conflict* (New York: Philosophical Library, 1955), 1.
27. Alexander, *Armenian and American*, 117.
28. Karekin Nejdeh, "What Is Racial Patriotism to the Armenian Younger Generation in America," *Hairenik*, January 7, 1934, quoted in Alexander, *Armenian and American*, 167–168. "New York Rally for Tricolor Attracts 1200," *Armenian Spectator*, August 31, 1933.
29. "Minor Riot at Chicago Mars Observance," *Armenian Spectator*, July 6, 1933.
30. "Archbishop Assassinated in Procession to Altar: Dies as Murderers Flee," *Armenian Spectator*, December 28, 1933; "Slain in 187th St. Church, Assassins Swarm about Armenian Prelate and Stab Him," *New York Times*, December 25, 1933.
31. "Worcester Flooded with Placards," *Armenian Spectator*, January 19, 1934; "The New York Murder," *Hairenik Weekly*, December 29, 1933.
32. "Five Hurt in Clash of Armenians Here," *New York Times*, February 26, 1934.
33. "Armenians in Wild Riot Near Common, Score Hurt," *Daily Boston Globe*, April 9, 1934.
34. Phillips, *Symbol, Myth and Rhetoric*, 228–229.
35. "The War of the Tri-Color," *Armenian Spectator*, February 1, 1934.
36. Louis Fischer, *Soviet Journey* (Westport, CT: Greenwood, 1935), 272.
37. Arthur Koestler, *The Invisible Writing* (London: Hutchinson, 1969), 107.
38. Aghavni Yeghia Yeghenian, *The Red Flag at Ararat* (New York: Womans Press, 1932), 170.
39. Interview with Suren Manukian, Yerevan, July 4, 2013.
40. Hakobyan, *Armenians and Turks*, 153–154.

41. Marc Nichanian, *Writers of Disaster Armenian Literature in the Twentieth Century*, vol. 1 of *The National Revolution* (Princeton and London: Gomidas Institute, 2002), 45–46.

42. Felix Corley, "The Armenian Church under the Soviet Regime, Part 1: The Leadership of Kevork" in *Religion, State & Society*, vol. 24, no. 1 (Oxford: Keston Institute, 1996), 10.

## Chapter 5

1. "Twenty Five Years After," *Hairenik Weekly*, June 2, 1943, 2.

2. Among those veterans of the 1918 republics who negotiated with the Nazis (with different outcomes) were the leader of the Azerbaijani First Republic, Mammed Amin Rasulzade, the Dagestani leader Said Shamil, and the former governor general of Tbilisi, Shalva Maglakelidze.

3. In his book *From Beirut to Damascus*, the anti-Dashnak journalist John Roy Carlson writes, "I met General Dro Ganayan, follower of the Nazi armies, a notorious Dashnag officer who told me that he had advanced with the Wehrmacht in their penetration of the Caucasus region and had retreated with them after Stalingrad." John Roy Carlson, *Cairo to Damascus* (New York: Alfred A. Knopf, 1951), 436.

4. "The Northern Uncle," *Hairenik Weekly*, August 2, 1945, 2.

5. Reprinted in Charles A. Vertanes, *Armenia Reborn* (New York: Armenian National Council of America, 1947), 173.

6. Vertanes, *Armenia Reborn*, 178–179.

7. Felix Corley, "The Armenian Church under the Soviet Regime, Part 1: The Leadership of Kevork," *Religion, State, & Society*, vol. 24, no. 1 (1996), 16.

8. Pargev Georgyan, "V bor'be z sushchestvovaniye" [In a struggle for existence], *Zhurnal Moskovskoi Patriarkhii*, no. 4 (1994), 45–56, quoted in Corley, "The Armenian Church under the Soviet Regime, Part 1," 16.

9. Corley, "The Armenian Church under the Soviet Regime, Part 1," 19.

10. Corley, "The Armenian Church under the Soviet Regime, Part 1," 19.

11. Arman Kirakosian, ed., *Armenia i Sovetsko-Turetskie Otnosheniya v Diplomaticheskikh Dokumentakh 1945–46 gg.* [Armenia and Soviet-Turkish Relations in Diplomatic Documents, 1945–46] (Yerevan: National Archive of Armenia, 2010), 256–258.

12. Harry Truman, *Year of Decisions*, vol. 1 of *Memoirs* (New York: Doubleday, 1955), 375.

13. Anita Burdett, ed., *Armenia: Political and Ethnic Boundaries, 1878–1948* (London: Archive Editions, 1998), 1030.

14. Quoted in Ronald Grigor Suny, *Looking Toward Ararat: Armenia in Modern History* (Bloomington and Indianapolis: Indiana University Press, 1993), 173.

15. Republished in John Kirakosian, *Aleksei Dzhivelegov i ego Istoriko-Publitsisticheskoye Nasledie* (Yerevan: Natsional'naya Akademiya Nauk,

2007). Accessed in March 2014, http://www.genocide.ru/lib/kirakosyan/jivelegov/4-230.htm, 232–251.

16. Kirakosian, *Armenia i Sovetsko-Turetskie Otnosheniya v Diplomaticheskikh Dokumentakh 1945–46 gg., 252.*

17. A. C. Sedgwick, "New Armenia Bid By Soviet Is Seen," *New York Times,* January 2, 1946.

18. Jamil Hasanli, *Stalin and the Turkish Crisis of the Cold War, 1945–1953* (Lanham, MD: Lexington, 2011), 192–195.

19. "Turkey Talks Fight Against Red Demand," *Times of London* (quoted by UPI), December 22, 1945.

20. Hasanli, *Stalin and the Turkish Crisis of the Cold War,* 200.

21. "Allah! I thought I finished them off thirty years ago," cartoon, *Hairenik Weekly,* September 12, 1946, 2.

22. Mirtad H. Tiryakian, "Towards the Fatherland," September 28, 1946.

23. Ara Shirinyan, *My Unfamiliar Fatherland* (Armenia), documentary film. Directed by Ara Shirinyan. Yerevan.

24. Tom Mooradian, *The Repatriate: Love, Basketball, and the KGB* (Detroit: Wayne State University Press, 2008), 150.

25. Mihran H. Exerjian, "The Repatriation Issue: An Opinion," *Armenian Mirror-Spectator,* vol. 15, no. 37, March 6, 1948.

26. Armen Amadian, "Leftists Attempt at Derogation of Escapees a Failure," *Hairenik Weekly,* vol. 15, no. 12, May 13, 1948. Bold font in original.

27. Hasanli, *Stalin and the Turkish Crisis of the Cold War,* 272–273.

28. Personal e-mail to the author from Azerbaijani historian Jamil Hasanli, March 5, 2014.

29. Nicola Migliorino, *(Re)constructing Armenia In Lebanon and Syria: Ethno-Cultural Diversity and the State in the Aftermath of a Refugee Crisis,* Studies in Forced Migration, vol. 21 (New York: Berghahn, 2008), 101. Phillips, *Symbol, Myth and Rhetoric,* 145. Nikola Schahgaldian, *The Political Integration of an Immigrant Community into a Composite Society: The Armenians in Lebanon, 1920–1974* (PhD diss., Columbia University, 1979), 221.

30. "Editorial: The A.Y.A.," *Hairenik Weekly,* vol. 16, no. 8, April 14, 1949.

31. Reuben Darbinian, "Our Neutrals," *Armenian Reveiw,* no. 4 (Winter 1954).

32. *Archbishop Khoren Paroyian's Holy Mission to America* (Boston: Armenian National Apostolic Church of America, 1957), 7. More than one Armenian expert told me that the ARF began collaborating with the OSS/CIA from 1944. The name of James Mandalian was mentioned as the intermediary. I have not seen any written confirmation of this.

33. *Investigation of Communist Take-Over and Occupation of the Non-Russian Nations of the U.S.S.R.,* Eighth Interim Report of Hearings Before the Select Committee on Communist Aggression, United States House of Representatives, 83rd Cong. 227 (1954).

34. *Investigation of Communist Take-Over,* 154–155.

35. *Investigation of Communist Take-Over,* 172.

36. *Investigation of Communist Take-Over,* 175.

## Chapter 6

1. *Until Justice is Done, The Armenian Mirror-Spectator,* June 25, 1966.
2. Muriel Mirak-Weissbach, *Through the Wall of Fire* (Reading, UK: Ithaca Press, 2013), 46.
3. Natasha May Azarian, *The Seeds of Memory: Narrative Renditions of the Armenian Genocide Across Generations* (PhD diss., University of California, Berkeley, 2008), 227.
4. Azarian, "The Seeds of Memory," 123.
5. Surmelian, *I Ask You, Ladies and Gentlemen*, 310.
6. Surmelian, *I Ask You, Ladies and Gentlemen*, 307–308.
7. "Antranik of Armenia" in *Essential Saroyan*, edited by William E. Justice (Berkeley, CA: Santa Clara Heyday Books, 2005), 32.
8. Quoted in William Saroyan, *An Armenian Trilogy*, edited by Dickran Kouymjian (Fresno: The Press at California State University, 1986), 105–106.
9. George Mardikian, *Song of America* (Salt Lake City: Utah Printing Company, 1956), 91.
10. Mardikian, *Song of America*, 227.
11. *UN Casebook with Quincy Howe.* (CBS-TV Channel 2, February 12, 1949). Accessed March 2014 at http://www.youtube.com/watch?v=uCebMq-GmH4.
12. Raphael Lemkin, *Totally Unofficial: The Autobiography of Raphael Lemkin*, edited by Donna-Lee Frieze (New Haven, CT: Yale University Press, 2013), 20.
13. A dozen or so national groups whom Stalin had deported en masse in the 1940s and whose culture he had erased, from the Chechens to the Volga Germans to the Crimean Tatars, would have had a strong case had they had the ability to bring a case. However, their stories were barely known at the time.
14. Lemkin, *Totally Unofficial*, 200–201.
15. "Genocide," *Hairenik Weekly*, vol. XIII, no. 49, January 30, 1947, 2.
16. "Exit Genocide," *Hairenik Weekly*, vol. XV, no. 45, December 30, 1948, 2.
17. "Written Statement of the Government of the United States of America," International Court of Justice, *Reservations to the Convention on the Prevention and Punishment of the Crime of Genocide, Advisory Opinion of May 28th, 1951*, 25.
18. "Hearings before a Subcommittee of the Committee on Foreign Relations United States Senate," *Eighty-first Congress, Second Session on Executive the International Convention on the Prevention and Punishment of the Crime of Genocide. January 23, 24, 25 and February 9, 1950*. (Washington, DC: Government Printing Office, 1950), 96.
19. Aron Traynin *Zashchita mira i bor'ba s prestupleniyami protiv chelovechestva [The Defense of World and the Struggle with Crimes Against Humanity]* (Moscow: Academy of Sciences of USSR, 1956), 226–227, 228.
20. "More Deportations," *Hairenik Weekly*, vol. XVI, no. 47, January 12, 1950, 2.

21. "Senator Lehman Calls for Liberation Program in New York Address," *Hairenik Weekly*, vol. XXII, no. 16, June 2, 1955.

22. Lou Ann Matossian, "Armenians Started Using the Word 'Genocide' in 1945, Khatchig Mouradian Shows," *Armenian Reporter*, June 26, 2009. *Memorandum on the Armenian Question Presented to the Council of Foreign Ministers* (New York: Armenian National Council of America, 1947), 3.

23. Interview with Richard Hovannisian, March 7, 2013.

24. Efraim Sicher, "The Future of the Past: Countermemory and Postmemory in Contemporary American Post-Holocaust Narratives," *History & Memory*, vol. 12, no. 2 (Fall/Winter 2000). Quoted in David B. MacDonald, *Identity Politics in the Age of Genocide* (Abingdon, UK: Routledge, 2008), 21.

25. Interview with Zaven Messerlian, September 24, 2013.

26. Leon Surmelian, "Mourning Is Not Enough," *Armenian Mirror-Spectator*, vol. XXXII, no. 42, April 24, 1965.

27. Nikita Zarobian, *Yakov Zarobian i ego epokha [Yakov Zarobian and his Era]* (Yerevan: Izdatel'stvo RAU, 2008), 128.

28. Interview with Suren Manukian, July 4, 2013.

29. "Rubikon-65," *Yerevan* journal, no. 4 (2006). Accessed at imyerevan.com/ru/society/view/2256.

30. Copy of letter given to author by Ophelia Injikian.

31. Razmik Panossian, *The Armenians: From Kings and Priests to Merchants and Commissars* (New York: Columbia University Press, 2006), 321.

32. Interview with Ophelia Injikian, July 4, 2013.

33. Haig Sarkissian, "50th Anniversary of the Turkish Genocide as Observed in Yerevan," *Armenian Review*, no. 4 (Winter 1966), 25.

34. Sarkissian, "50th Anniversary of the Turkish Genocide as Observed in Yerevan," 25. Interview with Ophelia Injikian, July 4, 2013.

35. Sarkissian, "50th Anniversary of the Turkish Genocide as Observed in Yerevan," 26.

36. Interview with Sashur Kalashian, July 5, 2013.

## Chapter 7

1. Vehig S. Tavitian, "The Rights of the Armenian People Are Again Denied," *Armenian Mirror-Spectator*, vol. 34, no. 28, February 11, 1967.

2. "Armenian Guilty of Killing Turks," *New York Times*, July 3, 1973, 9.

3. Tigran Kalaydjian, *Sentinel of Truth: Gourgen Yanikian and the Struggle Against the Denial of the Armenian Genocide* (Houston, TX: Strategic, 2013), 40.

4. "Out of Their Element," *Armenian Mirror-Spectator*, vol. 40, no. 32, March 3, 1973.

5. Belig Berkoz, "Letter to Honorable Judge," court affidavit, Santa Clara, California, August 29, 2000, published at http://www.ataa.org/reference/topalian/VIS6_Berkoz_Affidavit.pdf.

6. Gerard J. Libaridian, *Modern Armenia: People, Nation, State* (New Brunswick, NJ: Transaction, 2004), 40–41.

7. Monte Melkonian, *A Self-Criticism*, edited by Gregory Topalian, translated by Seta Melkonian (London: Gomidas Institute, 2010), 12–13.

8. Melkonian, *A Self-Criticism*, 19, 20. Hagop Hagopian was a *nom de guerre*. His real name was Harutiun Takushian.

9. Interview with Alec Yenikomshian, Yerevan, July 5, 2013.

10. Interview with Alec Yenikomshian.

11. "Armenian Secret Army Claims Responsibility for Athens Deaths," *Armenian Mirror-Spectator*, vol. 48, no. 4, August 9, 1980.

12. Markar Melkonian, *My Brother's Road: An American's Fateful Journey to Armenia* (London: I. B. Tauris, 2007), 85.

13. "'Justice Commandos' Address Communication to 'All Peoples and Governments,'" *Armenian Weekly*, vol. 42, no. 40, December 4, 1975. In 2001, more evidence of the link emerged when a leading ARF representative in the United States, Mourad Topalian, was given a 37-month jail sentence for keeping explosives in a storage locker in Cleveland, Ohio. Investigators said he been a leading member of the Justice Commandos in the 1980s. See David E. Kaplan, "Following Terror's Forgotten Trail," *US News and World Report*, January 28, 2001.

14. Interview with Ilter Turkmen, Istanbul, September 26, 2013.

15. Interview with Volkan Vural, Istanbul, September 27, 2013.

16. Interview with Antranik Boghossian, Yerevan, July 5, 2013. In Belgrade, he operated under a pseudonym, Harutyun Krikor Levonian.

17. "Five ARA Members Sacrifice Their Lives to 'Altar of Freedom,'" *Armenian Weekly*, vol. 50, no. 68, August 20, 1983.

18. Marvine Howe, "Most Armenians in Beirut Support Attacks on Turks," *New York Times*, March 1, 1980, 4.

19. Edward N. Costikyan, "An Insult to the Armenian Martyrs," *New York Times*, October 20, 1980, A18.

20. Anny Bakalian, *Armenian-Americans: From Being to Feeling Armenian* (New Brunswick, NJ: Transaction, 1993), 153.

21. Melkonian, *My Brother's Road*, 159.

22. Nathan M. Adams, testimony before the US Senate Committee on Human Resources, Subcommittee on Alcoholism and Drug Abuse, August 2, 1984, 107–108.

23. The Orly bombing caused the final split in ASALA, with Monte Melkonian denouncing it as a "fascist act."

24. William Echikson, "Armenian Bombing at Orly Ends Pact Between Socialists and Terrorists," *Christian Science Monitor*, July 19, 1983. The French authorities were accused of not actively pursuing the assassins of Ambassador Ismail Erez in 1975.

25. Attacks were staged in Ottawa and Melbourne by an organization calling itself the Armenian Revolutionary Army, which appeared to be a successor to the

Justice Commandos. James Ring Adams, "Lessons and Links of Anti-Turk Terrorism," *Wall Street Journal*, August 16, 1983; Jonathan Marshall writes that the CIA had earlier armed the Dashnaks, quoting CIA director William Colby that this was "part of a Cold War policy of using pro-Western minorities in the anti-Communist struggle." Jonathan V. Marshall, *The Lebanese Connection: Corruption, Civil War and the International Drug Traffic* (Stanford, CA: Stanford University Press, 2012), 154.

26. In interviews, neither Turkish ambassador to the UN and later foreign minister Ilter Turkmen nor the man who was undersecretary in the foreign ministry at the time, Şükrü Elekdağ, said they knew about the initiative. The Armenian writer Harut Sassounian is writing a book about the meeting, which will shed further light on it.

27. Interview with Oktay Aksoy, Ankara, October 2, 2013.

28. Interview with Tatul Sonentz, Boston, September 10, 2013.

29. *Ararat* periodical, Beriut, January 1995, quoted in Hakobyan, *Armenians and Turks*, 205.

30. Aksoy says that Abrahamian was also at the meeting, but others do not say so.

31. Haig Naccashian, "The First Armeno-Turkish Dialogue," *Armenian Reporter*, September 22, 2001.

32. Hakobyan, *Armenians and Turks*, 207.

33. Hakobyan, *Armenians and Turks*, 207.

34. Interview with Ilter Turkmen, September 26, 2013.

35. *Armenian Terrorism, Its Supporters, the Narcotic Connection, the Distortion of History*, Symposium on International Terrorism (Ankara: Ankara University Press, 1984), 14. One of the former Armenian militants, Alec Yenikomshian, agrees that they wanted to exploit Turkey's weakness. He says, "Until the '80 coup d'état in Turkey, Turkey was in internal turmoil, very deep instability, the scenery there was positive for the Armenian armed presence and struggle in Turkey, especially the historic Armenian homeland."

36. "Turkish President Blasts Armenian Goals," *Armenian Mirror-Spectator*, vol. 51, no. 9, September 17, 1983. On the issue of the Turkish "deep state" and the anti-Armenian campaign, see Nathan M. Adams, Subcommittee on Alcoholism and Drug Abuse, 127; Gareth Jenkins, "Susurluk and the Legacy of Turkey's Dirty War" *Jamestown Terrorism Monitor*, vol. 6, no. 9, May 1, 2008, http://www.jamestown.org/articles-by-author/?no_cache=1&tx_cablanttnewsstaffrelation_pi1%5Bauthor%5D=436.

37. I am grateful to Fatma Müge Göçek for sharing the manuscript of her book *Denial of Violence: Ottoman Past, Turkish Present and Collective Violence against the Armenians, 1789–2009* (New York: Oxford University Press, 2014), whose insights have shaped this section of the book, as well as many others.

38. Uras, a speaker of Armenian, served as an intelligence official in 1915–1916 and interrogated Armenian prisoners.

39. Jennifer M. Dixon, "Education and National Narratives: Changing Representations of the Armenian Genocide in History Textbooks in Turkey," *International Journal for Education Law and Policy*, Special Issue on "Legitimation and Stability of Political Systems: The Contribution of National Narratives" (2010): 109.

40. Interview with Omer Lutem, October 2, 2013.

41. Kamuran Gürün, *The Armenian File: The Myth of Innocence Exposed* (Nicosia: K. Rustem, 2001), 217–218, 220.

42. Jennifer M. Dixon, "Defending the Nation? Maintaining Turkey's Narrative of the Armenian Genocide," *South European Society and Politics*, vol. 15, no. 3 (September 2010): 472.

43. Dixon, "Education and National Narratives," 112–113.

44. Notes from a visit to the Military Museum, Istanbul, September 26, 2013.

45. "Terrorism: Will It Turn His American Dream into a Nightmare?" *New York Times*, April 26, 1982.

46. Lowry's close relationship with the Turkish embassy in Washington was revealed when academic Robert Jay Lifton received a letter from Ambassador Nüzhet Kandemir in 1990, in which the embassy had mistakenly included a briefing note from Lowry to the ambassador, detailing how he should respond to Lifton's arguments. See Roger W. Smith, Eric Markusen, and Robert Jay Lifton, "Professional Ethics and the Denial of Armenian Genocide," in *Remembrance and Denial: The Case of the Armenian Genocide*, edited by Richard G. Hovannisian (Detroit: Wayne State University Press), 1998.

47. Interview with Şükrü Elekdağ, October 3, 2013. Previously, Stanford Shaw and his wife Ezel Kural Shaw had taken refuge in Turkey for a time after their house was attacked by a crude homemade bomb.

48. Interview with Şükrü Elekdağ, October 3, 2013.

49. Aydin Yalcin, Hearing before US Senate, Committee on the Judiciary, Subcommittee on Security and Terrorism, June 25, 1981, 5.

50. *The Role of Cuba in International Terrorism and Subversion*, US Senate, Committee on the Judiciary, Subcommittee on Security and Terrorism, 1982, 94.

51. Ronald Reagan, "Proclamation 4838: Days of Remembrance of Victims of the Holocaust" (speech, August 22, 1981). Accessed at Ronald Reagan Presidential Library and Museum website, http://www.reagan.utexas. edu/archives/speeches/1981/42281c.htm.

52. On October 6, 1980, Hampig Sassounian's brother Harut had also tried to assassinate Arikan and was sentenced to six years of jail.

53. William Mihrtad Paparian, "A Candid Conversation Between an Armenian and a Turk," *Armenian Mirror-Spectator*, vol. 49, no. 36, March 20, 1982.

54. "Secretary Visits Turkey, Greece; Attends North Atlantic Council, Ankara, May 15, 1982," *Department of State Bulletin*, vol. 82, no. 2065, August 1982.

55. Andrew Corsun, "Armenian Terrorism: A Profile," *Department of State Bulletin*, August 1982, 35.

56. *Department of State Bulletin*, April 1983, 300.

57. Interview with Van Krikorian, October 17, 2013.

58. Bobelian, *Children of Armenia*, 190. Amb. Morton Abramowitz, then US ambassador to Turkey, says he lobbied 60 senators to oppose the resolution. See Morton Abramowitz, "The Never-Ending Armenian Genocide Resolution," *The National Interest*, March 19, 2010, http://nationalinterest.org/article/the-never-en ding-armenian-genocide-resolution-3411.

59. Interview with Omer Lutem, Ankara, October 2, 2013.

60. Caspar Weinberger, Statement before US House of Representatives, Foreign Affairs Committee, February 21, 1985. Accessed at http://www. disam.dsca.mil/pubs/Vol%207-3/Weinberger.pdf.

61. "Peres: Armenian Allegations are Meaningless," *Turkish Daily News*, April 10, 2001.

62. Bernard Lewis, *The Emergence of Modern Turkey* (London: Oxford University Press, 1961), 350.

63. Bernard Lewis, *Notes on a Century: Reflections of a Middle East Historian* (New York: Viking, 2012), 288.

64. Yusuf Halaçoğlu, "Realities Behind Relocation," in *Armenians in the Late Ottoman Period*, edited by Türkkaya Ataöv (Ankara: Turkish Historical Society, 2001), 140.

65. Bakalian, *Armenian-Americans*, 356–357.

## Chapter 8

1. Sebnem Arsu, "Seminar on 1915 Massacre of Armenians to Go Ahead," *New York Times*, September 24, 2005.

2. *BBC News* website, "Turks Protest at Armenian Forum," September 24, 2005.

3. Suny, Göçek, and Naimark, *A Question of Genocide*, 7–8.

4. "Armenian Conference Protesters Target Inönü," *Hürriyet Daily News,* September 25, 2005.

5. Derya Sazak, "Ermeni Tabusu [The Armenian Taboo]," *Milliyet,* September 27, 2005.

6. Bekir Coşkun, "My Armenian Matter," *Hürriyet Daily News,* September 27, 2005, accessed at http://www.hurriyetdailynews.com/default.aspx?pa geid=438&n=bekir-coskun-my-armenian-matter-2005-09-27.

7. Dixon, "Defending the Nation?," 477.

8. Interview with Halil Berktay, September 28, 2013.

9. Interview with Cengiz Aktar, June 4, 2013.

10. Taner Akçam, "To Study the Armenian Genocide in Turkey," paper presented at the Hrant Dink Memorial Workshop (Istanbul, June 1, 2013).

11. Gerard Libaridian, "A Report on the Workshop for Armenian/Turkish Scholarship," unpublished manuscript prepared on behalf of the organizers (Ann Arbor: University of Michigan, October 31, 2006), 7–8.

12. Donald Quataert, "The Massacres of Ottoman Armenians and the Writing of Ottoman History," *Journal of Interdisciplinary History*, vol. 37, no. 2 (Autumn 2006), 250, 258.

13. Interview to Ellen Rudnitsky and Mirko Schwanitz of the International Organization of Journalists, January 17, 2007. Accessed at http://crs.bilkent.edu.tr/hrantdink.htm.

14. Interview with Cengiz Aktar, June 4, 2013.

15. Interview with Tuba Candar, May 31, 2013.

16. Interview with Dikran Altun, May 31, 2013.

17. Interview with Tuba Candar.

18. "To Unlock and Transcend History," *Agos*, May 27, 2005. Translation provided by Hrant Dink Foundation.

19. Ulgen, *Sabiha Gökçen's 80-Year-Old Secret*, 109–111. A subsequent article also alleged that Gökçen was Armenian, but with a different background in the town of Bursa. According to this story, she even went to Beirut to meet her Armenian relatives.

20. Ulgen, *Sabiha Gökçen's 80-Year-Old Secret*, 119.

21. Ulgen, *Sabiha Gökçen's 80-Year-Old Secret*, 123.

22. Ulgen, *Sabiha Gökçen's 80-Year-Old Secret*, 131.

23. Şahin Alpay, "Sabiha Gökçen'in 80 yıllık sırrı [Sabiha Gökçen's 80-year-old secret]," *Zaman*, February 28, 2004.

24. Ulgen, *Sabiha Gökçen's 80-Year-Old Secret*, 125–126, 127.

25. Hrant Dink, "Writings for the 90th Year: My State of Mind," *Birgün*, November 1, 2004. Translation provided by the Hrant Dink Foundation.

26. Harut Sassounian, "Brief Comments on Many, Farcical Turkish Missteps," *California Courier*, October 12, 2006.

27. Sebnem Arsu, "Editor of Turkey's Armenian Paper Is Killed," *New York Times*, January 19, 2007.

28. Asbed Bedrossian and Asbed Kotchikian, *Hrant Dink: The Martyr for Many Causes*, Armenian News Network / Groong, February 2, 2007. Accessed at http://www.groong.org/ro/ro-20070201.html.

29. "Ex-Turkish Envoys Slam Campaign Apologizing to Armenians," *Hürriyet Daily News*, 2008. http://www.hurriyet.com.tr/english/domestic/10574703.asp?scr=1.

## Chapter 9

1. Nora Dudwick, "The Karabagh Movement: An Old Scenario Gets Rewritten," *Armenian Review*, vol. 42, no. 3/167 (Autumn 1989), 64. April 24 was only adopted as an official day of mourning in November 1988.

2. Interview with David Hovhannisian, July 7, 2013.

3. Gerard Libaridian, ed., *Armenia at the Crossroads: Democracy and Nationhood in the Post-Soviet Era* (Watertown, MA: Blue Crane, 1991), 129.

4. In *Droshak* newspaper, January 4, 1989. Quoted in Hakobyan, *Armenians and Turks*, 215.

5. In *Azg* newspaper, March 20, 1991. Quoted in Hakobyan, *Armenians and Turks*, 222.

6. Interview with Volkan Vural, September 27, 2013.

7. Hakobyan, *Armenians and Turks*, 272.

8. Hakobyan, *Armenians and Turks*, 217–219.

9. Interview with Gerard Libaridian, September 9, 2013.

10. Interview with Volkan Vural, September 27, 2013.

11. Interview with Volkan Vural, September 27, 2013.

12. In the end, 52,000 tons were delivered on behalf of the Europeans, as well as 6,000 tons from Syrian president Hafez Assad. Interview with Gerard Libaridian, September 9, 2013; Hakobyan, *Armenians and Turks*, 240.

13. Thomas de Waal, *Black Garden: Armenia and Azerbaijan Through Peace and War* (New York: New York University Press, 2013), 212.

14. Interview with Gerard Libaridian, September 9, 2013.

15. Interview with Vartan Oksanian, July 8, 2013.

16. Text from the Armenian presidential website, www.president.am, is no longer available but was republished on http://armenians-1915.blogspot.com/2006/08/954-president-robert-kocharians.html.

17. Interview with Vartan Oskanian, July 8, 2013.

18. Gerard Libaridian, "Erdogan and His Armenia Problem," *Turkish Policy Quarterly*, vol. 12, no. 1 (Spring 2013), 56, 57.

19. Quoted in "Armenia-Turkey: A Difficult Rapprochement Timeline 1990–2007," *European Stability Initiative*, August 2009, http://www.esiweb.org/index.php?lang=en&id=322&debate_ID=2&slide_ID=1. The letter was in fact the result of a joint initiative with Turkey's main opposition party, the CHP, and was promoted by the veteran former Turkish ambassador in Washington, Şükrü Elekdağ, now a CHP parliamentarian. Interview with Elekdağ, October 3, 2013.

20. "Armenia-Turkey: A Difficult Rapprochment."

21. Rice told Rep. Adam Schiff of California, a leading supporter of the Armenian lobby in Congress, "What we've encouraged the Turks and the Armenians to do is to have joint historical commissions that can look at this, to have efforts to examine their past, and in examining their past to get over it" (Desmond Butler, "Rice Avoids Questions on Armenian Deaths," *Associated Press*, March 21, 2007). Mesrob II, Armenian Patriarch of Constantinople also supported the idea of a joint commission.

22. Interview with Van Krikorian, October 17, 2013.

23. David L. Phillips, *Unsilencing the Past: Track Two Diplomacy and Turkish-Armenian Reconciliation* (New York: Berghahn, 2005), 107.

24. Phillips, *Unsilencing the Past*, 56–57, 61.

25. *The Applicability of the United Nations Convention on the Prevention and Punishment of the Crime of Genocide to Events which Occurred During the Early Twentieth Century* (International Center for Transitional Justice, 2003), http://ictj.org/sites/default/files/ICTJ-Turkey-Armenian-Reconciliation-2002-English.pdf, 14.

26. *The Applicability of the United Nations Convention* . . . , International Center for Transitional Justice, 7.

## Chapter 10

1. Zerin Elci and Jeff Mason, "Armenia-Turkey Sign Peace Deal, Pitfalls Ahead," *Reuters*, October 10, 2009.
2. David Phillips, *Diplomatic History: The Turkey-Armenia Protocols* (New York: Institute for the Study of Human Rights, Columbia University, 2012), 27–18. Interviews in Bern, November, 2013.
3. John Kirakosian was one of the three signatories of the 1964 letter calling for commemorations of the Armenian Genocide in 1965, as related in Chapter 3. He was given his name in honor of the American Communist journalist John Reed.
4. Phillips, *Diplomatic History*, 30.
5. Emil Danielyan, "IMF, World Bank See Quick Impact from Turkish-Armenian Border Opening," *Radio Liberty*, October 6, 2009.
6. Tatul Hakobyan, "Armenia Receives Turkey's President for Six-Hour Visit," *Armenian Reporter*, September 12, 2008.
7. Emil Danielyan and Ruzanna Khachatrian, "'Genocide' Question Still Haunts Armenia-Turkey Relations," *Radio Free Europe/Radio Liberty*, July 10, 2008.
8. Gerard Libaridian, "Erdoğan and His Armenian Problem," *Turkish Policy Quarterly*, vol. 12, no. 1 (Spring 2013): 43–64.
9. Khatchig Mouradian, "'Leave It to the Historians': Scholars from the Diaspora Reflect on the Commission," *Armenian Weekly*, October 19, 2009.
10. ICG, *Opening Minds, Opening Borders*, 7.
11. Interview with Bryza, September 16, 2013.
12. Phillips, *Diplomatic History*, 47; "Azerbaijan: President Aliyev Reasonable on N-K Options, Still Furious with Turkey," *Wikileaks*, April 7, 2009.
13. "Barack Obama on the Importance of US-Armenia Relations," January 19, 2008. http://web.archive.org/web/20090220125958/http://www.barackobama.com/2008/01/19/barack_obama_on_the_importance.php.
14. "Remarks by President Obama to the Turkish Parliament," *WhiteHouse.gov*, April 6, 2009. http://www.whitehouse.gov/the_press_office/Remarks-By-President-Obama-To-The-Turkish-Parliament.
15. "Statement of President Barack Obama on Armenian Remembrance Day," *WhiteHouse.gov*, April 24, 2009. http://www.whitehouse.gov/the_press_office/Statement-of-President-Barack-Obama-on-Armenian-Remembrance-Day.
16. "President Obama Retreats from Armenian Genocide Pledge," *Armenian National Committee of America Press Release*, April 24, 2009. http://www.anca.org/press_releases/press_releases.php?prid=1701.
17. Afet Mehtieva, "Turkey Seeks to Ease Azeri Worries on Armenia Ties," *Reuters*, May 13, 2009.
18. Phillips, *Diplomatic History*, 55; Conversations with Swiss and US officials.

19. Hakobyan, *Armenians and Turks*, 366–367; "Sen. Menendez Blasts Armenia-Turkey Protocols," *Armenian Reporter*, October 10, 2009.

20. "'All the countries that have not yet recognized the Armenian Genocide will do so sooner or later': An Interview with President Serge Sargsian," *Armenian Reporter*, October 1, 2009. Accessed at http://www.reporter.am/go/article/2009-10-01--all-the-countries-that-have-not-yet-recognized-the-armenian-genocide-will-do-so-sooner-or-later-an-interview-with-president-serge-sargsian.

21. Phillips, *Diplomatic History*, 56; Hakobyan, *Armenians and Turks*, 371–372; Matthew Lee, "Turkey, Armenia Sign Historic Accord after Last-Minute Talks to Salvage Pact," *Associated Press*, October 10, 2009; Vladimir Solov'ev and Igor Sedykh, "Armenia i Turtsia dogovorilis' molcha po sovetu Sergeya Lavrova [Armenia and Turkey agreed silently on Sergei Lavrov's advice]," *Kommersant*, October 12, 2009.

22. Hakobyan, *Armenians and Turks*, 374.

23. Seto Boyajian, "Davutoglu's Chicanery on the Eve of Signing the Protocols," *Asbarez.com,* October 9, 2009. http://asbarez.com/71753/davutoglu%E2%80%99s-chicanery-on-the-eve-of-signing-the-protocols; Levon Marashlian, "Maybe One of the Biggest Blunders in Armenian History," *Asbarez.com*, October 30, 2009. http://asbarez.com/72728/maybe-one-of-the-biggest-blunders-in-armenian-history/.

## Chapter 11

1. Interview with Armen Demirjian, Diyarbakir, September 29, 2013. All the conversations in this chapter date from September 29–October 1, 2013. I am grateful to Serra Hakyemez for being an excellent interpreter and guide.

2. A pioneering collection of oral histories of Diyarbakir Armenians has been published by the Hrant Dink Foundation. *The Sounds of Silence II, Diyarbakir's Armenians Speak*, prepared by Ferda Balancar (Istanbul: Hrant Dink Foundation, 2013).

3. Interview with Leyla Neyzi, Istanbul, September 27, 2013.

4. Interview with Dikran Altun, Istanbul, May 31, 2013.

5. Fethiye Çetin, *My Grandmother*, translated by Maureen Freely (London and New York: Verso, 2008), 66.

6. Interview with Fethiye Çetin, Istanbul, June 3, 2013.

7. *My Grandmother*, 62.

8. *My Grandmother*, 101–102.

9. On this phenomenon, see Ayşe Gül Altinay and Yektan Türkyilmaz, "Unravelling Layers of Gendered Silencing, Converted Armenian Survivors of the 1915 Catastrophe," in *Untold Histories of the Middle East*, edited by Amy Singer (London and New York: Routledge, 2008).

10. Christopher de Bellaigue, *Rebel Land: Among Turkey's Forgotten Peoples* (London: Bloomsbury, 2009), 109.

11. De Ballaigue, *Rebel Land*, 50.

12. De Bellaigue, *Rebel Land*, 111.
13. De Bellaigue, *Rebel Land*, 55.
14. Leyla Neyzi, Hranush Kharatyan-Araqelyan, *Speaking to One Another: Personal Memories of the Past in Armenia and Turkey* (Bonn: DVV International, 2010), 42.
15. Interview with Abdullah Demirbaş, Diyarbakir, September 30, 2013.

## Chapter 12

1. Elise Antreassian, "The Time for Crying Has Passed," *Armenian Mirror-Spectator*, April 16, 1977.
2. Michael J. Arlen, "Armenians vs. Turks—Again," *New York Times*, March 11, 1980.
3. Ulgen, *Sabiha Gökçen's 80-Year-Old Secret*, 126, quoting Hrant Dink, "About Armenian Identity (6), The Turk of the Armenian," *Agos*, January 23, 2004.
4. Interview with Dikran Altun.
5. *Twenty Voices*, Araz Artinian Productions, 2013.
6. "UNESCO's Ottoman Celebration Protested," *Asbarez*, September 29, 1997.
7. Mann, *Dark Side of Democracy*, 103–107.
8. Israel W. Charny, "Toward a Generic Definition of Genocide," in *Genocide: Conceptual and Historical Dimensions*, edited by George J. Andreopoulos (Philadelphia: University of Pennsylvania Press, 1994), 91–92.
9. Tzvetan Todorov, "The Lunchbox and the Bomb," *Project Syndicate*, August 2, 2003. Accessed at http://www.project-syndicate.org/commentary/the-lunchbox-and-the-bomb#zUeYp8zGPaBbsygW.99.
10. "Statement of President Barack Obama on Armenian Remembrance Day," *The White House*, April 24, 2010.
11. "President Obama Fails to Honor Armenian Genocide Pledge Once Again," *Armenian National Committee of America*, April 24, 2010.
12. Interview with Halil Berktay, Istanbul, September 28, 2013.
13. David Kazanjian and Marc Nichanian, "Between Genocide and Catastrophe," in *Loss: The Politics of Mourning*, edited by David L. Eng and David Kazanjian (Berkeley and Los Angeles: University of California Press, 2003), 127.
14. Schabas, *Unimaginable Atrocities*, 122–123.

# INDEX